Genealogical Records
of
BUCKINGHAM COUNTY, VIRGINIA

96- 1253

EARLY MAP OF
BUCKINGHAM COUNTY, VIRGINIA
BASED ON BISHOP MADISON'S MAP OF 1807

Genealogical Records
of
BUCKINGHAM COUNTY, VIRGINIA

By Edythe Rucker Whitley

CLEARFIELD

Reprinted for
Clearfield Company, Inc. by
Genealogical Publishing Co., Inc.
Baltimore, Maryland
1994, 1996

CONTENTS

DEDICATED TO

Elia Haseltine Jones Rogers
(Mrs. Asa Scobey Rogers, Jr.)
and
Mary Lillian Eubank Sullivan
(Mrs. Wiley Hampton Sullivan, Jr.)

*whose ancestors, like those of the compiler, came
from Buckingham County, Virginia, to Tennessee*

CHAPTER ONE

BUCKINGHAM COUNTY, VIRGINIA

Buckingham County was formed in 1761. It was probably named in honor of the Duke of Buckingham, but there is a record of a land tract called "Buckingham," in Albemarle County. A part of Appomattox County was added about 1859 or 1860.

Research on Buckingham County and its families is difficult for several reasons. The records were destroyed in 1869. Unless one is familiar with the section one cannot identify in the records of Albemarle County those families living south of the James River. Only those families designated in "Tillotson Parish" can be placed with any certainty in Buckingham County.

A few records for the county do exist. Although most of the records of Tillotson Parish have not survived, the Virginia State Archives has photostats of a few items, which may have been copies made by the clerk of the vestry of that parish for use of the Vestrymen in rendering aid to the parish poor. There are seven such items dated 1773 to 1776 and 1783, and there are three receipts of the years 1788, 1793, and 1796. From these papers we learn the following facts about the religious life of the county:

> Minister: Rev. William Peasley.
> Churches and Chapels: Buck and Doe, Goodins, and Maynards.
> Churchwardens: John Bernard, John Cabell, Rolfe Eldridge, and Harden Perkins.
> Vestrymen: Henry Bell, William Cannon, Dolphin Drew, John Fearn, Samuel Jordan, Thomas Miller, John Mosley, John Nicholas, and Samuel Taylor.
> Readers at various churches: William Binion, Charles Maxey, John Patterson, and William Hensley.
> Clerks of the vestry: Charles May.

The University of Virginia Library has made an effort to collect materials dealing with Buckingham County and its families from private owners and other sources. These materials are in the University Library.

The Virginia State Archives in Richmond has a land and personal property and poll tax for the year 1782. The list has been published in Augusta B. Fothergill and John Mark Naugle's Virginia Tax Payers, 1782-1787, (Repr. Baltimore: Genealogical Company, 1971). The first Federal Census that is available is that for 1810.

In 1825 a large and imposing courthouse was built on the public square in Maysville, the county seat of Buckingham. It was planned by Mr. Jefferson and modeled after a Greek temple. This building with all the records was destroyed by fire about midnight the 26th of February 1869, and the life works of Col. Bell, Rolfe Eldridge, Sr., and Rolfe Eldridge, Jr., passed away into ashes. Johnston, in his Old Virginia Clerks says, "There was not a paper left to bear witness to their skill and fidelity for one hundred years."

The first clerk of the county was a Col. Bell (probably Henry Bell). He lived until about 1770. William M. Cabell described him as having been "a man of fine character, good attainments, and an excellent clerk." He served the county from 1761 until his death. He left an honorable name and many descendants (See Johnston, Old Virginia Clerks, p. 112).

Bell was succeeded by Rolfe Eldridge, Sr., whose career is described in the Chapter on Family Sketches. Eldridge was clerk from 1770 until 1806.

The next clerk was Rolfe Eldridge, Jr., son of the preceding clerk, whose career is detailed in the Chapter on Family Sketches also. He served from 1806 until 1858, a total of fifty-two years.

In 1852 the laws were changed and Virginia county officials were no longer appointed. The old clerks as well as new candidates or aspirants had to pass in review before the electors. Although Mr. Eldridge had some opposition he received all of the votes except thirty-four. His own comment on his almost unanimous election by the people was, "that while it was highly gratifying as a testimony of the estimate in which he was held by his fellow-citizens, he preferred the smaller constituency of a court of justice."

Mr. Eldridge declined re-election in 1858, and he was succeeded by his son-in-law, Robert K. Irving, Esq., who filled the office until Virginia became "Military District No. 1," some eight years after Irving took office. The old clerks were ordered out, and strangers filled the places of those whom the citizens respected and loved.

In 1866 Bryce M. Pratt, a military appointee, served as clerk of Buckingham until 1870. He was succeeded by Peter A. Forbes, who enjoyed the tenure of the clerkship from 1870 to 1887. In 1887 he was reelected for a six year term.

It would be impossible to replace all of the destroyed records of history of Buckingham and her peoples, but in this compilation the author hopes to preserve those items which are becoming more and more difficult to locate as the years pass. The items presented here have been collected over a fifty year span as the author searched for her own ancestors in early Buckingham and adjoining counties.

CHAPTER TWO

TAX LISTS

The 1764 tax list was found in the records of Prince Edward County. It is titled "A List of All the Tithes, Lands and Wheel-Carriages in Buckingham County for the year Anno Domini 1764." The names in parentheses following some of the names are probably those of slaves. Following each name are three numbers; the first is for the number of tithes in the household; the second is the number of acres; and the third stands for the number of wheel carriages.

Adria Anglea; Constable; 0;400;0

Anthony Agee and Matthew Agee; 2;200;0

Matthew Agee; 1;150;0

John Agee; 1;0;0

Matthias Ayres and Matthias Ayres, Jr.; 0;0;0

Edmond Ayres and Nathan Ayres (Jamey; Jean); 6;2155;0

William Hunt Allen and William Easley (Bob, Tom, Tomboy, Jamey, Joe, Phillis, and Kate); 9;650;0

Adler Arrington; 1;0;0

William Anglea's list and Nathan Ashworth; 1;500;0

William Akers, Jr.; 1;200;0

William Akers, Sr., and John Akers; 2;0;0

Joseph Adcock (Edmund, Jack, and Genne); 4;400;0

Anderson Adcock; 1;100;0

John Adcock (Flora); 2;200;0

Henry Adcock; 1;0;0

George Hunt Allen (Jacob, Joe, and Moll); 4;394;0

James Agee (Seasor); 2;900;0

Blackburn Akers; 1;245;0

Benjamin Arnold (Dick, Easter, and Lucy); 4;250;0

Isaac Agee; 1;0;0

William Anderson, Benjamin Anderson, and Moses Kidd (Winey, Cate, and Hannah); 6;0;0

James Anderson and Sharp Spencer (Dennis, Peter, Phillis, and Judath); 6;1535;0

Joseph Adcock (Lucey); 2;200;0

Philip Anlen(?) (Lucy); 2;630;0

James Amos; 1;0;0

Benjamin Arthur; 0;175;0

William Anderson; 1;660;0

David Anderson; 1;220;0

Charles Anderson; 0;400;0

Jesse Atkins and Jobe Atkins; 2;0;0

William Baber (Cesar, Searey); 3;25;0

John Bunderant; 1;200;0

David Bell and Henry Bell; 0;0;0

William Horsley, Jesse Christian, and David Morris (Joe, Stephen, Charles, Bob, Hannah, Flora, Ben, Richmond, Charles, Moll, Sara, and Bess); 17;0;1

Thomas Batton (Sam, Phillis, and Peter); 4;400;0

Richard Bunderant; 1;200;0

John Bunderant; 1;800;0

Col. Robert Bolling and Josiah Wood (overseer) (Frank, Joe, Ben, Boss, Dilsey, Patt, Cloe); 8; 8727;0

William Binion and Martin Binion (Cesar and Pompey); 4;265;0

Terry Bradley (Bridget); 2;298;0

Henry Beard and John Beard; 2; 400;0

John Bramer and James Bramer; 2;0;0

Hickerson Barksdale and Abraham Chalton (overseer) (Sarry); 3; 270;0

Hardiman Beard; 1;0;0

Robert Bolling, Thos. Jeffres (over-
seer) (America, Bristol, Tom,
Lewey, Sifax, Bob, Jr., Hanah,
Isabel, Maria, Hagar); 13;0;0

William Barksdale; 0;200;0

William Bradley (Mingo, Robin,
Phillis, Such, and Jeany); 6;210;0

John Beazley and Sarah Daubings; 2;
325;0

Elizabeth Burks, David Burks, Rich-
ard Burks, John Burks, Charles
Burks (Jupiter, Moses, Pompey, and
Cate); 9;190;0

Charles Burnett; 1;0;0

Lambeth Blackburn; 1;200;0

John Bostick (Voll, Rose); 3;200;0

William Buxton (Commidore); 2;300;0

Joseph Burnett; 1;200;0

William Blackburn (Benj. and Jean);
3;290;0

Catherine Brooks' tithes (Moll); 1;
392;0

James Blackburn; 1?;200;0

James Baber and James Baber, Jr.;
2;177;0

Joseph Benning and Bohannon Kitchen
(Will, Jack, and Caesar); 5;1916;0

Griffin Burnett; 1;0;0

Thomas Boaze, Edmund Boaze, and
Daniel Boaze; 3;500;0

Thomas Boaze, Jr.; 0;100;0

Thomas Brooks; 1;0;0

Robert Burton (Cate); 2;0;0

Peter Bunderant for his son, John
Bunderant; 1;0;0

John Bunderant; 1;0;0

James Brown; 0;300;0

Isaac Berryman (Dick, Bob, and
Bruce); 4;200;0

Elizabeth Bates, William Burnett
(overseer) (Pompey, Agg, and Betty)
4;250;0

Thomas Bradley, Cumberland Co.; 0;
371;0

Daniel Boatwright; 0;100;0

John Baley; 1;200;0

Thomas Baley; 1;0;0

James Benning, Robert Jones (overseer (Coffey, Dick, Bob, Bachus,

Saterday, Fillip); 8;1440;0

John Benning and Lewis Christian
(overseer) (George, Tom, Pompey, Robin); 6;1200;0

William Burton (Simon, Peter);
3;400;0

Robert Bailey; 1;375;0

Thomas Blakey (Nutt, Amey); 3;
500;0

Isaiah Burton, Sr. (Sipyon, Dick,
Sarah, Masse?); 5;200;0

Nathaniel Burton (Corey); 2;800;0

James Bennett; 1;0;0

John Brothers (Hannah); 2;0;0

Joseph Bradley; 1;0;0

John Birk; 1;185;0

James Beckham; 1;0;0

James Burnett; 1;0;0

William Bumpass (Nett, Jack, and
Amos); 4;160;0

Richard Bailey; 1;0;0

Col. Archibald Cary's list; Jos.
Fuqua (overseer); (Jack, Tom,
Cesar, Atlas, Rose, Betty, Sara,
Cate); 9;0;0

Samuel Peak (overseer) (Harry,
Kitt, Wolly, Harry, Jude, Pompe,
Boatswain, Jamey, Tom, Betty,
Patt, Mariah); 13;0;0

Nathaniel Morris (overseer)
(Daniel, Sangle, Harry, Jack,
Branch, Dick, Ben, Lucy, Young
Lucy); 10;0;0

Liley Colman (Nan, Dinah, Jane,
York, Hector); 7;13,688;0

Joseph Callands; 0;200;0

Joseph Callands and Alex'r.
Banks; 0;3270;0

James Cunningham; 1;315;0

Anthony Charoon (Charles, Hana);
3;679;0

Abraham Childers; 1;250;0

Joseph Carter; 1;100;0

George Carter; 1;0;0

Francis Childers; 1;200;0

John Carner; 1;100;0

John Childers (Hannah); 2;415;0

Rane Chastain and Isaac Chastain
(Betty, Mary, and Betty); 5;
745;0

Joseph Curd (Sarah and Such); 3;400;0

William Curd (Joe); 2;400;0

George Chambers and Littleberry Epperson (Peter, Luis, and Cate); 5;477;0

Bayley Carter; 1;0;0

Edward Casson; 0;400;0

John Cabell and Nathaniel Woodroff, Jr. (Jubiter, Sapeo, Jack, Nan, and Jude); 7;910;0

Joseph Cabell, Samuel Burks, and John Cooley (Tom, Cupit, Will, Arob, Jamey, Peter, Sarah, Violet, Betty, Bess); 13;3975;0

Edward Pye Chamberlain and John McKenney (London, Bristol, Peter, George, Phillis); 6;600;0

Richard Chamberlayne's list and Benjamin Fambrough (Jack, Sam, Jeffry, Bobb, Sam, Jack, Jeane, Rachell, Tom, Jean, Betty, John Webster, Will, Bristol, Tom, Sam, Bessfortune, Bess, James, Monday); 22;3950; 0

Richard Cornwell; 1;0;0

Nicholas Corner; 1;200;0

William Cary, Jr. (Nancey); 3;0;0

William Corners; 1;100;0

Thomas Coleman and Henry Coleman (Ned and Gilbert); 4;0;0

John Cannon, William Cannon, Henry Amith, and William Smith (Will, Jobe, Esbill, Beck, Mersey, Mutt, Readman, Sam, Judath, James, Sam, Nedd, Bess, and Lucey); 18;3433;0

William Cannon Childers' list and Abraham Childers, William Rowland and Robert Jones; 3;0;0

John Cannafax and William Cannafax; 2;250;0

Col. George Carrington and Joseph Palmer (Simon and Moll); 3;1596;0

Col. Richard Cock's list and Charles Mores (York, Gully, Betty, Doll); 6;485;0

William Chambers (Peter, Sarah, Gean, Tamer); 5;390;0

Archer Christian; 1;0;0

William Cannaday; 1;200;0

John Cox; 1;0;0

Patrick Conner; 1;208;0

Col. John Cobbs and John Cobbs (overseer) (Glasgow, Sam, Jacob, Will, Frank, Moll, Rachell, Wine, Phebee, Betty); 13;520;0

John Coleman, Sr. (Cuffey, Jude, Nan); 4;606

Zachariah Coleman; 1;0;0

Peter Chastain and Rene Chastain; 2;496;0

John Chiles; 0;300;0

John Coleman, Jr.; 1;0;0

William Davison; 1;0;0

John Douglas and John Worley (Sam, Jack, Will, Phillis, and Cate); 7;557;0

John Worley (Sam, Jack, Will, Phillis, Cate); 7;557;0

Edward Davidson (Constable) and Charles Davidson; 1;400;0

William Durham; 1;0;0

Sarah Daubings; 0;200;0

David Davidson and William Davidson; 2;400;0

Richard Dodd; 1;0;0

Bryant Dolling (Fillis and Hanah); 3;200;0

Anthony Dibrall and Jinkins Jinkins (Sarah and Hannah); 3;800;0

John Davis, Benjamin Davis, Joel Davis, and Matthew Davis (Lewis); 5;0;0

George Daniel and William Hardwick 2;0;0

Abraham Daniel, Christopher Baltimore (Harry, Ben, Caesar, Mingo, Sarey, Nan, Phillis, and Cate), and James Daniel; 11; 1120;0

William Davidson, Jr.; 1;0;0

John Dunkin; 1;116;0

Mark Doss; 1;275;0

Alexander Davidson; 1;334;0

Anne Duiguid, Charles Patteson, Richard Bennett, and David Via (Squire, Harry, Doll, Sarah, Chloe, and Lucy); 9;1750;0

George Dameron, Michael Dameron, and Joseph Epperson (Tom, Dick, Sall, Dolsha),, and Matthew Hutcheson (overseer); 6;1411;0

John Edens (Dick); 2;0;0

Joseph Evans (shoemaker); 1;0;0

Joseph Evansson(?); 1;380;0

John Evett; 1;0;0

Warsham Easley; 0;600;0

Susanna Epperson (Cumberland);
0;400;0

Henry Evans and Ambrose Evans;
2;0;0

James Edins; 1;0;0

Thomas Evins; 1;0;0

James Ford (Gilbert); 2;700;0

Peter Ford; 0;405;0

James Ford, Jr.; 1;0;0

Col. John Fry; 0;1968;0

John Flood (Patroler); 0;200;0

William Fuqua; 1;583;0

Andrews Flowers; 1;187;0

William Flowers; 1;187;0

Mace Freeland and Richard Phillips
(London, Cate, Nancy, and Saul);
6;790;0

John Franklin's; 0;300;0

William Fallwell and Henry Fallwell;
2;0;0

John Fearn (Tom, Will, Daniel,
Winey; Venus); 6;1890;0

Stephen Forsee (Cumberland); 0;
200;0

John Flowers; 1;0;0

Jeremiah Farmer; 1;0;0

James Fitz Jarrell; 1;0;0

Francis Guilley (Toby and Jude);
3;200;0

William Gates and John Taylor;
2;500;0

John Goff; 1;200;0

Hugh Green (Jack); 2;500

James Goss and Shelton Bayley
(foreman) (Charles, Caesar,
and Phillis); 6;250;0

Peter Guarrant (Cate and Patt);
2;400;0

John Geveden (Will, Luis, and
Genne); 4;400;0

John Gannaway, Sr. (Abraham, Nero,
Jupiter, Jeffery, Moll, and Alis);
7;900;0

John Gannaway, Jr. (Roger, Famus,
and Champpin); 4;0;0

Stephen Garrot; 1;398(51); 0

Thomas Garrot; 1;100;0

Charles Garrot (Adam and Hannah);
3;300;0

William Griggory (Harkelas, Frand,
Hannah); 4;300;0

George Holms Givin (Sell, Lucy,
and Phillis); 4;560;0

Robert Glover and Archibald McNeill
(Caesar, Frank, George, Lucy,
Patt, and Fann); 8;1250;0

John Glover (Hall, Christmas, Bob,
Peter, Benjamin, Hannah, and Moll);
8;900;0

Samuel Glover and Anthony Dibrall
(Pompey, Sipyear, Moll, Jack,
Fortune, Jo, Sach, Nan, Bell,
and Phillis); 12;2245;0

Edward Gibson and John Gibson
(George, Edmund, and Flora);
5;907;0

Daniel Guarrant; 1;600;0

Knotley Gordan; 1;0;0

Thomas Gibson (Buck, Priss, and
Jansy); 4;0;0

William Gilliam, Sr., and William
Gilliam, Jr. (Harry, Primus, Nan,
Hanner); 6;200;0

Thomas Godsay; 1;400;0

(The list ends here - ED).

BUCKINGHAM COUNTY, VIRGINIA, TYTHABLES IN 1773 AND 1774

These records were found in the Virginia State Archives, Richmond, Virginia.

NAME	TYTHES IN 1773	TYTHES IN 1774
Abbot, George	1	1
Adcock, Anderson	2	2
Adcock, George	3	3
Adcock, John	3	4
Adcock, John (includes Joseph Adcock)	4	4
Adcock, Joseph	4	5
Adcock, Joseph	-	1
Adcock, Joseph, Jr. (levy: 1 free negro)	-	-
Adkins, Peter (John Hillard)	-	1
Agee, Anthony	1	-
Agee, Anthony (William Agee)	2	3
Agee, Anthony, Jr.	-	1
Agee, Isaac	1	1
Agee, James, Sr. (James Agee, Jr.)	4	-
Agee, James, Sr. (James Agee, Jr.)	-	5
Agee, John	1	1
Agee, Joshua. See Anthony Agee.		
Agee, Mathew (Jno. Ligon)	1	2
Agee, Wm. See Anthony Agee.		
Akers, John	1	1
Akers, Wm.	1	1
Akers, Wm., Jr.	2	2
Allen, Mrs. Elizabeth (Benja. Coleman)	3	4
Allen, George Hunt (Wm. Kidd)	12	12
Allen, John (Kinsman Allen)	2	2
Allen, Wm. Hunt (Wm. Smith)	9	8
Ammonet, John	-	1
Amos, Frank	1	-

Tythables in 1773 and 1774

Name	Tythes in 1773	Tythes in 1774
Anderson, Mrs. Ann (Henry Anderson)	4	1
Anderson, David	1	-
Anderson, Henry	-	2
Anderson, Micajah	1	1
Anderson, Nathaniel	3	3
Anderson, William	8	7
Anglin, Adran (or Adrian) (Jos. Anglin, Adrain Anglin, Jr.)	2	2
Anglin, Philip	1	-
Anglin, William (Isaac Anglin)	2	2
Arnold, Benjamin (Edward Arnold)	8	6
Arnold, Edward	-	1
Arrington, Adler	-	1
Arrington, Samuel	1	-
Asheworth, Thomas	-	1
Atkins, Peter	2	-
Austin, Archelus (Elijah Austin, Elisha Carter)	7	8
Axley, James	1	1
Ayres, Matthias (John Ayres)	5	4
Ayres, Samuel (Henry Flood)	2	2
Ayres, Nathan	4	4
Baber, Wm.	3	3
Bagby, Robt.	-	3
Bailey, Richard	1	1
Bailey, William (Thomas Bailey)	4	4
Baird, Archibald	-	1
Baird, Archibald. See Henry Baird.		
Baird, Hardeman	-	1
Baird, Henry (Archibald Baird, Henry Baird, John Taylor)	4	1
Baird, John	1	-
Baker, Henry (Henry Baker, Jr.)	3	-
Ballon, William Cabell	-	1
Bellow, Leonard	1	1
Ballow, Thos. (Wm. Breedlove)	-	4

8

Tythables in 1773 and 1774

Name	Tythes in 1773	Tythes in 1774
Barksdale, Hickerson (John Barksdale, Hawkeler Dangerfield)	7	6
Barksdale, William	2	2
Bates, John (Cannon Bates, Wm. Scruggs, James Stevison)	9	6
Beak, John	-	1
Beazley, John (Jonathan Beazley, Wm. Beazley)	5	6
Beckham, James	-	2
Bell, Henry (Charles Spencer)	6	7
Bell, Judith (Benja. Harrison)	-	17
Benning, James	6	-
Benning, John (John Worley, Joel Bondurant)	9	10
Benning, Capt. Joseph	6	-
Benning, Joseph (Hickerson Hicks)	-	5
Bernard, John (John Pryer)	10	-
Bernard, John, Jr.	1	-
Bernard, John, Sr. (John Bernard, Jr., Robert Bernard, Robt. Smith)		11
Bernard, Robert	1	-
Berryman, Isaac (Christopher Berryman, son)	5	5
Berryman, Isaac (William Berryman, son)	-	2
Berskerville, John	-	1
Beskerville, Geo.	-	-
Binon, Martin	-	1
Binon, William	6	6
Binns, John	-	-
Birks, Charles	2	2
Birks, John	2	2
Blackburn, John	-	1
Blackburn, Lambuth (Jacob Blackburn, Thomas Blackburn)	4	3
Blackburn, Thomas	-	1
Blakey, Robert	2	-
Blakey, Thomas (Thomas Blakey, Jr., Wm. Blakey, Alexr. Edens)	11	14
Blanks, Richard	5	7
Boatwright, Jesse	-	1
Boaz, Archibald	1	-

Tythables in 1773 and 1774

Name	Tythes in 1773	Tythes in 1774
Boaz, Daniel	1	1
Boaz, Thomas (Meshack Boaz)	2	2
Bocock, John	1	-
Bolling, Archibald	7	-
Bolling, Archibald (Anderson Woodson, John Garrett, John McLoud)	7	11
Bolling, Col. Robert (William Shaw, Peter Roy, John Asher, Jacob Cooper)	20	24
Bondurant, Darby	1	-
Bondurant, David	1	-
Bondurant, John, Jr.	1	-
Bostick, John	4	4
Bowles, David	-	1
Bradly, Wm.	1	2
Bradley, Wm. (John B. Garland)	-	3
Brady, Jos.	1	-
Brammer, James	1	-
Brammer, John	1	-
Brammer, John, Jr. (David Manning)	-	1
Bristow, James	10	8
Brothers, John	2	2
Brown, Allen, Sr.	-	1
Brown, I(s)hum (Wilson Brown)	-	2
Brown, James (James Neville Brown)	2	1
Brown, John (Allen Brown)	2	-
Brown, John, Jr.	1	1
Brown, John, Sr.	-	1
Brown, John, son of John, Sr.	-	1
Brown, Joseph	-	1
Browne, John	-	1
Bryant, Isaac	2	3
Bryant, John	-	2
Bryant, William	1	-
Buford, Milton	1	-
Buford, Thomas	1	-
Bumpass, William	1	-
Bunderant, Joel	1	-
Bunderant, Darby	-	1

Tythables in 1773 and 1774

Name	Tythes in 1773	Tythes in 1774
Bunderant, John	-	1
Bunderant, John, Jr.	-	1
Bunderant, John, Sr.	1	-
Bunderant, Joseph (Joseph Bunderant, Jr.)	-	3
Bunderant, Richard	1	1
Bunderant, Thomas	3	-
Burk, George (Tillotson Parish) (Thomas Wright)	5	-
Burnet, Joseph	1	-
Burnett, Griffin	-	1
Burnett, James	2	2
Burnett, Joseph	-	-
Burnit, David (Tillotson Parish) (James Edward Burnett, mut.)	2	-
Burton, Isaiah	-	6
Burton, Josiah	6	-
Burton, Nathaniel (Wm. Burton)	6	6
Burton, Robert (Isaac Burton)	2	2
Burton, William	1	1
Buxton, Wm. (George Buxton)	5	4
Bynion, Martain	1	-
Cabell, John (Tillotson Parish)	8	-
Cabell, Col. John (Isaac Hill)	-	8
Cabell, Col. Joseph (James Bootwright, William Johnson, overseers; David Reynolds, overseer)	17	-
Caniday, William	1	1
Cannon, John (Joel Davis, Charles Goldsby)	12	9
Cannon, William (Joel Meggs, James Stanard)	17	13
Carner, John	1	1
Carner, William (John Carner, John Carner son)	2	2
Carter, George	2	1
Carter, John (Huddleston Carter)	-	2
Carter, Joseph	2	1
Carter, Stephen	1	1
Cary, Col. Archibald (John Nelson, William Byram, Henry Garrott, Jesse Edwards, miller, Daniel Sanguila)	35	21

11

Name	Tythes in 1773	Tythes in 1774
Cary, Robert (Asaph Walker, overseer)	15	13
Cason, Seth (Edward Cason)	3	3
Chamberlane, Capt. Richd. (Benja. Morris)	29	29
Chambers, George	4	-
Chambers, John (John Chambers, Jr.)	4	7
Chambers, (?), Sr. (John Chambers, Jr., Edmond Chambers)	-	8
Chambers, Joseph	-	1
Chambers, Wm.	7	7
Chandler, Abram	-	1
Chastain, A-O Berham	-	1
Chastain, Archer	-	1
Chastain, Isaac	2	-
Chastain, John	1	-
Chastain, Peter (Abraham Chastain)	2	-
Chastain, Rene	4	4
Chastain, Rene (Eane), Jr.	2	2
Childress, Francis	2	2
Childress, Jno. (Alex'r. Stinson)	2	2
Childress, Willis (William)	1	1
Christian, Archer	1	1
Christian, Lewis	-	1
Cloar, John ("at Moses Goings")	-	1
Cobb, John (Tillotson Parish) (Waddy Vines)	2	-
Cobb. River Tom	-	4
Cobb, John (Lewis Kidd, overseer)	-	8
Cobbs, Thomas (at Walton's Fork) (Henry Coupland, Thos. Mayo)	7	15
Cocke, Col. Hartwell, estate (Shadrack Oglesby)	10	-
Coleman, John	-	1
Coleman, John, estate (Littleberry Coleman)	-	3
Coleman, Samuel	3	2
Conner. Nicholas	-	1
Cornwell, Richard	1	1
Cotterel, Charles	1	-

12

Tythables in 1773 and 1774

Name	Tythes in 1773	Tythes in 1774
Cottrel, Benjamin (Jacob Cottrel, Jno. Saunderson)	8	7
Couch, James	1	2
Couch, John	5	-
Cox, John	10	10
Cox, John ("The John Cox, the estate of William Moseley, dec'd.," Thomas Spoldin or Spalding)	-	7
Cox, John Hartwell	-	10
Cox, Matthew (John Chitwood)	6	6
Creasey, William (Charles Creasey)	7	8
Crews, Gideon	-	1
Crews, Walter (Gideon Crews, James Crews)	2	2
Crouch, John	-	5
Cumminger, John	1	-
Cunningham, James (Valentine Cunningham)	2	3
Curd, Joseph (Charles Curd, John Bradley, George Clack)	9	10
Curd, William, estate of (Joseph Epperson, dec., George Epperson, Yancey Bailey)	5	-
Curd, Wm. (Peter Word, Ambrose Ambruse)	6	6
Damerson, Thena	-	-
Daniel, Abraham	7	7
Davenport, Richard	-	2
Davidson, Edward, Jr.	-	1
Davidson, Stephen	-	1
Davie, Peter (Isaac Davie, son)	3	2
Davie, Peter (Peter Davie, Jr.)	3	-
Davie, Peter, Jr.	-	1
Davis, Mrs. Ann (Thos. Davis)	2	2
Davis, Benja.	-	1
Davis, Champness	1	-
Davis, Henry (Tillotson Par.)	1	-
Davis, Joel	-	1
David, Matthew	1	-
Davison, Charles	1	-
Davison, Edward, constable	1	1

Tythables in 1773 and 1774

Name	Tythes in 1773	Tythes in 1774
Davison, Edward, son of David	-	-
Day or Gay, John	1	1
Day, Lewis	1	1
Deal, James	1	-
Dibrel, Anthony (Charles Dibrel, John Dibrel)	5	7
Donald, James (Tillotson Par.)	1	-
Doss, Edward	1	1
Doss, James	1	1
Doss, Mark (John Doss)	3	3
Doss, Thomas (one place called unr. in 1774)	1	1
Douglas, James (Jesse Cobbs)	2	3
Douglas, John	-	8
Douglass, John	7	-
Drew, Dolphin, Col. (Thomas Haynes Drew)	9	9
Duiguid, Ann (Thos. Tucker)	5	4
Duiguid, Wm.	4	5
Dunkin, John (James Dunkin)	-	2
Durham, John	1	-
Durham, William	1	1
Easley, William	2	5
Easley. Wm.	-	5
East, Ezekiel	-	1
Edens, James	1	-
Edens, John	-	-
Eldridge, Rolfe (David Miller)	2	-
Ellett, Zachariah, constable	-	-
Ellsome, Thomas	-	1
Epperson, Francis	-	1
Epperson, George. See Curd, Wm. Estate of Joseph Epperson, dec.		
Epperson, Joseph, dec. See estate of William Curd.		
Epperson, Littleberry (Jeremiah Woodward)	3	3
Evans, Robert	1	1
Evins, Thomas	1	-
Evitts, Nehemiah	1	-
Evitt, Thomas	1	-

Tythables in 1773 and 1774

Name	Tythes in 1773	Tythes in 1774
Falwell, Wm.	-	2
Farguson, Edward	1	-
Farguson, Joel	1	-
Farguson, John	1	2
Farguson, Moses	1	-
Farguson, Wm.	1	-
Fearn, John	8	7
Fearn, Thomas (John Furlong)	4	5
Ferguson, Joel (1771?)	1	-
Ferguson, John	-	1
Ferguson, Moses	-	1
Fields, Joh (or John?) (mulatto)	-	1
Flood, John	-	1
Flud, John	1	-
Flowers, Andrew (Tillotson Par.)	1	1
Flowers, Ralph (Tillotson Par.)	1	2
Foard, Rich'd.	-	1
Ford, Boaz	1	1
Ford, Eliza. See John Fird.	-	-
Ford, James (levy free)	1	1
Ford, James, Jr.	1	1
Forde, Richard	1	-
Francis, Wm.	-	1
Freeland, Mace (Ben Pendleton, Mace Freeland)	5	5
Freland, Rob't. (John Harris)	4	-
Fuqua, Joseph	-	1
Fuqua, William (Wm. Fuqua, Jr.)	-	3
Fuqua, Wm. (Joseph Fuqua, Wm. Fuqua)	4	3
Gallaway, Wm.	-	1
Galle, Terry	-	1
Gannaway, John, Jr. (Gregory Gannaway)	7	6
Gannaway, John, Jr. (younger) (John Woodson, Edward Morgan, Rich'd Johnson)	-	4
Gannaway, John, Sr.	7	-
Gannaway, Wm. (Henry Byram)	-	3
Garratt, Charles, dec.; est. of (Richard Pasley)	-	5

15

Tythables in 1773 and 1774

Name	Tythes in 1773	Tythes in 1774
Garratt, Stephen (John Garratt, Charles Rakes)	3	2
Garratt, Thomas	1	-
Garrott, Charles (Wm. Thomson)	6	-
Garthard, John B. See Wm. Bradley	-	-
Gates, Charles (Hezekiah Gates)	1	2
Gates, William (Elijah Gates)	4	4
Genkins, John	-	1
Genkins, Joseph, Jr.	-	1
Genkins, Joseph, Sr.	-	1
Gibson, Edward (Terry Gallahon, John Gibson)	5	5
Gibson, John (John Cousins)	2	-
Gibson, Miles	-	2
Gibson, William	2	1
Gibson, Wm.	-	4
Gilley, Francis (Charles Gilley, Francis Gilley)	5	-
Gilliam, Charles	-	1
Gilliam, John	4	5
Gilliam, Wm.	-	3
Glover, John (John Glover, Jr.)	8	9
Glover, Edmond	-	2
Glover, John, Jr. (James Harris)	3	3
Glover, Joseph	1	-
Glover, Robert (Edmond Glover)	10	10
Glover, Samuel (Zachariah Griffin, Anthy. Glover)	12	12
Glover, Samuel, Jr.	-	1
Godfree, (-)	-	1
Godsey, Thomas (Austin Godsey)	2	-
Godsey, Thomas (Augustine Godsey)	2	-
Godsey, Thomas	-	2
Gott, William (Samuel Glover)	2	-
Gordon, Motley (mulatto)	-	1
Gordon, Northly (prob. same as above)	1	1

16

Name	Tythes in 1773	Tythes in 1774
Goss, Benjamin	1	–
Goss, James (Shelton Railey)	6	6
Gregory, William (Thomas Gregory)	6	6
Grisham, Lee (Henry Franklin)	–	2
Guanaway, John, Sr. (prob. intended for Gannaway)	–	7
Guerrant, Peter (Jno. Guerrant)	3	4
Guillery, Francis (Charles Guillery, Francis Guillery)	–	5
Haincock, Robert	1	–
Hall, Charles	–	1
Hall, William	1	–
Hall, William, Jr.	–	1
Hamelton, Morris	1	1
Hamelton, Samuel	4	4
Hammon, John	3	3
Hancock, Samuel (Tillotson Par.) (William Hancock, Richard Hancock)	5	5
Hancock, Thomas (Tillotson Par.)	1	1
Hancock, Robert	–	1
Hansard, Archelus	1	–
Hansard, Archer	–	1
Hansford, John	1	–
Hardeman, Baird	–	–
Hardeman, John	–	1
Hardwick, George	2	–
Hardyman, John	1	–
Harmon, Edward	1	1
Haris, John's, quarter (William Meglason, overseer)	3	–
Harvey, Thomas	2	1
Harvey, Thomas, Jr.	1	1
Harvey, William	1	2
Hatcher, Archibald	–	1
Hay, Wm.	1	–
Henslee, Wm.	1	1
Henslee, Zachariah	1	1
Hews (?), John (Robert Hughes)	–	–
Harvey, William	1	2

Tythables in 1773 and 1774

Name	Tythes in 1773	Tythes in 1774
Hatcher, Archibald	-	1
Hay, William	1	-
Hillard, John	1	-
Hines, Caleb (Thomas Hines)	2	1
Hines, Thomas	-	1
Hobson, John, at his quarter (Archer Hatcher)	5	-
Hodges, Benjamin	1	-
Hodnett, Ayres	8	-
Hodnett, John (Philip Hodnett)	8	8
Holt, William (Tillotson Par.)	1	-
Hood, John	-	1
Hooper, George	7	7
Howard, Est. of Maj. Benj.	-	18
Howe, James	2	-
Howerton, Thomas (James Howerton)	-	4
Hoy, John Booker	1	-
Hoy, William (Edward Davison, overseer)	10	4
Huddleston, Robert	1	1
Hudson, Simon	2	2
Hughes, John	1	2
Hughes, Robert (Tillotson Par.) (John Hughes)	5	-
Hundly, James	1	1
Hundley, John	1	-
Ingle, George	1	1
James, Richard (Tillotson Par.) (Daniel Harris, Phill. Hannabell)	11	10
Jefferies, Nathaniel (Thomas Jefferies, Nathaniel Jefferies)	5	6
Jefferson, Randolph (Tillotson Par.) (John Bowles, Stephen Slatery)	13	14
Jenkins, John	1	1
Jenkins, Joseph	1	1
Jennings, Anderson	1	1
Jennings, John	1	-
Jennings, William	1	1
Jinnings, John	-	1
Johns, James (Edward Garnett)	5	6

Tythables in 1773 and 1774

Name	Tythes in 1773	Tythes in 1774
Johns, John	1	-
Johns, John (Henry Hines, Stanup Richardson, and John Moss)	8	8
Johns, Josiah	1	2
Johns, Mallory (mulatto) (of Tillotson Parish)	1	-
Johns, Sally	1	-
Johns, Thomas	3	3
Johns, William (Thomas Wood)	2	4
Johns, William, Jr. (Ambrose Day)	2	4
Johnson, Wm.	-	1
Jones, Abraham	-	1
Jones, Daniel	3	4
Jones, Elias	1	2
Jones, John (John Jones, Jr., Thomas Jones, William Burton, Thomas Jones)	10	9
Jones, Josiah (John Williams and Robert Smith)	5	6
Jones, Robert	3	3
Jones, William (Tillotson Parish)	6	7
Jordan, Reuben (at his quarter) (Archer Hamblet)	5	-
Jordan, Reuben (Tillotson Parish) (Archer Hamblet)	6	-
Jordan, Samuel (Wm. Jones)	13	13
Kersey, Edward (Tillotson Par.) (Edward Kersey, Jr.)	2	-
Kidd, Benjamin	1	-
Kidd, James	1	-
Kidd, John (Tillotson Par.)	1	1
Kidd, Moses	1	1
Kidd, Samuel	1	1
King, (?) (his quarters) (John Bush, Robert Page)	21	-
King, Mr. Walter (Robert Boage, John Bush)	-	25
Kitchen, Bohannah	1	1
Kyle, Robert (David Kyle, Robert Kyle)	5	5
Lambath, William (Peter Jones, Benja. Meggison)	3	-
Landers, Robt.	-	1

Tythables in 1773 and 1774

Name	Tythes in 1773	Tythes in 1774
Langhorn, Morris (Robert Furlong)	9	-
Lax, James	1	1
Layn (Layne), Charles (Jesse Layn)	2	1
Layne, Jesse	-	1
Lee, Arthur	2	-
Lee, Evan	-	1
Lee, Gresham (Hen. Franklin)	2	-
Lee, John	1	-
Lee, Richard	1	2
Lee, Young	1	-
Leseure, Samuel	-	2
Lesure, Chastain	-	2
Lesure, James	-	2
Lesure, (?)	2	-
Locket, David	5	5
Low, Alexander	1	-
Low, Daniel Johnson (David Low)	6	6
Low, Jesse	-	1
Low, Wm. (Larkin Rutherford, John Williams)	7	7
Mackashane, Richard	1	-
Macmanawy, John	-	1
Maddox, Jacob	1	1
Maddox, Wm. (Stephen Maddox)	5	5
Malcom, James	1	-
Maloid (Malloid), David (John Blackburn)	4	4
Mannin, William	1	-
Manning, Samuel	-	1
Martin, John (James Martin, John Martin)	3	-
Martin, Wm.	2	-
Martin, Wm., Jr.	-	2
Martin, Wm., Sr.	1	1
Mase, Silvanus, ferry keeper (also spelled Massie)	1	1
Masters, James	-	1
Masters, John (Wm. Masters, John Masters)	-	3

Tythables in 1773 and 1774

Name	Tythes in 1773	Tythes in 1774
Mathews, Thomas	2	-
Matthews, Gregory	7	4
Matthews, James (Joel Matthews)	4	4
Matthews, Samuel	-	1
Matthews, Thos.	-	3
Maxey, Charles	-	2
Maxey, Edward (John Maxey)	2	2
Maxey, Nathaniel	1	1
Maxey, Sampson (Samson)	1	1
May, Charles (John May)	5	7
May, John	1	1
Mayo, Valentine	2	2
Mayes (Mays), John (Tillotson Par.)	1	-
McCormack, (?)	-	1
McCormack, David	1	-
McCormack, Hugh	1	-
McCormack, John	1	-
McCormack, (?)	-	1
McCormack, Sherwood	-	1
McCormack, Thomas (David McCormack, his son)	1	2
McFadeen, Farrel	1	-
McGasson, Matthews	-	1
McGlasson, Wm. (James McGlasson)	-	3
Meredith, James (James Meredith, Jr.)	4	-
Millam, Edmond	-	1
Miller, Frederick	-	1
Millon, William (Edmon Millom)	2	-
Milton, Absolom	1	-
Mims, Drury	8	6
Moore, Robert (Alex'r. Moore)	-	2
Morris, Nicholas (William Morris, John Morris)	5	4
Morris, Wm.	1	-
Morris, Wm., Jr.	-	1
Morris, Wm., Sr.	-	1
Morrow, John (Francis Giddeon, Jno. Morrow, Jr.)	5	5

Tythables in 1773 and 1774

Name	Tythes in 1773	Tythes in 1774
Moseley, Charles	4	4
Moseley, Francis (Joseph Evans, Benjamin Payne)	9	12
Moseley, John (Henry Hodsey)	7	-
Moss, James, Sr. (May Moss)	4	4
Moss, James, Jr. (Thos. Moss, Jr.)	3	5
Moss, Thomas (John Moss, Thomas Moss, Henry Falwell)	5	3
Moss, William	2	2
Muckelroy, John	-	1
Murphey, Thomas Truman (John Murphey, Thomas Murphey, Richard Murphey)	3	4
Murrel, Thomas	3	-
Murry, Anthony (Joh. Saunderson, John Hencan)	14	14
Murry, Laurence	-	1
Neighbors, Francis	-	1
Nicholas, John (John Johnston, Randolph Jefferson, Patrick Campbell, Daniel McCallum, Samuel Taylor, Jr., Walker Perkins, Jesse Bootwright, Peter Campbell, Dan'l. McCallum)	38	34
North, Richard	2	2
Northcutt, Richard	1	1
Northcut, William (Terry Northcutt)	-	2
Nowlin, James (Thomas Elsom)	3	-
Nowling, Francis (Richd. Nowling)	-	2
Nucum, John	1	-
Obruan, Matthias	1	-
Obrian, Patrick	1	-
Page, John	1	1
Palmer, George (Wm. Palmer)	2	-
Palmer, James	1	1
Palmer, Nixon	1	-
Palmer, Wm.	-	2
Palmor, James	2	-
Palmor, John (Isaac Palmor)	4	5
Palmor, Jun.	1	-

Tythables in 1773 and 1774

Name	Tythes in 1773	Tythes in 1774
Palmor, John	-	3
Pamplin, James (Tillotson Par.)	5	-
Pasley, Richard	1	-
Patterson, Charles (Le-? Patterson)	6	-
Patterson, Charles (Tillotson Par.)	4	4
Patterson, Charles (Landis Patterson)	-	6
Patteson, David (Tillotson Parish) (John Edins)	9	10
Patteson, David, estate (John Patteson)	-	6
Patteson, James	2	4
Patteson, John, clerk	8	1
Patteson, John	-	1
Patteson, John	5	-
Patteson, Littleberry	-	1
Patteson, Peter (Ben Patteson)	4	3
Patteson, Thomas (Arch. Gilliam, Wm. Lee)	5	6
Patteson, (?) (Wm. Shepherd)	7	7
Patteson, Wm., Jr.	-	1
Payne, Barnett	1	1
Payne, Joseph	1	1
Peak, Henry	3	3
Peak, Jeffery	1	2
Peake, William	1	-
Peasley, Wm.	-	3
Peasley, Rebent, William	3	-
Peek, John (Aaron Peek, Jonathan Peek, Absalom Peek)	3	3
Peek, Wm.	-	1
Pen, Rawly (mulatto)	-	1
Pendleton, Benja.	-	1
Pendleton, John	1	-
Perkins, Hardin (David Oglesby)	9	10
Perkins, William (John Watkins Perkins)	4	-
Perkins, William, Jr.	4	-
Perkins, Wm.	-	5
Perkins, William, Sr. (John W. Perkins)	-	4

Tythables in 1773 and 1774

Name	Tythes in 1773	Tythes in 1774
Perrow, Charles	7	7
(David Perrow, Charles Perrow, Jr.)		
Perrow, Daniel	6	6
(Daniel Battersby Perrow, Stephen Perrow)		
Peters, Edmund	-	5
(Edmund Moss)		
Phelps, John	4	5
(Adrain Anglin, Jacob Burton)		
Phelps, Thomas	4	3
(Josiah Phelps)		
Phelps, Wm.	4	4
(Richd. Phelps)		
Pretchard, John	1	-
Pride, Francis	-	4
Prichard, John	-	1
Pryer, David	3	1
(James Murrel)		
Pryer, Edmond (or Edwd)	-	2
Pryer, Edward	3	-
(N? Smith)		
Pryer, Sarah	3	2
(William Jennings)		
Pryer, William	1	1
Puckett, Robert	1	-
Qualls, David	-	1
Qualls, John	1	1
Radford, John	-	1
Railey, Philip	-	1
Rakes, Charles	-	1
Rakes, David	1	-
Rakes, Henry	-	1
(David Rakes)		
Rakes, William	1	1
Ransone, Flamsteed	-	6
(Henry Ransone)		
Rayley, Wm.	1	-
Redd, Thomas	6	10
(John Redd)		
Renne, Stephen	-	1
Renolds, Archer	2	2
(Moses Reynolds; also shown as Archelus Reynolds)		
Renno, Stephen	2	-
(John Renno)		
Reves, John	1	-
Reynolds, Charles	-	1

Tythables in 1773 and 1774

Name	Tythes in 1773	Tythes in 1774
Ridgeway, James	-	2
Ridgeway, Phebe (Harry Fanning)	3	3
Ridgeway, Richard	2	2
Ridgeway, John	-	-
Right, Augustine	1	-
Right, John	1	-
Rippy, Richard	-	3
Robertson, Mary	1	1
Robertson, Richard	1	-
Robertson, Zachariah	-	1
Roseberry, William	1	-
Routon, John (Robin Williams)	3	4
Rutherford, Larkin	-	1
Sally, John	-	1
Salle, Isaac	-	1
Salle, Isaac	-	1
Salle, Jacob	-	2
Salle, John	-	1
Salle, Olive	-	1
Salle, William, Sr. (Martha Ayres)	-	7
Salle, Wm, Jr. (Hunt Salle)	-	2
Salley, Jacob (James Durram)	3	-
Salley, Moses	1	-
Salley, William, Jr.	1	-
Sallye, William, Sr. (Mathias Ayres)	8	-
Sanders, Daniel	1	-
Sanders, Daniel	4	-
Sanders, Robt., Jr.	2	-
Sanders, Thomas (George Baber)	8	8
Sanders, James	-	2
Saunders, (?) el	-	6
Saunders, Daniel (Nixon Pamer)	-	6
Saunders, Robert (James Dunham, Thompson Bristow)	8	10
Saunders, Samuel (Griffin Burnet)	6	-

Tythables in 1773 and 1774

Name	Tythes in 1773	Tythes in 1774
Saunders, Stephen (James Aunders, John Saunders)	14	16
Scott, Hugh (Tillotson Parish) (Joseph Scott)	2	2
Scrugs, James (Tillotson Par.) (Jesse Scrugs, Allen Scrugs, Isham Scrugs)	4	5
Scruggs, John	5	6
Scruggs, Theodorick	-	3
Scruggs, Thos. (Jos. Scruggs)	2	-
Scruggs, William (Ambros Beaber, Thomas Baber, Ambrose Beaver, Thomas Beaver, Edward Beaver)	6	7
Sharp, Richard (Richard Sharp, Jr.)	2	2
Shelton, Francis	1	1
Shoemaker, James	-	1
Shoemaker, John (James Shoemaker, Orlander Shoemaker)	3	-
Shoemaker, John	-	1
Shoemaker, Leander	-	1
Smther (?), John (Garratt Smetheir(?).)	2	-
Smith, Alexr.	2	2
Smith, Henry	3	2
Smith, James	1	-
Smith, Robert	1	-
Smith, Robert	1	-
Smith, Thomas (Ambrose Inge)	-	3
Smith, Wm.	1	-
Smith, William (Thomas Smith, William Smith, Jr.)	3	2
Snoddy, James	-	1
Snoddy, John (Cary Snoddy, John Snoddy, Jr.)	3	3
Southern, James	1	1
Southern, James	-	1
Southern, Joseph	-	1
Southern, Samuel	1	-
Southern, Wm. (Reubin Southern)	2	2
Spears, John	-	5
Spears, John (Em. Spears)	-	-
Spencer, (?)	1	-

26

Tythables in 1773 and 1774

Name	Tythes in 1773	Tythes in 1774
Spencer, Francis	5	5
Spencer, Francis West (Job Atkins)	6	7
Spencer, Samuel (William Worley)	9	9
Spencer, William	-	1
Staples, Isaac	1	1
Staples, John	-	1
Staples, Saml. (Jno. Staples, David Coleman)	9	9
Statin, William	2	-
Staton, George	1	1
Staton, James	-	1
Staton, John (George Dameron)	2	3
Staton, Reubin	1	1
Staton, Wm. (Joseph Staton)	-	3
Stephens, John (Joseph Green)	2	2
Stephens, Thomas (George Vest, Jno. Stephens)	2	4
Still, Thos.	1	1
Still, Wm. (Henry Still)	5	5
Stinson, Alexander	10	-
Stinson, Alexr., Jr.	-	3
Stinson, Alexander, Sr. (George Stinson, Cary Stinson)	-	11
Stinson, David (James Maluim)	1	-
Stinson, John (Edmund Adcock, Benja. Payne)	9	8
Stinson, Joseph	1	1
Strange, John (Jesse Strange)	2	2
Sublett, James	1	1
Swiney (Swinney), Thomas	1	1
Taylor, Daniel (Richard Taylor, son)	2	2
Taylor, George	-	1
Taylor, Joseph (James Robertson)	-	3
Taylor, Joshua	1	-
Taylor, Richard (Joshua Taylor, Jno. Taylor)	5	5

Tythables in 1773 and 1774

Name	Tythes in 1773	Tythes in 1774
Taylor, Richard, Jr. (Joshua Taylor)	3	6
Taylor, Saml. (Richard Taylor, John Snord(?).)	6	8
Taylor, Samuel, Jr. (James Roberson)	3	-
Terry, John (Stephen Terry)	2	-
Thomas, Henry (John Legan)	2	1
Thomas, James (Jeremiah Shoemaker)	4	5
Thomas, John	-	3
Thomas, Joseph (Wilkerson Murrel)	-	5
Thomas, Thomas	1	-
Thompson, Robt. (constable)	1	-
Thornhill, Thomas (Tillotson Par.) (Thomas Thornhill, Jr., Garrison Hawkins, David Walker)	5	5
Thornhill, William	1	1
Thurman, Elisha	-	1
Tibbs, John	1	1
Tindal (Tindall), Benjamin (Olivin(?) Lewis, overseer)	6	6
Toney, Charles	3	3
Toney, John	4	4
Toney, Wm. (Wm. Toney, Jr.)	2	2
Trent, Peter (Daniel Pryde)	6	-
Trent, Col. Alexr. (William Pride Daniel)	-	6
Freeman, Wm.	1	1
Turpin, Col. Thos. (William Harris)	-	6
Turpin, Thos. (Benja. Bailey, overseer)	4	4
Tyre (Tyree), David (constable) (Ben Tyre)	1	1
Tyre, Wm.	-	1
Urquhart, Walter (Christopher Macrae)	-	2
Vest, John	1	1
Vest, Rich'd.	-	1
Via, David	-	3
Walker, Asop (Baily Carter)	-	3

Tythables in 1773 and 1774

Name	Tythes in 1773	Tythes in 1774
Walter, David	-	1
Walker, Elmore	1	1
Walker, James (Thomas Brooke)	6	5
Walker, John	1	-
Walker, John	1	-
Walker, John (Richard Hodges)	5	5
Walker, John	-	1
Walker, Thomas (John Walker)	1	1
Walker, William	1	-
Warrin, William	1	-
Warters, Charles	-	1
Watkins, Joel (Wm. Naile)	1	2
Watt, William (Rich'd Dean)	11	11
Weakland, Wm. K.	5	5
Weaver, David	1	1
Webb, John	-	2
Webb, Martin	1	1
Webb, Samuel	1	-
Webb, Theodrick (Thodrick) (John Garratt, John Radford, John Fitxhjawald)	11	14
Webb, Wm. (Wm. Francis)	4	3
Welch, James (?)	1	1
West, Richard	3	4
Wever, John	1	1
Wheeler, Benjamin	-	1
Wheeler, Charles (John Wheeler, son)	-	2
Wheler, Aech	-	1
Wheler, Charles (Joe Wheler)	2	-
Wheler, Sary	-	1
White, Henry (Tillotson Par.) (Henry Page White)	2	2
White, John (Tillotson Par.)	1	1
White, John (Tillotson Par.)	1	-
Whitney, Jeremiah (Richard Bauldock)	11	11
Wilkenson, Major	1	-

Tythables in 1773 and 1774

Name	Tythes in 1773	Tythes in 1774
Wilkerson, William (Turner Wilkerson)	3	5
Wilkeson, Joseph Thomas	-	-
Williams, Richard	1	1
Williams, Robt. (Wm. Gowing)	-	4
Williamson, Thomas	-	1
Williamson, William	4	4
Willis, Meshack (Jno. Jones)	-	2
Winfree, George	1	1
Wingo, John	-	1
Winston, Anthony (Anthony Winston, Jr., John Balkins)	34	33
Witt, Ben (Ben Witt, Jr.)	-	-
Wood, Thomas	2	1
Woodall, David	1	1
Woodall, James	1	-
Woodall, William	1	1
Woodson, Jacob (George Buxton)	4	5
Woodson, John (Alexr. Wm.)	-	7
Woodson, Shadrack	4	-
Woodson, Tucker	1	-
Woodson, William (Jesse Woodson)	3	4
Wooldridge, Henry	3	3
Wright, Augustine	-	1
Wright, George (Henry Perkins, Tom Scott)	4	-
Wright, (?) (Thos. Wright)	2	-
Wright, Peter	-	1
Wright, Randolph	1	1
Wright, Thomas (Tillotson Par.)	4	4
Wright, Thomas	1	-
Zachary, Bartho. (John Zachary)	4	5

The first number after each name indicates the white male tithables. The second number shows the number of horses owned. The third and fourth numbers indicate the number of negro tithables, and the number of negroes between the ages of 12 and 16. In some cases the white male tithable is identified in parentheses of a connection with another person. The compiler cannot explain this, but copied the records exactly as they are given.

Agree, James, Sr.; 1-8-7-2

Agee, James, Jr.; 1-6-3-1

Amos, James; 1-1

Anderson, Capt. Charles; 1-6-1-0

Amos, Clough (A. Shep'd.); 2-1

Amos, Reuben (Obe A.); 2-1

Amos, Frank (S.T. & A.S.); 3-1

Ayres, John, (SN); 1-3-2-1

Akers, John, Sr. (Jno. & Elija); 3-4-1-0

Akers, Susanna; 0-2

Akers, Lewis; 1-3-2-0

Agee, Joseph; 1-3-0-2

Adcock, William; 1-1

Ayres, John, Jr. (Ed. A.); 2-3-4-1

Agee, Jacob; 1-4-3-1, one stud horse

Adcock, George, const.; 0-3-1-0

Adcock, Carter; 1-1

Agee, Hercules; 1-5-1-1

Allen, Samuel; 1-2

Anderson, Richard; 1-3-3-1

Ayres, Nathan (Watt A.); 2-8-8-1

Anderson, Edmund; 1-1-2-0

Anderson, Thomas, Est(ate); 1-17-18-6

Anderson, John; 1-1-1-2, ordinary license

Anderson, Jeffry (M); 1-0

Adcock, Joseph (s. of And'n); 1-1

Adcock, John (s. of And'n); 1-2

Anderson, William, Sr. (W.A., Jr.); 2-12-8-2

Ayres, Matthias; 1-2-2-1

Adams, William; 2-2-1-0

Allen, William (SG); 1-3-3-2

Allen, Mary; 0-3-8-0

Archer, Charles; 1-1

Ayres, Edmund (W. Maxy); 2-3-5-2

Allen, William Hunt (Th. Hu.); 2-12-18-4

Apperson, Jacob; 0-4-4-0

Amonet, Reuben; 1-0

Amonett, William; 1-5-2-0

Allen, William (estate); 0-7-10-1

Anderson, Matthew (Ja. A.); 2-4-4-0

Anderson, Henry; 1-5-7-0

Armistead, Thadeus; 2-3

Agee, John; 1-3-1-1

Akers, William; 1-3

Adcock, John, Sr.; 1-2-3-0

Adcock, Henry (s. of John); 1-2

Allen, Samuel, Colo.; 9-13-22-4

Amos, Francis (s. of Fra.); 1-0

Anderson, David; 1-4-2-2

Adcock, Joseph (s. of Jno.); 1-4-3-0

Anderson, James; 1-3-3-0

Akers, John (SB); 1-3-1-0

Bridgewater, Chesley; 1-0

Branch, Bolling; 1-1-2-0, one chair

Brooks, Dudley, const.; 0-2-3-1

Brown, Lewis; 1-0

Brooks, Wilson; 1-3-1-1

Banton, William (Jno. B.); 2-5-2-0

Bryant, Austin (AB); 2-3

Burton, Benjamin; 1-2-2-0

Bryant, Anthony; 1-1

Brown, R. Woods; 1-1

Baber, Isaac; 1-5-1-0

31

Bransford, Benjamin;
 1-3-3-1

Bondurant, Thomas (Jno. and
 Th.); 3-6

Brooks, Read; 1-1

Branch, Matthew; 1-1-5-2

Ballowe, Thomas (s. of Th.);
 1-1

Ballowe, Chloe; 0-1-5-0

Burton, Nathaniel; 1-6-4-1

Bolling, Lenaeus (G. Perry);
 2-8-18-4

Baber, George (W.B.); 2-5-1-1

Baber, James; 1-2

Bondurant, Darby (Ja. B.);
 1-4-1-1

Beazley, William; 1-2

Burton, Robert (Doug. B.);
 2-5-5-2

Berryman, Isaac; 1-4-3-0

Berryman, William Johnson;
 1-5-5-1

Berryman, Anderson; 1-4-2-0

Blanks, Robt., estate; 0-1-1-1

Baber, Edward; 1-3-1-1

Bagby, John, Sr.; 1-4-5-0

Bagby, James; 1-1

Burton, John; 1-2-1-0

Bolling, Jesse; 1-1

Burton, Jesse; 1-2-2-0

Bagby, Daniel; 1-4-6-2

Bagby, Capt. Henry (Ja. B.);
 2-6-6-0

Bransford, Thomas; 1-2-2-1

Ballowe, Leonard; 0-5-5-2

Ballowe, John; 1-1

Blankenship, Gad (Elijah & J.);
 3-3-1-0

Bernard, John, estate; 0-6-18-5

Bernard, Wm. R.; 1-1

Boatright, Reuben; 1-3-2-0

Baber, Caleb; 1-1

Bernard, George; 1-1

Bryant, John; 0-2-1-0

Bransford, John, Jr.; 1-2-1-0

Bransford, (John?), Sr.;
 1-7-7-1

Brown, Benajah; 1-6-9-1

Brown, John; 1-3-1-0

Baber, Thomas; 1-4-4-1

Barnes, James; 1-0

Bell, Henry C.; 1-3-6-0

Benning, Joseph; 1-7-7-4

Baird, Archibald (P. & W.);
 3-3-4-2; 1 stud horse

Ball, Isham; 1-1-1-1

Buxton, Charles; 1-1-3-0

Bell, Henry (J. S. D. B.);
 3-11-24-1

Brown, Jno. Stanford; 1-4

Bagby, Cleyton; 1-1

Bolling, Powhatan; 1-4-10-2

Baird, Hardiman (H. & D. B.);
 3-2

Boaz, Elizabeth (Jas. B.); 1-4

Boaz, Meshack; 1-1

Bishop, Stephen (Ro. Carter);
 2-3

Baker, John; 1-0

Brooks, William; 1-0

Buckhanan, John; 1-3-6-0

Blackborn, James; 1-4-6-0

Cobbs, Thomas (Jr.); 1-5-7-1

Curd, Edward (B. Eds.); 2-7-5-2;
 1 stud horse

Chambers, John (C. & Geo.);
 3-7-7-0

Couch, John, Jr.; 1-2-4-1

Chamberlayne, William; 0-3-7-2

Chambers, Alleway; 1-1

Couch, Daniel; 1-7-7-1

Couch, James (Jesse C.);
 2-6-11-0

Couch, Jas. Bartlett; 1-1-6-0

Call, Charles, constable
 (M.C.); 1-2-1-0

Carter, Joseph; 2-2-3-0

Christian, Thomas; 1-1

Christian, Archer; 1-0

Chastane, Stephen; 1-5

Carter, George (W. M.); 1-3-5-0

Childres, John (D.C.); 2-4-5-0

Childres, Francis Ware;
1-1-1-0

Coupland, David (Th. H.);
2-4-12-3

Carter, Joseph, Jr.; 1-3

Chambers, Josias; 1-3-6-1

Carter, Thomas (Jno. C.); 2-2

Cottrell, Jacob; 1-2-3-2

Cottrell, James, free n.; 1-1

Cottrell, Ford; 1-0

Cottrell, Harry; 1-1

Craig, Robert (B.B.); 1-12-16-4

Cunningham, Joseph; 1-4-1-0

Charlton, John G.; 1-2

Charlton, Jacob; 1-3

Carter, Henry (S.G.); 1-1-1-0

Cottrell, Richard (3 apps.);
4-3-2-1

Cunningham, William; 1-3-1-0

Cayce, Shadrack; 1-1-1-0

Cox, Henry; 1-5-3-0

Cox, Edward; 1-1

Cox, Matthew, estate; 1-10-9-4;
1 r. chair

Carter, George (S. G.); 1-1-1-1

Carter, Joseph (do.); 1-2

Curd, Joseph; 1-6-1-0

Cousins, Josias; 1-0

Cunningham & Guerr't.; 3-2-8-0

Cox, John, per Wm. Ross; 1-0

Carden, Youen; 1-0

Couch, John, capt.; 1-6-11-1

Cloptpn, Benjamin (Anthy. C.);
2-2-3-0

Cox, George (Th. Alk.); 2-5-3-0

Chaudoin, David; 1-1

Chaudoin, Francis, estate; 0-1-1-0

Cobbs, Thomas (R.) (Wm. C.);
2-9-16-0

Chastane, Rane (S.P.) (Jno. C.);
2-4

Cox, Thomas; 1-0-1-0

Chastane, Rev. Rane (Jno. Wat.
or Wst.); 1-4-1-0

Chastane, Martin (W. Ayres); 2-2

Chastane, Elijah; 1-2

Chinault, James; 1-1

Coleman, Julius; 1-4-4-1

Coleman, Daniel; 1-0

Coleman, Parmenus; 1-2-3-0

Cary, Robert; 1-6-13-1

Childres, Thomas, estate; 0-3

Curd, John; 1-1-1-0

Curd, Anne (Cha. Curd); 1-2-0-1

Cason, William; 1-4-2-0

Cannon, William; 1-6-14-2

Day, William; 1-0

Drake, Joel; 1-3-2-0

Duncan, Fleming W.; 1-2-1-2

Davis, William; 1-4-3-0

Duncan, George (A. S.); 2-3-3-1

Davis, Peter; 1-1

Davis, Matthew, estate (Z 7 M);
2-1

Davis, William Fleming; 1-0

Duncan, Jesse; 1-3-1-0

Duncan, Edw'd, estate; 0-2-3-1

Duncan, Charles; 1-0

Duncan, Jacob (Jac'b D.); 2-5-1-0

Duncan, John; 1-0

Davis, Benjamin; 1-0

David, Robert; 1-3

David, Bartlett (Chap. D.);
2-5-7-1; 1 chair.

Dibrell, Anthony; 1-4-3-0

Dobson, Richard (W. Ws.);
2-24-32-2; 1 phaeton

Donoho, Edward; 1-1-1-0

Druen, William; 1-1

Druen, Samuel; 1-1

Daniel, Hezekiah (Prince Edwd.);
0-1-2-0

Edwards, Archibald (A. North);
2-3

Evans, Robert; 1-3-1-0

Evans, Capt. William; 1-10-6-3

Epperson, John (Th. Akers);
2-7-6-0

Eldridge, Rolfe (Ro. & Geo.);
5-5-11-3

Edwards, Nehemiah; 1-0

Elcan, Lion (Jno. Morris);
2-7-5-0

Ford, Joseph; 1-4-1-0

Fuqua, Gabriel; 1-4

Francis, John; 1-3

Ferguson, Robert1 1-2-2-0

Filbates, Edward; 1-1

Flowers, Rowland; 1-2

Fuqua, William (Mo. F.);
2-8-6-0

Faris, Charles; 1-1-1-0

Farrow, Thomas; 1-1

Ford, Boaz (A. & B.); 3-2-4-0

Ford, Elisha; 1-1

Ford, Salley; 0-1

Fuqua, Joseph (Wm. F., Jr.);
2-5-4-0

Fuqua, Robert; 1-1-1-0

Flournoy, Silas; 1-12-10-3

Ferguson, Edmund; 1-3-1-0

Fearn, George; 1-1

Fuqua, Stephen (St. Howl.);
2-5-2-0

Ford, Joel; 1-5-1-1

Forbes, Alexander; 1-1

Flowers, James; 1-3

Flowers, Joseph; 1-1

Ferguson, John (B. S.); 1-1

Fitch, Samuel; 1-1-1-0

Garrott, Stephen, Sr., estate;
0-3-2-2

Garrott, Elijah; 1-1

Gregory, William; 1-6-6-1

Gregory, Samuel; 1-2

Gannaway, Robert (Wm. G.); 2-4-3-0

Garrott, William; 1-2

Garrott, Isaac; 1-5-3-0

Grizle, William; 1-1

Gilliam, John (s. John); 1-2-2-0

Gilliam, William; 1-3-2-0

Garrott, Charles; 1-5-4-2

Glover, Thomas; 1-1-1-1

Goff, John, Jr.; 1-1

Garland, Jesse; 1-2-3-0

Gates, Allen; 1-3-3-1

Goff, William (W. G., Jr.);
2-5-3-0

Glover, Samuel; 1-10-14-1

Gipson, William (Th. G.);
2-6-3-1

Garnett, Nathaniel (W. G.);
2-4-2-2

Gilliam, Susanna; 0-1

Glover, John; 1-2

Glover, William; 1-1

Guerrant, Peter, Jr. (S. W. C'd);
2-2-2-2

Guerrant, Peter, Sr.;
1-5-8-0

Guerrant, Stephen; 1-3-3-1

Guerrant, Capt. John; 1-9-5-1

Gardner, James; 1-1

Gilliam, Richard; 1-3-1-0

Garrott, Anthony; 1-1

Galleway, Terry (Wm. G.); 2-1

Gannaway, John, Sr.; 1-3-5-0

Gannaway, John, Jr.; 1-0

Gannaway, Marmaduke; 1-0

Gannaway, Thomas; 1-1

Gipson, John, Sr. (Wm. G.);
2-5-2-0

Gunter, Thomas; 1-1

Gevodin, Thomas; 1-0-1-0

Garrott, Jno. D., estate
(Wm. G.); 1-4-7-1

Grizle, Henry; 1-0

Gilliam, Richard Curd; 1-3-1-1

Gilliam, Isham; 1-1

Garrett, Thomas; 1-2

Galding, Freeman; 1-1

Gills, William; 1-4-4-0

Garrott, Joshua; 1-0

Hinion, William; 1-0

Herring, Pitt; 1-0

Hall, Edward (Edw'd. M.);
2-5-8-0

Hall, Thomas; 1-2-2-1

Hall, William; 1-3-3-0

Hicks, Anthony; 1-1

Hicks, Hickerson; 1-3

Huddleston, Jarratt; 1-1

Hudgins, James, Sr. (H.H.);
2-5-2-1

Holman, Tandy, estate (Allen
S.); 1-6-6-1

Harris, Joseph (Ja. H.); 2-2

Hudnal, Lawson; 1-2

Hudnal, James, estate; 1-4-3-2

Hudnal, Richard; 1-3-1-0

Howl, James, Sr.; 1-1-1-0

Hooper, Stephen; 1-2-2-1

Holright, William; 1-1

Huddleston, George; 1-3-2-0

Huddleston, Thomas (s. Ro.);
1-2-0-2

Halsal, Thomas; 1-1-0-2

Hervey, Ellison; 1-1-4-0

Hervey, Stephen; 1-1

Hardwick, Harman; 1-0

Howard, Isham; 1-1

Hocker, Adam; 1-1

Hobson, William (M. H.); 2-8-13-3;
1 chair

Howl, Gideon; 4-5-4-0

Hendrick, John; 1-6-5-0;
1 chair

Hodnet, Philip (P. B.); 2-6-7-0

Hopkins, Benjamin; 1-1-3-0

Hooper, James; 1-3-2-0

Harris, John; 1-6-8-4

Harris, Francis; 1-6-2-0

Hambleton, John (S.M.); 1-3-0-1

Hansford, William; 1-2-0-3

Harris, William (W. H., Jr.); 2-1

Hardy, John; 1-2

Hill, Robert; 3-9-8-4

Hinson, John; 1-1

Hinson, John, Jr.; 1-2

Hobson, Lawson (D. B.); 2-3-5-0

Hamilton, Samuel; 1-3-1-0

Hatcher, Barnett; 1-1

Hatcher, Arthur, estate; 0-1

Huddleston, Thomas, Sr. (Wily
H.); 2-4-2-0

Hambleton, Maurice (Wm. H.);
2-7-1-2

Hambleton, John (S.S.); 1-3-2-0

Haynes, William; 1-2

Harris, Will'm (s. of Jos'h);
1-0

Harris, John, cooper (Ja. H.);
2-0

Howerton, Thomas; 1-2

Howerton, Fill; 1-1

Howerton, Riley; 1-0

Hambleton, Henry (S.M.); 1-1-1-0

Hall, William (S. Me.); 1-2-1-0

Hopper, John; 1-8-6-1

Heath, John; 1-3

Hendricks, Elijah & Bernard
(Wm. Kerr); 3-1-0-1

Hudgins, James, Jr.; 1-2

Hooper, George; 1-3-5-0

Hooper, George, estate (Wm. H.);
1-9-8-2

Hervey, Jeffry; 1-0

Johns, Glover; 1-3-4-0

Jones, William (B. L.) (D. Jones)
2-2

Jones, Davison; 1-1

Jackson, Henry; 1-3-2-1

Jones, William (s. Ro.); 1-1-1-0;
1 stud horse

Isoms, James; 1-3-1-0

Jeffris, William; 1-2-1-1

Jeffris, Mary; 0-3-6-0 (per
son Will. - scratched out)

Jeffries, Jesse; 1-0-1

Johnson, David; 1-0

Jefferson, Randolph (Jno. Jeff'r);
2-8-12-0

James, James (Mullato); 1-1

James, James, Jr. (Mullato); 1-1

James, Francis (ditto); 1-1

Johnson, Nicholas; 1-0-1-0

Johnson, William, s. of Nichol's;
1-2

Johnson, Pumfrett; 1-2-1-0

Jones, Abraham, Jr.; 1-3

Jones, William, estate;
0-6-6-1; ordinary lic.

Jones, Robert; 1-8-8-0

Jones, William, Jr.; 1-7-5-4

Johnson, Philip; 1-1

Jones, Anthony (s. Wm.); 1-0

Jeffris, James; 1-1

Johnson, William (Appamattox); 1-1

Johns, Abner; 1-1

Johns, John, Jr. (incl. his mother); 1-3-3-0

Johns, Edmund; 1-1-1-0

Johns, John, Sr. (Sam. J.); 2-8-9-2

Johns, William (s. Jno.); 1-2-2-0

Kidd, Lewis; 1-0

Kidd, Sherwood; 1-0

Kidd, Wm. (near N. Canton); 1-2-1-0

Kidd, Absalom; 1-2-1-0

Kidd, John, Sr.; 1-3-2-2

Kidd, Archer; 1-1

Kidd, Wm. (s. Jno.); 1-0

Kincaid, Robert; 1-7-11-1

Kidd, William, Sr.; 1-2

Kidd, Moses, estate; 1-2-5-2 (Wm. T.)

Kidd, Joseph; 1-0

Lain, Gabriel; 1-3-0-1

Lipscomb, Col.; 1-2-5-2

Lewis, William (carp'r); 3-1-1-1

Liggon, John; 1-0

Lackland, John; 1-3

Lowe, Reuben; 1-0

Lackland, Zadock; 1-3-2-2

Lackland, Margery; 0-6--5-1

Lesueur, Chastane (M. L.); 2-5-3-2

Lumpkin, Anne (Obed'h); 1-3-3-0

Langhorne, Maurice M.; 1-4-6-1

Lipscomb, Hezekiah; 1-1

Land, John; 1-4-7-1

Land, John Braxton; 1-1-2-0

Lesueur, Samuel (S. L.); 2-5-3-2

Loyd, Joshua; 1-1-0-2

Lipscomb, Anderson; 1-0

Lancaster, William; 1-2-2-0

Lesueur, Peter (Dav'd L.); 2-5-5-1

Lipford, John; 1-2-1-0

Loyd, Benjamin; 1-1

Maxey, Samson; 1-1

Murrel, Cornelius; 1-1

Matthews, Thomas; 1-1

Maxey, John; 1-5

McNeel, Charles; 1-1-0-1

May, Charles, Colo.; 1-3-2-1

Maxey, James; 1-2

Moseley, Capt. Francis; 1-8-8-1

Murphy, Richard, estate (D.M.); 1-2

Maxey, Edward, estate; 0-2

Maxey, Edw'd, s. of Edward; 1-3-1-0

Murray, William O.; 1-2-5-1

Murray, Anthony; 1-4-6-1

Minton, William (Jesse M.); 2-3-6-0

Mosby, Benjamin, estate; 0-1-2-2

Morris, Nathaniel; 1-8-11-2

Mire, Dr. Jacob; 1-2

Moseley, Benjamin, estate; (N. Ayres, Jr.); 1-9-17-3

Morrow, John; 1-5-8-0

May, Peter; 1-0

May, William; 1-0

Moseley, William; 1-4-4-1

Moss, Anne (M.) (Dr. & Jx.); 2-3

Moss, William; 1-1

Moss, James (carp'r.); 1-1-1-0

Moss, Thomas (s. Jas.); 1-1

Moss, James, Sr. (Ja. M., Jr.); 2-3-6-0

McCormac, John (Th. McC.); 2-3-2-0

Maxey, Nathaniel (Jac'b M.); 2-1-1-1

Maxey, Thomas; 1-2

Murphy, Thomas Truem'n; 1-2-1-0

Molloy, Daniel; 1-2

Miles, Isham; 1-2-1-0

McGlassan, William; 1-4-3-0

McGlassan, John; 1-2-1-0

Marshall, John (per Apperson) (Jac. A.); 1-9-10-2

Moss, Francis; 1-4-4-0

Moss, Thomas, Sr. (Wm. M.); 2-5-2-0

Marshall, John (per Talley) (Ch. T.); 1-8-14-0

Moss, Fanny, per W. Jones; 0-3-5-1

Miller, John (P. tan); 0-2-2-0

Mosby, Benjamin; 1-7-14-0; 1 coach

Matthews, Charles; 1-3-4-0

Matthews, William; 1-3-1-2

Merideth, James; 1-3-5-1

Molloy, William; 1-3-3-1

Moseley, Peter, merch't (J. R.); 2-4-3-1; 1 coach

Morrison, Dr. James; 1-1

McGehe, Jacob; 1-1

Molloy, William; 1-3-1-1

Morris, Benjamin (Ja. P.); 2-7-5-1

Moseley, John (S. W.); 1-5-4-2

Miles, William; 1-2-1-1

Moss, Benja. (Free N.); 1-1

Molloy, Rhoda; 0-5-5-3

Madox, William; 0-4-5-2

Madox, Michael; 1-4-3-1

Madox, David; 1-2

Nunally, John (B. N.); 2-3-3-2

Nixon, William; 1-1

Nixon, Hurriah; 1-1

Nelson, Abraham; 1-3-1-1

Nunally, Josiah; 1-2

Nunally, Arthur; 1-3-2-1

Nicholas, George; 1-8-11-3

Nunally, Barnett; 1-3; 1 stud horse

Newton, Joseph; 1-3-1-1

Nicholas, Robert; 1-15-19-4

Nowlin, David; 1-4-4-0; 1 stud horse

Newton, William; 1-2-0-1

Nicholas, Joshua; 1-4-5-4

Nelson, Elijah; 1-1-1-0

Oliver, John (Pl. R.); 2-1

O'Bryant, Glen; 1-0

Oglesby, David; 1-1-0-1

O'Bryant, Patrick, estate; 0-2-2-0

O'Bryant, William; 1-2

O'Bryant, Patrick; 1-0

Pattison, Charles; 1-4-2-2

Prince, John (F. & W.); 3-2

Pryar, David (L. & Z.); 3-2-2-0

Pryar, Langston;. 1-1

Pryar, Banister; 1-0

Pucket, Cheatham; 1-1-2-0

Pattison, Capt. David (S. P.); 2-6-6-1

Pattison, John, surveyor; 1-6-7-3

Perkins, Capt. Hardin (D. Cont.); 2-6-7-2

Perkins, Hardin, estate; 0-5-10-2

Perkins, Price (Jno. G.); 2-4-7-2

Palmer, Isham; 1-1-2-0

Palmer, Elizabeth; 0-5-4-0

Pattison, Thomas; 1-3-6-1

Price, Dr. Wilson; 1-2-0-1

Perrow, Charles; 1-5-4-0

Perrow, Charles, estate (Thad. A.); 1-5-6-2

Perrow, Guerrant; 1-0

Pollard, Benjamin; 1-1-1-1; ordinary license

Palmer, Joseph, tailor; 1-0

Pryor, David; 1-0

Price, Thomas Johnson; 1-3-3-1

Putney, Ellis (Jno. P.); 2-6-10-4

Puryear, Reuben; 1-1-2-0

Pace, Joseph; 1-2-1-1

Palmer, John (Cal. Branc); 1-5-2-0

Palmer, Isaac; 1-2-1-0

Palmer, William; 1-0-2-0

Price, John; 1-1-1-0

Pucket, Douglas; 1-1

Peak, Jeffry, estate (Jno. Sm.); 1-3

Ridgway, Richard; 1-3-5-1

Rice, Davenport; 1-1

Ripley, Richard; 1-3-1-0

Raglin, James; 1-0

Ramsey, James; 1-3

Ross, William; 1-15-16-4; 1 phaeton

Richardson, Ruchard; 1-6-6-3

Rawlins, Henry (Jno. L.); 2-2-6-1

Reece, William; 1-1

Riddle, Peyton & Co. (Th. W.); 2-1-1-0; 1 chair

Read, Clement (S. Rudder); 1-3-4-1

Robertson, Nicholas; 1-7-5-0

Robertson, Nicholas, Jr.; 1-2-1-1

Ransone, Jno. D.; 1-1-2-0

Ransone, William; 1-3

Ransone, Flemstead, estate; 0-2-5-0

Reynolds, David; 1-0

Self, Robert; 1-3-2-0

Smith, Thomas (B.); 1-3

Staton, John; 1-1-2-0

Staton, Rane; 1-2-1-0

Staton, George; 1-0

Staton, Reuben; 1-1

Staton, Benjamin; 1-0-1-0

Staton, William, estate; 1-2-2-1

Staton, Cornelius; 1-0

Self, Thomas; 1-1

Stanton, William, Jr.; 1-1

Suddearth, John; 1-1

Sanders, Daniel; 1-5-6-1

Scrugs, Capt. William; 1-7-7-0

Scrugs, Finch (S.W.); 1-2-0-1

Seay, Abney (Jas. S.); 2-2-3-0

Smith, William (S. Ro.); 1-0

Salle, Jacob; 1-5-1-0

Settliff, John; 1-1

Salle, Isaac; 1-4-1-0

Salle, Magdalene; 0-1-1-0

Stuart, John (Jno. S., Jr.); 2-5-3-1

Shepherd, William; S.D.; 1-2

Stinson, Alexander; 1-2-4-2

Stinson, David; 1-4-2-0

Stinson, Archer; 1-1

Scott, John (M.); 1-3

Scott, Benjamin (M.); 1-0

Scrugs, Allen (Ish. S.); 2-3-5-1

Scruggs, Isham; 1-1-2-0

Scruggs, Valentine; 1-4-2-1

Scruggs, James, estate; 0-1-3-0

Scruggs, Finch (S.V.) (Morgan); 2-1-0-1

Scrugs, Thomas; 1-1-1-1

Sadler, Thomas; 1-1-1-0

Smith, George; 1-3-1-0

Scrugs, Nathan; 1-1

Scrugs, Keziah; 0-2-6-1

Scrugs, Drury; 1-1-1-1

Stanton, Matt; 1-1-1-1

Sweeny, Malachi; 1-2-2-0

Sanderson, Thomas; 1-1

Smith, Henry, Jr.; 1-0

Smith, Henry, Sr., estate; (Ja. S.); 1-2-1-0

Shelton, Richard; 1-1

Scrugs, Drury (S. Th.); 1-1

Smith, William (Allen's); 1-1

Shirley, John; 1-2

Stanton, James, Sr.; 1-4-3-0

Stanton, James, Jr.; 1-1

Sanders, Rev. James; 1-8-8-0

Smith, Benjamin; 1-1

Smith, Robert (Jno. S.); 2-1

Sanderson, John, estate (Ro. S.); 1-5-5-0

Sanderson, John, Jr.; 1-1

Snoddy, Cary; 1-3-2-1

Snoddy, James (Dav'd S.); 2-3-3-0

Snoddy, Daniel; 1-2-1-0

Southeren, Samuel; 1-2-2-0

Shelton, Clough, estate; 0-11-9-3

Sanders, John, estate; 0-6-7-1

Sanders, Judith, widow of J.S.; 0-2-3-0

Salle, Edward; 1-1

Sanders, Robert; 1-2-5-1

Sanders, Robert; estate; 0-4-5-1

Sanders, Thomas; 1-3-3-0

Sanders, Edward; 1-4-2-1

Stinson, John; 1-3-6-0

Stinson, Asa; 1-1

Shelton, John; 1-1-0-1

Stinson, Cary (Ja. S.); 2-3-4-0

Stinson, Alexander, Jr. (S.C.); 1-0

Scott, Saymer; 1-1

Sanders, Samuel, Jr.; 1-1

Smith, John; (S. Ro.); 1-0

Seay, Reuben; 1-2-1-0

Taylor, John; 1-1-1

Thomas, Thomas (Dav'd Th.); 2-6-3-1

Turner, John; 1-6-6-0

Tindall, John; 1-7-3-1

Taylor, Samuel; 1-4-2-0

Thomas, Daniel; 1-2

Thomas, John; 1-1

Thomas, Philip; 1-0

Taylor, James (B.S.); (R. N.); 2-4-3-0

Toler, Absalom; 1-1

Tindall, Hatcher; 1-0

Taylor, Edward; 1-3-1-1

Toney, Edmund (s. Jno.); 1-1

Tabscott, James; 2-2-2-0

Toney, Charles (Edm'd. T.); 2-2-6-1

Toney, John (S. Ch.); 1-1-1-0

Toney, John (S. Jno.); 1-0

Talley, Charles; 0-1-3-1

Tandy, Smyth; 1-3-2-0

Toney, John, Sr. (Ja. T.); 2-5-8-3

Toney, William (Jno. T.); 2-4-4-0

Tindall, Thomas; 1-4-6-1

Tindall, Benjamin, estate; 0-3-9-1

Tindall, Benjamin; 1-0-2-1

Tindall, William; 1-1-1-0

Tindall, Washington; 1-0-1-0

Tindall, Powhatan (an Inft.); 0-0-2-0

Tirpin, William (Cum'b.); 0-4-10-1

Thurman, John; 1-1-1-0

Vasser, John; 5-8-2-0

Vauter (or Vawter), Thomas; (L. V.); 2-3-3-0

Veat, William; 1-0

Vauter, Edward; 1-3-1-1

Venable, Josiah; 1-5-5-2

Winfrey, Henry; 1-3-3-1

Winfrey, Hill; 1-2-3-2

Wilkinson, Lewis; 1-7-7-1

West, Rowland; 1-1

Watkins, Robert Bolling; 1-1-3-0

Watkins, John; 1-2-1-0

Winfrey, Samuel; 1-6-11-1

Wooldridge, Charles; 1-1

Wooten, William; 1-0

Woodall, David (Jno. W.); 2-3

Woodall, Isaac; 1-1

Woodall, Obediah; 1-2

Woodall, William; 1-1

Woodall, William (s. Wm.); 1-1

Wooldridge, Thomas, Sr.; 1-5-4-1

Wooldridge, Thomas, carp'r; 1-2-2-0

West, Richard; 1-7-6-0

West, John (S. R.); 1-3-2-0

Wheeler, Robert; 1-0

West, John, const'l; 0-1

Williams, Nathaniel; (D.W.); 2-2

Word, Banjemin (E. Prinn); 2-2

Walton, Anthony (Josiah P.); 2-7-4-2

Wilson, James; 3-12-16-2

Walton, Edward (Cumb.); 0-2-3-1

Wheeler, Charles, Sr.; 1-1

Watkins, Spencer; 1-2-4-1

Wadmore, William; 1-3-3-0

Wadmore, James; 1-1

Williams, Thomas; 1-1

Wood, Owen (R.Q.); 2-3

Wootten, Joseph; 1-1

Wilkerson, Turner (R. Scrugs);
   2-5-5-0

Wilkinson, William; 1-3-5-1

Wilkinson, Francis; 1-2-3-1

Witz, John; 1-0

White, William; 1-0

Winniford, Judith; 0-2-2-0

Word, George Washington; 1-1

Wright, Archibald; 1-4-7-2

Walston, Joseph; 1-1

Whorley, Peter; 1-1

Williams, John; 1-3-2-0

Walton, Langhorne; 1-2; 1 stud
   horse

Word, Thomas; 1-3-6-0

Wooldridge, Joseph; 1-2-2-0

Warriner, David; 1-1-2-0

Winston, Anthony; 2-9-8-2 (C.
   Bethel)

Wright, Gabriel; 1-5-3-1

Woodson, William; 1-3-1-1

Woodson, Jacob, estate; 0-1-3-0

Woodson, Jacob; 1-5-3-0

Watkins, Pleasant; 1-3-2-1

Watkins, Charles; 1-4-1-0

Walthal, Francis; 1-4-4-1

Walthal, James; 1-1

Wilborn, Thomson; 1-1-0-1

Whealer, Charles, Jr.; 1-1

Wooten, William; 1-0

Wilcox, Susanna; 0-9-15-5

Wooldridge, John; 1-0-1-0

Wooldridge, Henry; 1-0

Wilborn, Jane (R. W.); 1-5-4-0

Watt, William; 1-8-10-3

Walker, Washington; 1-1-1-0

Watt, Maj. James; 1-9-11-1

Wood, Thomas (Jno. & Ro.);
   3-5-4-1

Wood, Edmund; 1-1

Walke, Thomas; 1-1-2-0;
   ordinary license

West, Claborn; 1-2-2-0

Winston, William; 1-2-5-2

Houses, Lots, etc., in New Canton

Hill, Robert, rents

Adams, William

Anderson, John, rents

Witz, John, rents

Pollard, Benja.

Shelton, Richard, rents

Smith, Henry, rents

Guerrant, Peter, Sr., owns

Palmer, Joseph, rents

Cunningham & Guerrant,
   rents

Moseley, Peter, rents

Moseley, Peter, owns

Licenses to retail establishments

Epperson, John

Riddle, Peyton

Hendrick, Elijah Bernard

Elcan, Lion

Moseley, Peter

Hocker, Adam

Cunningham & Guerrant

Scott, Saymer

Hill, Robert

Witz, John

Perrow, Guerrant

Scruggs, Oglesby, & Co.

Irving, Walter

District No. Two
Josias Jones, Commissioner

Alvis, Charles; 1-0

Allen, George; 1-4-3-0

Ambros, Henry; 1-1

Ambros, Ambrose; 1-1

Alvis, Ashley, & Son; 2-4

Arnold, Terry; 1-2-1-1

Abraham, Jacobs L.; 1-5-3-1

Alott, George; 1-2

Alott, Benjamin; 1-4-1-1

Alvis, David; 1-0

Alvis, David, Jr.; 1-1

Austin, Archelus, estate; 2-8-6-0

Austin, John; 1-1-1-0

Brothers, John, Jr.; 1-3-1-0

Burkes, Samuel, son of Jon.; 1-2

Beverly, Jonathan; 1-1

Beverly (or Benerly), William; 1-1

Burkes, Joseph (son Chas.); 1-0-1-0

Branch, Jonathan; 1-2

Bradley, Richard; 1-2

Branch, Olive; 1-3-0-1

Beckham, William; 1-2

Bradley, William, coop'r' 2-3

Bradley, Stephen (son of Do.); 1-1

Baley, William; 1-1

Brown, Joseph; 1-3

Brown, Jackey; 1-1

Belcher, Beverly; 1-1

Branch, Archerhel; 1-2-4-1

Burnett, James; 1-8-2-3

Bondurant, William & F.; 2-6-7-2

Brown, William; 1-4-3-0

Burkes, George; 1-6-7-0

Burkes, Samuel, s. of Geo.; 1-0

Burkes, George, Jr.; 1-1-1-0

Burkes, Charles; 1-1

Baley, Benjamin; 1-4-1-0

Baley, Philop; 1-2-1-0; ordinary licenses

Bradley, John, and son; 2-1

Bradley, Richard; 1-4

Burkes, John, and son; 2-6-4-0

Boaz, John; 1-0

Brown, Isham, & son; 2-2

Brothers, John; and son; 2-2-4-0

Beckham, James; 1-5-6-0

Beckham, James, Jr.; 1-0

Bocock, John, & son; 2-6-3-2

Brown, (?); 1-1

Bagby, Henry; 1-1-0-1

Burton, Dr. Robert; 1-1-1-0

Bagby, John (and sons?); 3-3-5-0

Brown, Stephen; 1-3

Brown, John, cooper; 1-3

Bigbie, William; 1-6-4-1

Brown, Nathaniel; 1-0

Bell, Joseph; 1-0

Brown, Frederick; 1-0

Boling, Archebald; 1-6-12-2; 1 stud horse; 1 riding carriage; 1 stage wagon

Blakey, Thomas; 1-7-7-1

Ballowe, Thomas; 1-1

Barskwild, John; 1-1-1-1

Bryant, John; 1-0

Blakey, Robert; 1-1

Colmon, Robert, & C. Burks; 2-3-3-1

Currey, Reubin; 1-1-1-0

Chandler, George; 1-2-1-0

Conner, Archer; 1-0

Colmon, Thomas; 1-1

Colmon, Jesse; 1-0

Conner, Nicholas, and sons; 3-3

Conner, Charles; 1-2

Conner, John; 1-0

Chick, William; 1-2-6-0; ordinary license

Christian, John (mart.: merchant); 1-1-2-1

Coatney, Samuel; 1-1-0-1

Childres, John; 1-2

Childres, James; 1-0

Cabell, John, col.; 1-16-12-2

Chandler, Jesse; 1-2

Carter, Daniel; 1-1

Carter, George, and son; 2-2

Carter, Hulsey; 1-3

Coalmon, James, and son; 2-5-3-0

Colmon, John; 1-2

Carter, Amon; 1-2

Cock, David P.; 1-2

Christian, George; 1-0-4-0·

Colmon, Samuel; 1-5-6-2

Coleman, John, son of Sam'l;
1-1

Creasy, William; 1-1

Christian, John (H.); estate;
1-7-9-1

Cabell, Capt. Joseph; 1-27-29-7

Clark, Joseph, & sons; 3-9-5-0

Doss, Edward; 1-5-4-0

Doss, Jacob; 1-1

Doss, Reaney; 1-1

Doss, John; 1-2

Doss, Jesse; 1-2

Davidson, Edward; 1-5-0-1

Davidson, Josiah; 1-2

Davidson, Mary, Wr. (widow);
0-4-7-1

Drinkerd, Dancey; 1-1

Drinkerd, Archibald; 1-1

Doss, Berry; 1-1

Doss, Stuart; 1-3-1-0

Doss, James; 1-2-1-0

Doss, Solomon; 1-1

Duval, Samuel S.; 1-5-15-2; 1
stud horse

Doling, John; 1-2

Doling, John, Jr.; 1-1

Davidson, Stephen; 1-4

Day, John, and son Jas.; 2-3

Davis, Jesse; 1-0

Dibrell, Anthony, estate; 0-4-6-0

Day, Anderson; 1-1

Diuguid (or Giuguid), William;
1-20-20-2; 1 stud horse

Diuguid, George; 1-4-3-0

Duval, Philop; 1-7-20-3

Elerson, Thomas; 1-3

Elgin, John, & bro.; 1-3

East, Thomas; 1-1-2-0

Frealand, Mace & son; 2-7-7-2

Flowers, Andrew; 1-4

Flowers, Samuel (son Mary); 1-1

Flood, Moses; 1-4

Flood, Noah; 1-6-3-0

Flood, William; 1-0

Flood, John; 1-0-4-2

Flowers, John; 1-1-2-0

Forsey, Francis, & son;
2-5-4-3

Farguson, Joel, & son;
2-2

Fitz, Charles; 1-1-2-0

Flowers, Ralph, & son;
2-3-2-0

Flowers, Rev. William; 1-4-1-0

Faris, Valentine; 1-0

Farguson, John, merchant;
1-8-11-1

Flood, Capt. Henry; 1-13-18-3;
1 "coche" (coach)

Freeman, Isaac, mulatto; 1-0

Freeman, Peater, mulatto; 1-0

Farguson, Dougald; 1-5-6-0;
1 riding chair

Forster, William; 1-0

Farguson, John, Jr.; 1-1

Farguson, Moses; 1-1

Farguson, John, & son; 2-7

Farguson, Robert; 1-0-1-0

Farguson, Archibald; 1-2

Farguson, Thomas; 1-2

Fawell, Elisha; 1-1

Fawell, William; 1-1-0-1

Fawell, Richard; 1-0

Faris, Silvanus; 1-1--2-0

Faris, Jacob; 1-0

Farley, David; 1-1

Gotherd, John B.; 1-2

Gotherd, Shadrick; 1-1

Grifin, Zachariah; 1-2

Goyan, William & son; 2-2

Grigory, Edmond; 1-1-1-0

Grigory, Thomas; 1-3-1-0

Gillom, James; 1-2

Gillom, John, son Ditto;
1-2-1-0

Gibson, Miles, and sons;
3-3-4-1

Gibson, Labon; 1-2-3-0

Gary, John; 1-3-4-1

Glover, Stephen; 1-3-3-1

Gunter, Thomas; 1-4-3-2

Gunter, John; 1-1

Gillom, Richard; 1-2

Gillom, David; 1-1

Glover, Anthoney; 1-11-0-1

Glover, Edmond; 1-9-12-1

Garnet, John; 1-1

Glover, John, Jr.; 1-2

Gannaway, Grigory, & son; 2-6-4-1

Glover, Chesley; 1-6-3-1

Goleher, Charles; 1-2

Godfrey, John; 1-1

Garnet, Amsted; 1-2-1-1

Gaines, Barnet; 1-4-8-1; ordinary license

Gunter, William, & son; 2-2

Gunter, Edmond; 1-1

Garrott, Stephen, Jr.; 1-2

Garrott, Thomas, Jr.; 1-1

Hughes, Powel; 1-2-5-0

Hughes, Littleberry; 1-4-2-0

Hughes, Stephen; 1-4-2-0

Hughes, John; 1-1

Harris, Edmond; 1-3-2-0

Hardeman, Richard; 1-2-1-0

Hardeman, John, & sons; 3-8-4-1

Hardeman, John, Jr.; 1-1

Harrison, Benjamin; 1-3-6-0

Harris, John; 1-4-3-0

Harris, John, Jr.; 1-3-2-0

Hood, Hobson, and Nathl. Hood; 2-4-2-2

Hardwick, Benjamin; 1-5-3-0

Hardwick, William; 1-1

Hatcher, Josiah; 1-8-4-1; 1 stud horse

Hartgrove, William, & sons; 3-5

Harris, Obediah; 1-3-2-1

Harvey, Daniel; 1-3-1-0

Hall, Samuel; 1-3-1-0

Harrington, John, & son; 2-2

Hubbard, John; 1-2-1-0

Harris, Robert, son Jon.; 1-0

Irving, Charles, estate; 0-14-31-6

Jones, William, merchant; 1-7-7-1

Johnston, Philop; 1-2-1-0

Jones, John, & son Jon.; 2-7-6-0

Jones, Thomas, son Jon.; 1-3-1-0

Jones, Samuel; 1-3-3-2

Jones, John, estate; 0-4-11-0

Johnston, Richard; 1-5-12-1

Johnston, Christopher; 1-1

Johnston, Lewis; 1-0

Jones, Charles, son Abm.; 1-3

Jones, Flemsted; 1-4-1-0

Johnston, Benjamin; 1-0-1-0

Jurdan, Benjamin; 1-1

Jones, Arthur; 1-7-4-1

Jones, Charles; 1-5-9-1

Jones, John A., & sons; 3-14-17-2

Jones, William; 1-7-11-1

Jennings, William, estate; 0-3

Jennings, Samuel, exempt; 0-3-0-1

Jones, Michael, & sons; 3-5-4-1

Jones, Edward; 1-4-6-1

Jones, Josias, & sons; 3-7-7-4

Jones, Samuel; 1-1

Killey, George; 1-0

Kitchen, Bohanah; 1-2

Kitchen, John; 1-1-1-0

Kitchen, Elijey; 1-1

Kyle, David, & son; 2-10-11-2; 1 stud horse

Lain, James; 1-1

Lee, Guy; 1-1

Lain, Jesse; 1-3

Lain, David; 1-0

Leualen, Charles, & son; 2-5-1-2

Lawhorn, William; 1-1

Lewis, Wm., & Jack B. Lewis; 2-1-1-0

Langford, John ; 1-2-1-0

Lewis, Edward; 1-1; ordinary
  license

Lee, Grisham; 1-5-4-1

Lee, Benjamin; 1-1

Linthicum, Edward, & son; 2-5-2-2

Macgehee, William; 1-1

McClaird, Daniel; 1-1

Morris, Hudson; 1-2

Morris, Edward; 1-3

McCormick, David, son of Shed.;
  1-2

McCormack, Sherwood, & son;
  2-3

McCormack, Stephen; 1-1

McCormack, Benjamin; 1-1

Moseley, Robert (DC); 1-6-4-0

McFagin, William; 1-2

Maxey, Claiborn; 1-1-1-0

Maxey, Tirbefield; 1-1

McCraw, William; 1-3-3-0

Moseley, Capt. Daniel; 1-8-9-0;
  1 riding chair

Maxey, Nathaniel; 1-2-1-0

Moseley, Robert, Jr.; 1-4-5-1

Moseley, John, estate; 0-5-4-1

Moseley, Matthew, wid'r (prob.
  Martha Moseley); 0-1-3-0

Maxey, Benjamin; 1-1

Moseley, Arthur; 1-5-6-1

Mullins, Joel; 1-1

Moses, Henry, & son; 2-4

Moses, Peater, & son; 2-4

Moses, Peater, Jr.; 1-0

McCraw, Francis; 1-1-1-0

Maxey, Charles; 1-5-4-0

Maxey, Jacob; 1-0

Mercy, Prittiman; 1-8-8-5

Moseley, Robert; 1-5-8-1

Moseley, Daniel, Jr.; 1-1

May, Hugh; 1-0

Moseley, William, Sr.; 1-3-4-1

McManeway, John; 1-2

Moseley, Benjamin, & son; 2-5-8-1

McCormack, John; 1-1

Miller, Capt. George; 1-4-8-0;
  1 phaeton out of repair

Miller, Thomas, estate; 1-2-4-2

Moss, John; 1-0

Moss, John; 1-0

Moss, David; 1-0

Migginson, Joseph C.; 1-19-9-3;
  1 phaeton

Moore, Benjamin; 1-7-18-3

North, Richard, & son; 2-4-5-1

North, William; 1--2-1-0

North, Canthoney (or Anthonney);
  1-1-2-0

North, Thomas; 1-1-1-0

Neighbours, Nathan; 1-1-1-0

Nowlin, James A., & sons;
  3-3--1-0

Nowlin, Abraham; 1-2

Neighbours, John; 1-1

Neighbours, Francis; 1-1

Neighbours, Abraham; 1-1

Osbern, Thomas; 0-0-2-0; 1
  stud horse

Penn, George; 1-6-3-2

Pendleton, Benjamin; 1-3-1-0

Patteson, Edward, & son;
  2-4-1-0

Pendleton, Mace; 1-4-1-0

Pendleton, James; 1-2-1-0

Patteson, William (B. & son);
  2-3

Peak, Philop, & son; 2-5

Pamplin, Nicholas; 1-0; 1
  stud horse

Patteson, John, son Jas.;
  1-2-0-1

Page, Edmond; 1-0

Pritchard, John; 1-1-1-0

Plant, James; 1-1

Phelps, William; 1-4-5-3

Phelps, Richard; 1-4-4-0

Phelps, Alexander; 1-2-2-0

Phelps, Robert; 1-1-1-0; 1
  horse

Phelps, James, son Wm.; 1-0-1-0

Patteson, John (lame);
  1-10-9-3

Phelps, Charles, son Wm.; 1-2-3-0

Phelps, Charles; 1-3-1-0

Pankey, John; 1-2-3-0

Patteson, John, estate; 0-6-5-0

Patteson, Rev. Davis, & son;
2-3-5-2

Patteson, James, waterman; 1-1-2-0

Patteson, Charles Mart.; 1-2

Perkins, Samuel; 1-0-2-0

Poore, Elisha; 1-4

Pittmon, John, & sons; 2-6-9-4

Patteson, James, & sons;; 3-11-8-0

Parish, David; 1-5-7-0

Palmore, Joseph; 1-5-4-1

Patteson, Peater; 2-5-8-1; 1
riding chair

Patteson, Tarleton; 1-1

Perkins, William, Colo.;
4-10-9-2

Perkins, John; 2-3-4-1

Perkins, William, estate; 0-3-3-0

Rice, John; 1-3

Radford, John; 1-3-5-2

Rakes, William; 1-3

Rakes, David; 1-0

Rakes, Henry; 1-1

Runnels, William; 1-0

Rakes, Elisha; 1-0

Robertson, Hugh, & son; 2-1

Rives, Robert; 0-1-1-0

Roberts, John; 1-0

Radford, James; 1-4-2-0

Radford, William; 1-3-3-0

Routon, James; 1-5-2-0

Routon, John; 1-4-1-0

Radford, Benjamin; 1-2-3-0

Radford, Reubin; 1-1-0-1

Richerson, Robert; 1-2

Rakes, John; 1-2

Rakes, Anthoney; 1-3

Raglin, John; 1-2

Rogers, Capt. Robert; 1-5-4-0

Smith, William, & Ed'd;
2-2-2-0

Spencer, Moses; 1-5-6-2

Smith, Euriah; 1-2-1-0

Smith, Richard (or hard'm);
1-2-1-0

Spencer, David; 1-3

Smith, Robert, & sons;
5-5-2-1

Spencer, William, & son;
2-6-2-1

Smith, John, Fish Pond; 1-1

Swiney, Moses, & son;
2-6-5-0; 1 stud horse

Stephens, John; 1-7-7-1

Smith, Robert, Fish Pond;
1-1-2-0

Still, Jacob; 1-0

Smith, Hilery; 1-0

Stephens, William, & father;
2-6-5-1

Sanders, Samuel, & sons;
3-6-7-2

Sanders, Thomas, Jr.; 1-2-3-0

Smith, Obediah; 1-3

Staples, William; 1-3-2-1

Smith, George; 1-3-1-1; 1
stud horse

Smith, Patrick; 1-3

Smith, Dianah; 0-2-1-0

Smith, Shadrick; 1-4-0-1

Smith, Jacob; 1-3

Smith, Samuel; 1-1

Spears, John, & son James;
2-4-5-0

Spears, Samuel, estate;
0-1-3-0

Spears, John; 1-2-1-0

Spears, William; 1-1

Sanders, Thomas, & son
Fr. S.; 2-7-13-3

Still, John; 1-0

Spencer, Samuel; 1-3-3-0

Smith, Ely; 1-1

Still, William; 1-4

Spinner, Jesse; 1-2-1-0

Stuart, John; 1-0

Sears, John; 1-4-3-1

Smith, William (son B.); 1-2

Staples, Charles; 1-2

Staples, Thomas; 1-3-3-1

Staples, Youel John; 1-2

Taliaferro, Charles; 1-2-3-1

Taylor, Jarrott; 1-1 (maybe Tarlor)

Trail, Ashford; 1-0

Thornell, William; 1-3-2-0

Thornell, Jesse; 1-3-4-1

Thornell, Abselom; 1-4-4-0

Thomas, John, son of James; 1-1

Thomas, John, Capn.; 1-6-3-1

Talor, Thomas; 1-1

Tommas, Joseph; 1-2

Turner, William; 1-2

Turner, Nicholas; 1-2-1-0

Turner, John; 1-1

Turner, James; 1-0

Turner, Andrew, Jr.; 1-0

Turner, Andrew, EX (prob. for estate); 0-2

Talor, Joshuay; 1-7-1-0

Terry, Thomas; 1-2

Terry, John; 1-2-0-1

Terry, James; 1-2-0-1

Terry, Joseph; 1-1

Trent, Thomas, Ex'p' 0-4-2-1

Thompson, Mathew; 1-4-2-0

Thomas, James; 1-2

Urquehaert, John; 1-2-1-0

Vier, William; 1-1

Vier, Robert; 1-0

Vier, Littleberry; 1-4

Visey, Andrew; 1-2

Vest, John; 1-1

Wright, John, & son; 2-3

Wright, William; 1-1

Wright, James; 1-1-1-0

Williams, Samuel; 1-0

Woodroff, Hardin; 1-4-1-1

Williamson, William; 1-3

Williamson, Thomas; 1-3

Wade, William; 1-2-1-0

Wright, Thomas, Jr.; 1-0-0-1

Wright, John, Jr.; 1-1

Wright, John; 1-3

Walker, John, son Jon.; 1-3-4-1

Walker, James, son Do.; 1-5-5-1

Woodroff, Cap. John; 1-3-6-2

Walker, James, & F. Lew's; 2-12-12-4

Watson, George; 1-1

Walker, John (J. Ri?); 1-3-5-1

Williams, Moses; 1-0

Whitlock, Thomas; 1-3-3-1

Winkfield, Thomas, Jr.; 1-0-1-0

Woody, Henry; 1-1

Walker, Randolph; 1-2

Watkins, Silas; estate; 2-4-5-2

Wright, Robert; 1-2-3-0

Walker, Dr. James; 1-4-6-2

Webb, William, Jr., & son; 2-5-7-0

Webb, William; 1-2-5-1

Webb, Abraham; 1-5-2-0

Webb, Wintworth; 1-2-1-0

Webb, Joseph; 1-1

Webb, John; 1-1

Watson, William, & son; 2-5

Wilkerson, John; 1-1

Wooldredge, John; 1-0

Winkfield, Thomas; 1-4-7-1

Walker, Thomas, exempt; 0-1-0-1

Wilkerson, James, & son; 2-5-4-0

Welch, James; 1-3

Welch, Richard; 1-1

Welch, Robert; 1-0

Yancey, Charles; 1-9-12-2

Store Licenses

Rives, Robert, & Co.

Wills, Willis, & Co.

Christian, George, & Co.

Christian, John

# # #

CHAPTER THREE

MARRIAGES

Most of the marriage records of Buckingham County were destroyed. These few were found in the Virginia State Library, in Richmond.

Benjamin Abbott   Sarah Flowers   12 June 1786
   John Christian, bondsman.

John Adcock   Sally Wheeler   13 February 1787
   Thomas Parley, bondsman.

John Akers   Anne Jefferies   21 March 1785
   Abner Lee, bondsman.

James Anderson   Janie Guerrant   16 April 1787
   Peter Guerrant (bride's) father.

Darby Bundurant   Lucy Hall   12 June 1786
   Thomas Hall, Jr., bondsman.

Jacob Burton   Ann Hambleton   26 Jan. 1785

John Carden   Cathajane Davis   25 Nov. 1791
   Benjamin Davis (bride's) father.

Stephen Christian   Mary Amonet   (?) (?) 1786
   Wm. Amonet (bride's) father.

William Clarke   Frances Taylor   (?) (?) 1791
   Thomas McCormack, bondsman.

Fleming Duncan   Martha Scruggs   17 Feb. 1787
   Pleasant Saunders, bondsman.

Alexander Forbes   Lucy Scruggs   28 Jan. 1787
   B. M. Bartlett Davis, bondsman.

Charles Garrot   Cloe Agle   11 Dec. 1785
   John Agee, bondsman.

William Goss   Dicey Kidd   30 October 1785
   Isaac Salle, bondsman.

Zechariah Griffin   Elizabeth Beverly   18 Sept. 1786.
   Wm. Fuqua, bondsman. The groom's name may be Techariah.

Robert Hill   Sally Anderson   22 March 1786
   William Anderson (bride's) father.

Philip Howerton   Susanna Smith   28 July 1792
   Henry Smith (bride's) father.

Simon Huddleston   Lucy Page   (?) (?) 1786
   James Page (bride's) father.

Holloway Hudges   Nancy Berryman   8 February 1787
   Matthew Branch, bondsman.

John Jamison   Sarah Palmer   17 Nov. 1786
   William Johnson Berryman, bondsman.

Absolom Kidd   Lettice Owens   29 December 1786
   Jesse Kidd, bondsman.

Elisha Lox (or Lax)   Mary Neighbours   12 June 1786
   William Phelps, bondsman.

Thomas McCormack Daniel Taylor (bride's) father.	Mary Taylor	7 Sept. 1791
Joseph Martin	Magdalene Lutteral	8 June 1787
Thomas Moss William Toney (bride's) father.	Betsey Toney	21 February 1787
Thomas Parley James Bristow, bondsman.	Winnie Adcock	17 Nov. 1785
James Price John Strong, bondsman.	Elizabeth Strong	15 Feb. 1794
James Taylor Thomas Harris, bondsman.	Nancy Wooten	16 December 1784
(?) Terry	Lucy Lax	date not given
Joseph Tomson Stephen Garrit or Garrot (bride's) father.	Susannah Garrit	15 June 1787
John Walker Edward Herndon, bondsman.	Mary Kidd	28 Jan. 1786
James Wheeler John Welch, bondsman.	Elizabeth Welch	20 June 1786
Stephen Wright Peter Ford, bondsman.	Peggy Brooks	1 Nov. 1784

CHAPTER FOUR

MILITARY RECORDS:

REVOLUTIONARY, WAR OF 1812, ETC.

COMPANY OF MINUTE MEN UNDER CAPT. NICHOLAS CABELL, 17 NOVEMBER 1775 THROUGH
6 DECEMBER 1775

(This list of Minute Men, in Battalion Duty at Pond Field Camp, was found in
Collection No. 5084, Box 1, at the Alderman Library, University of Virginia,
Charlottesville. The numbers in parentheses following the names of individ-
ual soldiers indicate "Distance" on the original list, and probably indicate
distance from soldier's residence to the place of muster or place of discharge-
ED.)

p. 1.　Lieut. John Gilmer (8)
　　　Ens. Benjamin Taliaferro (20)
　　　Sgt. Maj. James Barnett (20)
　　　Sgt. Maj. John Thomas (40)
　　　Joseph Neal (40)
　　　Ralph Jopling (40)
　　　James Becknett (40)

　　　George Phillips (40)
　　　Hezekiah Hartgrove (30)
　　　Edward Harper (20)
　　　William Cawthon (20)
　　　James M. (?) Alexander, Jr. (18)
　　　John Fitzgerald (20)

p. 2　George Hite (25)
　　　Benjamin Wright, Jr. (25)
　　　Reuben Nevill (40)
　　　Thomas Smith (20)
　　　Brannard West (40)
　　　John Patterson (40)
　　　John Bones (18)
　　　John Johnson
　　　Thomas Griffin
　　　William Powell
　　　Thomas Hawkins

　　　Joseph Dicken
　　　George Creasy
　　　Benjamin Clark (5)
　　　Azariah Martin (1½)
　　　William M. Ansley or Andley
　　　Littleberry Witt
　　　Henry Randolph (40)
　　　Clough Shelton (40)
　　　John Jordon (60)
　　　David Balloe

p. 3　Jno. Willis
　　　Jno. M. (?) Alexander (18)
　　　Robert Horsley (40)
　　　Walter Lockard (18)
　　　Austin Smith
　　　John Carpenter (16)
　　　Joseph Canterberry (16)
　　　John Willis (2)
　　　James Roark (40)

　　　John Dever (20)
　　　John Laine
　　　Minos Wright (30)
　　　Matthew Cartwright (30)
　　　Reuben Griffin (20)
　　　John Taylor (12)
　　　Elliot(?) Reed, Jr. (13)
　　　William Jones
　　　Isaac Hilt

p. 4　Daniel Dunimon (?)
　　　John Horsley
　　　Josias Jones
　　　John Wyatt Gilbert
　　　Julius Golden

　　　Allen Blair
　　　Samuel Staples, Jr.
　　　James Enix
　　　John Bowman
　　　Samuel Allen

MILITIA OFFICERS ASSOCIATED WITH BUCKINGHAM COUNTY

177-? Capt. William Duguid's Company of Guard at Albemarle Barracks (26).
1781 - Capt. Wm. Perkins' Company in Battle of Hot Water and Jamestown
　　　(26).

49

1781 - Capt. Silas Watkins' Company at the Siege of Yorktown (26).
1781 - Capt. Wm. Giles' Company at the Siege of Yorktown (26).

ABSTRACTS OF REVOLUTIONARY PENSION APPLICATIONS

(The originals are at the National Archives in Washington, D. C. - ED).

ARNOLD, BENJAMIN, b. 28 Jan. 1762 in Buckingham Co., Va., and d. after 1833 in White Co., Tenn.

He stated he was drafted in Laurens Co., S. C., and served as a private in Capt. Ford's Co., Col. Cleveland's Regt., S. C. Militia.

He was placed on the Pension Roll in West Tennessee under the Act of 1832. After the War he lived in Amherst Co., Va., for about 2 years, then for 15 years in Henry Co., Va., for 5 years in Rowan Co., N.C., and then he moved to South Carolina where he remained for about 12 years, then he moved to Warren Co., Tenn. (Pens. S.2920).

BEACKHAM, WILLIAM, applied for a pension in 1819, and gave his in 1821 as 63. He stated he was born in Amherst Co., Va.

At the time of his application, he and his wife Sally, aged 58, had a daughter Susanna, aged 14. (Pens. S.37738).

BISHOP, STEPHEN, drew a pension in Buckingham Co., for his service as a Revolutionary Soldier (Pens. S. 37770).

BLALOCK, JOHN, and wife POLLY; in 1822 he declared in Carter Co., Tenn., aged 70, that he enlisted in Buckingham Co., Va. He stated he was born in Brunswick Co., Va., on 4 Sept. 1762, and that he later moved to Burke Co., N.C. (Pens. W.1807; BLWt. 24979-160-55).

BROWN, LEWIS, was b. c.1761, and d. 14 Feb. 1815. He married in May 1787 in Buckingham Co., Va., Clarissa Smith, who was 71 in 1842 and 87 in 1855 when she applied for bounty land. She stated she and her husband were married by a Baptist preacher named Rene Chastain or Shelteen, and that the marriage was recorded in Buckingham Co.

Lewis Brown resided in Henrico Co., Va., with his father Joseph Brown before the War. He was a soldier in the Infantry in 1784, and was paid by the State of Virginia.

In 1842 when Clarissa applied for a pension, son John Brown, age 54, made a statement. She was placed on the Pension Roll in Nashville, Tenn., under the Acts of 1838, 1843, and 1848. In 1848 she applied for a continuance of the pension.

BROWN, STEPHEN, was b. c.1756 in Cumberland Co., Va., and d. by 31 Aug. 1837. He lived in Buckingham Co. during the Revolution, and served in the Virginia Militia under Capt. Redd, guarding British prisoners.

He moved to Bledsoe Co., Tenn., about 30 years after the War. His discharge was destroyed when his house burned about 1813, but he stated he could prove his service by Charles Thurman, also of Bledsoe Co., who served in the same Regiment. The arrears of his pension were paid on 31 Aug. 1837 to a child of his.

CHARLTON, JACOB, applied for a pension on 12 May 1834 from Hawkins Co., Tenn, stated he would be 92 years old next April, and declared he was b. in James City Co., Va., on 25 April 1743. A record was kept by the clerk of the Church of England either at Hickory Neck Church or Warnen Eye (Warrany) Church.

He was living in Powhatan Co., Va., when he entered service as a draftee under Capt. Isaac Porter in September 1777. He marched to Westham Ferry on the James River, where he was stationed to watch the river and prevent a British force from ascending the river. He was also to prevent the Tories from passing and repassing to the enemy. He served three months and returned home.

He was drafted again under Capt. Thomas Miller in Buckingham Co., Va., in the fall of 1779 (He thinks the month was September as he had pulled down some of his fodder but had not taken it up, and had to leave it in that condition) He returned home on Christmas Eve.

From Buckingham Court House his company was marched to Chesterfield Court House. They remained there a few days to rest and draw provisions, then they marched through Petersburg to Surry Church and Mackey's Mill. Here they joined the grand army. The morning after their arrival, they were preparing breakfast when they received information from an express that the British were landing below Suffolk Town, but when they reached Suffolk the British had taken alarm and had departed.

He remained there until his three months had expired, and returned to Petersburg where his company received thanks for the courage they had displayed in driving the British from the shore. After having his canteen filled with brandy, he received his discharge signed by Capt. Miller.

He was living in the same county when he was drafted under Capt. Richard Crump in the latter part of the Summer of 1781. From Buckingham Court his company marched through Petersburg to Nusum Spring on James River, where they were stationed about six weeks or two months, waiting for an express. They were to see that no one ascended the river. They remained in sight of the cannonade at Little York and could see the bombs bursting in the firmament. While stationed there they received an express that Wallis (i.e., Cornwallis) had surrendered. All the forces were marched into Yorktown where they were dismissed and he returned home. He served about three months.

He is now confined to his bed, probably with his last spell of sickness. He lived in Buckingham Co., then moved to Sullivan Co., Tenn., and later went to Hawkins Co., Tenn., where he has lived for the last fourteen years.

Jacob Charlton of Hawkins Co., Tenn., private in the company of Capt. Porter in the Virginia Militia for nine months, was placed on the Pension Roll at Jonesborough, Tenn., at $30.00 per annum, under the Act of 1832. Certificate was issued on 11 June 1834. (Pens. S.3149).

CHAUDOIN, or CHADDAIN, JAMES. (The name is also spelled Chadoin or Shaddain). On 3 Oct. 1832 in Franklin Co., Ill., John (X) Chaudoin of said county, age 71, stated he was b. in Chesterfield Co., Va., on 16 Nov. 1761. He has a record of age taken from a register kept by his father.

He was living in Buckingham Co., Va., in Feb. 1777 when he entered the service as a substitute for Peter Lashure who was drafted in a three month tour of duty as a militiaman. His service expired about the time of Cornwallis' surrender, but a portion of the militia was retained in service for about three weeks to guard some prisoners at Winchester.

Chaudoin died before 30 March 1848 when Sary (X) Chaddoin of Hamilton Co., Ill., gave her age as 82, and stated she was the widow of John Chaddoin, commonly called John Shaddoin. She stated she was married in February 1778 in Chesterfield Co., Va., and her maiden name was Sary Wilkerson, daughter of Thomas and Susanna Wilkerson. The marriage was performed by Rev. Eleazer Clay, minister of the Gospel. Her husband died 21 June 1843. She submits a leaf from the family record, each entry written about the time the child was born.

Malindy, b. 12 May 1812.
John Phenix, b. 13 May 1812.
William Phenix, b. 13 May 1814.
Morris Chaudoin, b. 11 Oct. 1832.
Mary Chaudoin, b. 23 Nov. 1834.
Claborn Chaudoin, b. 18 June 1836.
Sary Chaudoin, b. 16 Sept. 1838.
John Chaudoin, b. Nov. 1761.
(?), his wife, b. 1769.
(?) Chaudoin, b. Feb. 1789.
Susannah Chaudoin, b. 16 Aug. 1790.
(Sarah?) Chaudoin, b. 25 June 1792.
Mary Chadoin, b. 1 Dec. 179-?
Andrew Chaudoin, b. 25 Dec. 1795.
(Joh)n Chaudoin, b. 9 April 1798.
(Charity?) Chaudoin, b. 16 Aug. 1800.
(Jesse?) Chaudoin, b. 30 July 1802.
(Thurza?) Chaudoin, b. 6 July 1804.
Matthew Chaudoin, b. 13 (?) 1806.

The clerk of Chesterfield Co., Va., reported he could find nothing relative to the marriage of John Shaddoin and Sarah Wilkerson, except the certificate of Eliazer Clay setting forth that he had celebrated the rites of matrimony between them, and returned by Clay to the June 1778 Term.

On 18 Aug. 1848, Hamilton Co., Ill., Sarah (X) Chaudoin of said county, aged 83, applied for continuance of pension.

John Chaudoin of Franklin Co., Ill., a private in the company of Capt. Dugar, Col. Cavill's Regt., Va. Line, for nine months and twenty-one days, was placed on the Illinois Pension Roll at $32.34 per annum, under the Act of 1832. Cert. no. 7816 was issued 6 April 1833.

Sarah Chaudoin, widow of John (who died 21 June 1843), was placed on the Illinois Pension Roll at $32.34 per annum. Cert. no. 8319 under the Act of 1843 and 1844 was issued 18 July 1848. (Pens. W.22745).

CHENAULT, JAMES, aged about 61, declared in Buckingham Co., Va., on 22 April 1819 he enlisted with Capt. Henry Terrel in the 5th Va. Regt. of Col. Josiah Parker for two years, in 1776 or 1777. He was at the Battles of Brandywine and Germantown, and at the capture of Gen. Burgoyne at Saratoga. He was discharged at Valley Forge, and gave his discharge to an officer to obtain his pay.

James Chenault of Buckingham Co., Va., private in the Regt. of Col. Parker in the Va. Line for two years, was placed on the Va. Pension Roll at $8.00 per month from 22 April 1819, under the Act of 1818. Cert. no. 12540 was issued 21 July 1819. (Pens. S.39296).

CHILDERS, ABRAHAM, of Perry Co., Ky., aged 82 years on previous 15 Nov., on 17 Oct. 1832 declared he enlisted about six months before the Battle of Brandywine, in Amherst Co., Va., where he then lived, under Capt. Samuel Campbell (or Cavill or Cabell), in Col. Meriwether's Regt. He was placed in the 4th or 5th Va. Regt., made a cook, and served eighteen months. He was detached under Capt. Pamphlin, served three years, and discharged at Winchester, Va., about one month after Cornwallis' surrender. He was at Amherst, Bottom's Bridge, Morbin (Malvern?) Hill, and Four Mile Creek, and was never out of Virginia except for a trip to Guilford CourtHouse, where he could hear the guns, and except for his trip to Maryland, and the Battle of Brandywine, where he was wounded in the left thigh. He stated he was born in Buckingham Co., but had no proof of his age.

By 24 July 1834 he had moved from Perry Co. to Lawrence Co., Ky., where he made a statement.

Depositions were made by:

John Childers, aged 44, on 6 May 1849, Owsley Co., Ky.; grandson of Abraham Childers; stated his grandfather claimed to be a cook in the 5th Va., heard his grandfather mention Moses Fleetwood of the same company who was wounded while trying to pick some apples; stated his great-uncle Moseby Childers was killed at Brandywine; his grandfather Abraham died in what is now Letcher Co., Ky., on 6 May 1849.

William Childers, in Owsley Co., Ky., on 11 March 1854, stated his father, Abraham, died in April 1849 leaving children: William, Francis, Polly, Dicy, Abraham, Jr., Elizabeth, Goldsby, and Seley. William's mother, Elizabeth, died 17 Feb. 1833.

Patrick Masterson, 25 April 1855, Owsley Co., Ky., deposed he knew Abraham before he entered service. Masterson served under Col. Muhlenberg and Jonathan Langdon from about the 1st of June before the Siege of Stony Point, and stated he saw Childers in that desperate slaughter, and later saw him at Washington's encampment at Morristown. Masterson was discharged a little after the defeat of Yorktown.

Patrick Masterson, 18 April 1855, Owsley Co., Ky., stated that Abraham Childers was an enlisted soldier from the River Tiney or Pye, Amherst Co., Va., and got acquainted with Childers at Washington's stay at Williamsburg.

Alexander Patrick stated he took affidavits of Hiram Polly and Archilles Craft, but is unable to tell what became of the proof. He once attempted to take Childers' affidavit, but on all public occasions he would get intoxicated so his statement was neglected. At one time he proposed to go to Lawrence Co., Ky., to take the proof of Micajer Fresheur, Joseph Newman, Josiah Marcum, Adam Crum, and George Hardwick, all Va. soldiers.

Thomas Fleetwood (Fleatwood) was a soldier who claimed to have been at Gates' defeat at Camden.

Masterson enlisted under Jonathan Langlin and Col. Hughlinberg (or Muhlenberg).

Thomas Francis, 17 Sept. 1855, Letcher Co., Ky., aged 81, stated he had lived in the county for 29 years, and had known Abraham Childers for 60 years. He claimed to have served under Gen. Washington as a cook.

James (X) Collins, 21 Sept. 1855, Letcher Co., Ky., stated he had lived in the county for 35 years, and has known Abraham Childers for 50 years.

William Childers, in his 68th year, 6 Oct. 1855, Owsley Co., Ky., stated he was the son of Abraham Childers who employed Elisha Smith and Alexander Patrick to attend to his business. He (Abraham -ED) was addicted to drink and upon public occasions he most generally got so drunk he was not capable of attending to any business. The deponent often heard his father say that one Fleetwood, who served with him perhaps at the Battle of Camden, was wounded in the hand by a British musket ball while attempting to pull off a bunch of apples, during the American retreat. Col. Ephraim Mayfield was one of the officers. William Childers moved to Indiana in 1837 and never returned to Letcher Co. The balance of the children spread in different directions. Patrick started once to the Sandies to take the affidavits of Joseph Numan, Joseph Marcum, Adam Crum and Neager Fasher, who were in his company, but they are all dead. He was frequently requested to take the affidavit of Patrick Masterson who would identify him as being in service under Washington, at Stoney Point, Morristown, etc., and Col. Meriwether at Williamsburg while Washington was encamped there before the capture of Cornwallis. William Childers has been a member of the Reformed Church for many years.

Joseph (X) Mullins, 18 Oct. 1855, Owsley Co., Ky., stated he had known Abraham Childers, late of Perry Co., for 41 years, and that (Abraham) was "addicted to intoxication," but when he was sober he was a man of truth.

Stephen (X) Arthur, 18 Nov. 1856, Powell Co., Ky., stated he was born on 9 March 1760 and knew Abraham Childers, late of Perry Co., Ky.; Arthur was raised in Bedford Co., Va., and Childers was raised in the adjoining county of Amherst, but in the same neighborhood. After the conclusion of the War Childers moved to Buckingham Co., Va. Childers entered service some time before Arthur did, but Arthur was present when Abraham Childers, William Childers, Moseby Childers, Moses Fleetwood, John Fleetwood, Joseph Tuman and others enlisted. (Pens. R.1922).

CHILDERS (or CHILDRESS), PATTERSON, and wife NANCY. On 2 May 1844 in Jefferson Co., Tenn., Mrs. Nancy (X) Childress, aged 76 years, declared she was the widow of Patterson Childress who enlisted in 1778 in Buckingham Co., Va., under Capt. Leonard Boler for three years. She married Patterson Childress on 12 May 1784. Her husband died 12 September 1831.

Joseph (X) Janeway, aged 71, res. of Jefferson Co., Tenn., where on 3 May 1844 he stated he knew Patterson and Mary Childress from 1784 until Patterson's death in 1831. Janeway saw Patterson discharged from service in Surry Co., N. C., after Cornwallis surrendered, and understood that his (Patterson's) term as a regular soldier for three years had expired.

Nancy Hamilton, heir-at-law of Nancy Childers or Childress, widow of Patterson Childers, submitted a memorial in Knox Co., Tenn., where said Nancy resided at Mecklenburg. On 15 April 1853 Nancy Hamilton wrote from Knox Co. that her post office was now Flint Gap, Tenn. On 9 May 1853 Nancy Hamilton, as heir-at-law of Nancy Childress, gave a power of attorney from Sevier Co., Tenn., to prosecute her claim.

The State of North Carolina issued a specie certificate for £ 31.6.4 to P. Childers. (Pens. R.1928).

CHILDERS, PLEASANT, and wife SARAH. Pleasant Childers stated he was born in 1759 in Virginia, married Sarah Jeffries (or Jeffrey) on 16 April 1785 in Buckingham Co. Pleasant died in Pike Co., Ky., on 24 April 1839.

He enlisted for nine months about July 1780 in Warren Co., N. C., and was assigned to the 6th N. C. Regt., Continental Line. He was at the Battle of Guilford Court House on 15 March 1781. Soon after this battle, his term was up, and he was discharged by General "Linkhorn." He stated that he applied for a pension from Floyd Co., Ky., and on 25 Feb. 1822 was granted a pension of $96.00 per annum. His wife Sarah died 10 August 1843 in Pike Co., Ky., survived by children Lucy, Elizabeth, Sally, Jesse (who married Sallie Belcher in 1821 in Pike Co., Ky.), Nathaniel, Pleasant, and Flemon. Nathaniel was living in Pikeville, Ky., in 1851. Judge J. W. Childress, Judge of Pike County Circuit Court, wrote on 20 December 1928 to the War Department for the record of Pleasant Childers, doubtless the ancestor of Judge Childress. (Pens. R. 1924)

CHRISTIAN, THOMAS, and wife MARY. On 11 Oct. 1841 in Buckingham Co., Va., Christian, then 81 years, declared he entered service as a drafted militiaman in Buckingham Co., where he was born, and has since resided, in the Company Capt. Thomas Anderson. He marched to the barracks in Albemarle Co., Va., where he remained three months guarding British prisoners. He was discharged and returned home.

He was again drafted in Buckingham Co., in Capt. Charles Patterson's Company, Lieut. John Brookes and Ens. William Beckham, and marched to Blandford and then to Cabin Point, where the company drew their arms, and was placed under Col. Charles Fleming of Gen. Muhlenberg's Regt. Christian remained at Cabin Point for some time and then marched to Stoner Mills in Surry Co., and from there to Suffolk Town, where the army remained until he was discharged. Soon after he returned home and heard of the defeat of the British at Yorktown.

His discharge from Capt. Charles Patterson was kept for many years and was destroyed when his house burned. The affidavit of John Doland, filed in the pension papers of James Falwell, was taken jointly by him and Falwell.

James (X) Falwell, in Buckingham Co., 29 Sept. 1841, declared he was drafted as a private and militiaman under Capt. William Anderson, and that Thomas Christian of the said County marched in the same company and served the same time. He and Thomas Christian were again drafted as private militiamen under Capt. Charles Patteson, and marched to Blandford and Cabin Point and were put under Capt. Charles Fleming. They marched to Mackey's Mills or Stoner's Mill, and then to Suffolk Town, at which place they were discharged after a tour of three months.

Miles Gipson of Buckingham Co., on 24 Feb. 1842, declared that for several years he has been Steward of the Poor House, and that Christian never resided at the Poor House, but was permitted to reside in the neighborhood with his family. He sent Christian to the Court with Falwell. Christian is old, very poor and lame and can only get about a little on crutches.

Mary (X) Christian, 14 Aug. 1854, aged 56, declared she was the widow of Thomas Christian, whom she married on 6 July 1814 at her father's house by Rene Chastain, M. G., and that her name was Mary Adcock. Her husband died at home on 3 October 1853.

The clerk of Buckingham County certifies that Thomas Christian and Mary Adcock were married on 6 July 1814.

Mary Christian repeated her former deposition on 29 March 1855.

Sterling G. Apperson on 9 July 1855, also declared that Thomas Christian died on 3 October 1853.

Thomas Christian, of Buckingham Co., private in the company of Capt. Patterson of the Va. Line for six months, was placed on the pension roll at Richmond, Va., at $20.00 per annum under the Act of 1832. Certificate No. 31946 was issued 5 May 1842.

Mary Christian, widow of Thomas Christian, was placed on the pension roll at Richmond, Va., at $20.00 per annum. Certificate 5362 under the Act of 1853, to commence 3 October 1853, was issued on 22 July 1855. Bounty Land Warrant 28656 for 160 acres was issued 2 June 1856 (Pens. W. 25409; BLWt. 28656-160-55.).

CLAIBORNE (or CLIBORNE), LEONARD, and wife Frances. On 14 April 1834 in Chesterfield Co., Va., Claiborne, then of Buckingham Co., Va., stated he was born and raised in Chesterfield Co., and was a resident of that county when the Revolutionary War started, and for some time after the war. Now 73 years, he further stated that in April 1779 he entered service under Capt. Creed Haskins and Lieut. John Robertson and marched to Warebottom Church, and then crossed the James River, then to Byrd's to Westover and recrossed the river, then down the river and crossed and went to Williamsburg where he stayed some time in the barracks, then marched to York, where he was discharged. Col. Robert Goode commanded the regiment. Claiborne served two months, and in in the fall of 1780 joined a volunteer company assembled by Capt. Creed Haskins (he thinks John Trabue was a subaltern), and marched from Chesterfield Court House to Randolph's Mill in the said county, then through Petersburg, Price George, Nansemond, and the low counties, and returned to Smithfield and then to Cabin Point, and up to the Burnt Mills and then to Petersburg, where he was discharged, having again served two months.

In April 1781 he entered service again, as a substitute for Joel Foulks near Blackwater under Capt. Henry Cheatham and Lieut. John Farmer. Arnold and Phillips drove them up to Petersburg and there they had a fight with the British. The night before the fight they lay upon their arms. Major Holt prepared them for battle. The next day was April 25th. The battle commenced and they were taken from where they were and marched down the river below Pocohantas and again prepared for battle. Part of the company went down the river and fired at the British boats. Then they drove up to the courthouse. On the 26th, Col. Goode was called out with the militia and met them at Chesterfield Courthouse. About this time, Foulks took his place and he took his own under Capt. Creed Haskins. Then they marched to the coal pits and crossed the river at Tuckahoe, and went from there to Richmond and to Bottom's Bridge. While there, the pressment ried to take Capt. Haskins' horse. He was then discharged. Claiborne served fifteen days for Foulks as a substitute, and fifteen days for himself.

About 20 May 1781 they were called out under Capt. Creed Haskins, Lieut. John Robertson and Col. Goode. They marched to Manchester and formed on the hill and drew some guns. The British were then in Richmond and burned Rocky Ridge Warehouse. They marched from there to Col Cary's and passed Col. Cary's mills while they were burning, went to Swift Creek Mills and were stationed there until the British left Richmond, then marched to Petersburg, and from there to Mackey's Mills, and were discharged. He served about six weeks.

In the summer after Sudberry's defeat they were again called out under Capt. Archer Walthall, and met at Chesterfield Courthouse, and marched to Manchester, and crossed the river, then down to the Brick House or West Point and then to Hubbard's Old Field in Gloucester, where they were stationed for a while. At Gloucester an alarm was given and they were prepared for action. Two companies of light infantry and some riflemen were called to go down upon the lines. While there, the British came for Parson Price. They marched to the lines. The main army marched back to Hubbard's Old Field where they were discharged. As he was on the lines under Capt. Burk and Maj. Wicks he was kept three weeks longer. He served two months and twenty-one days.

William Goode, Sr., declared on 14 April 1834 in Chesterfield Co. that he served in the Revolutionary War on the two tours first mentioned by Mr. Claiborne. John (X) Condry declared he served the first tour with Claiborne in Capt. Creed Haskins' Company, and that they were all boys together.

Frances (X) Claiborne, declared in Buckingham County on 13 Sept. 1841, that she married Leonard Claiborne on 27 November 1788, and that he died on 9 December 1839. On 31 May 1843, at age 76 years, she declared the same information. On this latter date Thomas O. Claiborne also declared that Leonard Claiborne died on 9 December 1839.

Leonard Claiborne and Fanny Turner were married in Amelia County, with a marriage bond dated 13 Nov. 1788. Robert Tanner was security.

Frances Claiborne, aged 80, applied for a continuance of the pension in Buckingham Co., on 4 November 1848.

Leonard Claiborne of Chesterfield Co., Va., private in the Regt. of Col. Goode in the Va. Line for eight months and three days, was placed on the Virginia pension roll at $27.00 per annum under the Act of 1832. Certificate no. 23924 was issued on 21 April 1834. Frances Claiborne of Buckingham Co., widow of Leonard Claiborne, who died 9 Dec. 1839, was placed on the pension roll at Richmond, Va., at $27.00 per annum. Certificate 7556 under the Act of 1838 was issued 23 August 1843. Cert. no. 4318 under the Act of 1843 was issued 17 Jan. 1844, and Cert. no. 3557 under the Act of 1848 was issued on 31 January 1849. (Pens. W.3388).

COBB (COBBS), FLEMING, and wife SALLY. Cobbs stated on 11 June 1833 in Kanawha Co., Va., that he was 66 years old, was born in December 1767 in Buckingham Co., Va., in 1787 moved to Albemarle Co., and in 1789 moved to Kanawha County. In Feb. or March 1791 he enlisted as an Indian Spy under Col. George Clendenin; was a soldier defending Clendenin's Frontier or Elk Fort under Capt. William Clendenin; in spring of 1793 enlisted as a First Sgt. under Capt. Moses Mann; frequently went scouting with Col. Thomas Lewis, Maj. Leonard Cooper, and Capt. Mann; was drafted the last of February 1791, or the first of March 1791, and had as assistant spies Charles McClung, David Robinson, Joe Burrell, and Tom LeMasters. After his discharge in November he lived with Thomas Upton and family; later he had as companions John Young and John Morris.

Andrew Donnally deposed on 11 June 1833 in Kanawha Co. that he has known Fleming Cobb since 1790.

Martin Hammock deposed 11 June 1833, Kanawha Co. that he has known Cobb since March 1792.

Michael (X) Newhouse deposed 11 June 1833 he has known Cobb since 1790.

John Young deposed 11 June 1833 he has known Cobb since 1790.

Michael Newhouse deposed 11 August 1852 that Cobbs enlisted and served under Capt. William Clendenin.

Thomas Casdorph deposed 25 May 1854 that Cobbs served in the Indian Wars of 1791, 1792, and 1793, and that Cobbs died about 8 years ago at the age of 70.

Sarah (X) Cobbs, aged 79 years, deposed 12 June 1854 she was the widow Fleming Cobbs; that he served in the Indian Wars of 1791, 1792, and 1793; that as Sarah Morris she was married 10 January 1796; that her husband died at his residence on the Kanawha River near Charleston on 10 January 1846.

Thomas A. Cobbs deposed on 13 June 1854 that the entries on the book containing the family record are in the handwriting of Fleming Cobb, and that the book is now in the possession of his widow Sarah Cobbs. The Book states:

Fleming Cobbs was born 25 December 1767 and married
    Sally Morris 10 January 1796.
Sally Cobbs his wife was born
Fleming Cobbs his book bought out Arbuckle's store
    20 March 1806.

William Wood, justice of the peace for Kanawha Co., deposed on 27 Nov. 1854 that he has known Cobb since 1809.

Mrs. Katherine Venable deposed 20 November 1854 that she came to Kanawha Co. when 9 or 10 years of age and she knew Cobb as a soldier at the fort; that Cobb married a near relative of hers; and that he lived a close neighbor to her until he died.

A payroll of Lieut. Mann's command of volunteer militia embodied for the defense of Greenbrier and Kanawha for the year 1793 shows that Fleming Cobb served as a sergeant from 1 January 1793 to 27 September 1793 and received total pay of $28.25.

Sally (X) Cobb, aged 81, deposed on 3 November 1855 that she was the widow of Fleming Cobb who was a private in the Virginia militia in the Revolutionary War for 1 year.

The clerk of Kanawha County reports that among the marriage returns for 1796 prformed by James Johnson is: Fleming Cobb to Sarah Morris.

Bounty land warrant No. 83776 for 160 acres of land was issued 25 September 1858 to Sally Cobb, widow of Fleming Cobb. (Pens. No. BLWt. 83776-160-55; BLWt. 26996-160-55; O. W. Inv. File 2072).

CONNER, ARTHUR, and ELLENA his wife. On 20 December 1842 in Buckingham County, Va., Ellena (X) Conner, aged 85 years, stated she was the widow of Arthur Conner who was a sergeant in the Continental and militia service of Virginia. She knew when he enlisted and that he was gone a long time, at least five years. They lived in the same neighborhood at the time he entered service, although they were married subsequently to the expiration of the last period of his service. He was engaged in several battles and she recollects the battle of Charleston, South Carolina. She was married in October 1783, and her husband died 22 September 1831.

J. H. Routon wrote from New Store, Va., on 21 March 1843 that he has sent the certificates of exchange, and also an original discharge given at Camp Ashley Hill, S. C., as a Regular in the Va. Line to the Continental Establishment dated 9 Sept. 1782, signed by Jas. Harmar, Lt. Col. D. Adj. Gen.:

"This is to certify that Arthur Connor has been regularly Exchanged for one of the One Hundred & Ninety-Nine Continental Prisoners, as Specified in Major Edm'd Mass'bd Hyrn's Certificate, dated 30 June last. Charlestown, 10 Sept. 1781. Signed James Frazer, Com. Prisoners."

Edmond A. Conner of Prince Edward Co., Va., submitted the Register of the Births of the children of Arthur Conner and Ellena, alias Eleanor, his widow. It is in the handwriting of Meshack Boaz who died several years ago. The register has been in his possession for the last twenty-four or twenty-five years: submitted 6 April 1843 in Buckingham Co., Va.

"These are the children of Arthur and Eleanor Conner
John Conner was born 19 January 1784.
Edmund Archdacon Conner was born 19 November 1785.
Molley Conner was born 18 January 1788.
Elenor Conner, daughter of Arthur and Elenor, was born 13 December 1787.
Charles Conner, son of Arthur and Elenor, was born 27 December 1791.
Sallye Conner, daughter of Arter and Elenor Conner, was born 7 January 1794.
Luke Conner, son of Arter and Elenor, was born 19 February 1796.
Arter Conner, son of Arter and Elenor, was born 22 August 1798.

Meshach Boaz, aged 66 years, on 4 Jan. 1843 in Buckingham Co., Va., stated he remembered when Arthur Conner returned from the Revolutionary War and was married to an aunt of Boaz, and he thinks Arthur and Ellena were married about 1783. John Conner who was their oldest child was born in 1784, and Arthur died in September 1831 leaving several children and grandchildren.

Elizabeth (X) Boaz, aged 88 years, on 28 June 1843 in Buckingham Co., Va., stated she knew Arthur Conner before he went into the Revolutionary War. He lived in the family with her stepmother until he was married to his present widow, Ellinor Conner. He enlisted in 1778, and was gone until the fall of 1782.

Maj. Samuel Baldwin, aged 78, on 21 Sept. 1843 in Prince Edward Co., Va., stated he was raised in the same county and neighborhood with Arthur Conner. He enlisted under Capt. John Morton about 1777 or 1778, served out the time for which he enlisted and returned to the same county where he lived until he moved to Buckingham.

Ellena (X) Conner, aged 86 years, on 6 Aug. 1844, in Buckingham Co., Va., applied for continuance of pension. She was the widow of Arthur Conner who died 22 Sept. 1831, private in the Va. Line for two years, and who was placed on the Richmond, Va., Pension Roll at $80.00 per annum. Cert. no. 8572 under the Act of 1838 was issued 30 July 1844, and cert. no. 6024 under the Act of 1843 and 1844 was issued 22 Aug. 1844. (Pens. no. W.6733).

CORNETT (CORNIT), WILLIAM, and wife MARY. (Rev. Pension W. 6723; N.A. Acc. No. 874, 050036. Notation says "Not Half Pay." On 12 Aug. 1833 in Perry Co., Ky., William Cornett of said county, aged 71 years, stated he was born in Henrico Co., Va., enlisted in 1779 for six months in Buckingham Co., Va., under Capt. Anthony Winston in the regiment of Col. Skipper and Maj. Jones. His lieut. was Bostick under Gen. Lawson of Prince Edward Co. In 1780 he was drafted for six months in Buckingham Co., where he then lived. He served under Capt. Saunders, Maj. Gannaway and Col. Patterson, Lt. Anthony Hockett (Hackett?) and Ens. Thomas Gregory. He was discharged by Capt. Saunders at the White Oak Springs near Little York shortly before Lord Cornwallis was taken.

William (X) Cornett deposed on 14 Sept. 1835 in Perry Co., Ky., about 28 years, and previous to that had lived in Va. On 3 July 1843 in Letcher Co., Ky., the court certified that William Cornett died on 26 Nov. 1839, and

Mary Ann Cornett was his widow.

Mrs. Mary (X) Cornett, stated on 31 May 1850 in Letcher Co., Ky., that she was the widow of William Cornett who was pensioned in Perry Co., Ky. She and her husband were married in Washington Co., Tenn when she was 22 years old. She is now 80. Her husband died 14 years ago next 26 November. She had ten children; those now living included: Sally Macdanel, Polly Brashears, Robert Cornett, Nancy Combs, Rodger Cornett, Rachel Caudill, Samuel Cornett, Nathaniel Cornett, and Joseph Cornett.

Archable Cornett, aged 61 or 62 last 12 Jan., stated on 1 June 1850 in Perry Co., Kt., that his father William died 26 Nov. 1836. His father married Mary Etherage in Washington Co., Tenn. His father always told him he was three years old when his father married for the second time. Archable was by the first wife.

Other deponents in the pension application, their age, date of statement, and place of statement, included:

Robert Brashers, aged 57, 1 June 1850, Perry Co. He knew William Cornett's wife for over 50 years.

Margaret (X) Brashers, aged 88, 1 June 1850, Perry Co., Ky.

Elija (X) Corns, no age, 3 June 1850, Perry Co.

Robert B. (X) Cornett, aged 53, 12 April 1851, Perry Co. He is a lawful child of William and Mary, and was married in January 1822. Robert E. Cornett and Louvisa Combs were issued a marriage license in Perry Co., Ky., on 10 Jan. 1822, by Jesse Combs, Clerk of said co.

Samuel Cornett, aged 42, 24 Dec. 1851, Letcher Co. Ky. William and Mary were married in the spring of 1796 and had two children born by 1800: Robert B., born 7 Jan. 1797, and one child, now dead, born in 1799.

Elijah (X) Combs, 81, 13 April 1852, Perry Co., Ky.

Sampson Brashers, no age, 28 Sept. 1852, Perry Co., Ky. William and Mary's children were: Robert, m. Louisa Combs; Margaret, died in infancy; Roger, m. Polly Lewis; Nancy, m. Samuel Combs; Samuel, m. Polly Adams; Nathaniel, m. Lydia Caudle; Rachael, m. John Caudle; Joseph E., m. Sally Brown.

Sally (X) Stapleton, 90, 22 Jan. 1853, Owsley Co., Ky. Mary had two children before she married Cornett: Sally, m. Thomas McDaniel, and Polly, m. Robert S. Brashers, Probate Judge of Perry Co. These two children of Mary's were illegitimate and were not by William Cornett.

Thomas Cody, born 1783, 25 Jan. 1853, Perry Co. His grandmother, Judah Stacy, raised Mary as a child.

Archibald (X) Cornett, born 1789, 26 Jan. 1853, Perry Co., Ky. He is the reputed son of William Cornett, whose second wife, Mary Everage, raised him, and always treated him kindly.

Abel Pennington, no age, Probate Judge of Owsley Co., 14 March 1853, Ousley Co., Ky.

Samuel (X) Combs, 54, 30 May 1853, Owsley Co., Ky. He married Nancy Cornett.

W. M. Fulkerson, no age, 13 Oct. 1853, Owsley Co., Ky.

Jesse Combs, Clerk of Perry Co., Ky., states that Mary Cornett died 28 Jan. 1852 leaving heirs Robert, Nancy, Roger, Samuel, Nathaniel, Rachael, and Joseph E. Cornett.

William Cornett of Perry Co., Ky., private in the company of Capt. Anthony in the Regt. of Col. Skipper in the Va. Line for one year, was placed on the Kentucky pension roll at $40.00 per annum under the Act of 1832. Mary Cornett. widow of Private William, was placed on the Kentucky Pension Roll at $40.00 per annum. Cert. no. 1050 under the Act of 1848 was issued 23 Feb. 185?, to end 28 Jan. 1852.

CRAIN, THOMAS, Revolutionary Soldier and Pensioner. Pension no. S. 16352. On 9 Aug. 1832, Mercer Co., Ky., Crain, then about 77 years old, stated he was born in King William Co., Va., moved to Goochland Co. at age 15, where he lived during the Revolutionary War. In May 1778 he went out under Col. Morris to Valley Forge to see his brother, then in the army. There he enlisted under Capt. Burley for twelve months in the 7th Va. Regt. commanded by Capt. William Daingerfield. At other times he served under Capt. White, Capt. Miller, Col. Richardson, Captain Richardson, Capt. Smith, and Col.

Pleasants. After being discharged at Richmond he returned to Goochland Co. for two years, then moved to Powhatan Co. for five or six years, then to Buckingham Co. for about seven years, then to Mercer County where he died on 7 October 1833 leaving a widow Polly Crain.

Thomas Taylor, in his 64th year, on 28 Aug. 1832 in Mercer Co., Ky., deposed he knew Thomas Crain for many years and knew he served in the Revolutionary War.

Polly (X) Crain deposed on 10 October 1832 in Mercer Co. that she was the widow of Thomas Crain.

Thomas Crain of Mercer Co., Ky., a private in the regiment of Col. Morris of the Va. Line for 21 months from 1778 was placed on the Kentucky Pension Roll at $70.00 per annum under the act of 1832. Cert. no. 5014 was issued on 1 Feb. 1833. On 21 Oct. 1833 John A. Benton, attorney, gave a receipt for the pension of Polly Crain.

CREWS, GIDEON, Revolutionary Pensioner. No. 39371. Gideon (X) Crews, aged about 66 years, on 4 June 1818 in Knox Co., Tenn., deposed that he enlisted in Buckingham Co., Va., in the company of Capt. Thomas Patterson in the 6th Va. Regiment, and served about two years, until a few months after the capture of Burgoyne. He was at the Battles of Saratoga, Age Hill, and at other skirmishes, and was discharged at Valley Forge. Gideon Crews made statements about his service on 31 July 1819 (when he stated he served for about one year in the 6th Regiment, and was then placed under Col. Morgan for about one year), and 2 October 1820 (when he stated that he owned four old pewter plates, one piece of old pewter dish, one pot, one old pine table, one churn, one pair of cotton c ards, five chairs, one sow, and ten pigs, valued at $7.13½. His family consists of himself, his wife, two daughters at home, two grandchildren aged three and five. His wife if about 60).

James (X) Crews deposed in Knox Co., Tenn., on 4 June 1818.

John (X) Childers deposed in Knox. Co., on 31 July 1819 that he was present when Gideon Crews enlisted.

Shadrack (X) Maxey deposed in Knox Co. on 31 July 1819 that he saw Gideon Crews in service.

Gideon Crews of Knox Co., Tenn., private in the regt. of Col. Matthews in the Va. Line, for two years, was placed on the East Tennessee Pension Roll at $8.00 per month from 4 June 1818 under the Act of 1818. Cert. no. 17108 was issued 24 May 1820.

CREWS, JAMES, Revolutionary Pensioner. No. 39387. James (X) Crews, aged 60 years, in Knox Co., Tenn., on 4 June 1818 stated he enlisted in Buckingham Co., Va., in the company of Capt. Thomas Patterson in the 6th Regiment, and served about two years. He was at the taking of Burgoyne, at the Battles of Saratoga and Age Hill, and at many other battles and skirmishes, and was discharged at Valley Forge, Penna. On 31 July 1819 James (X) Crews added that he served one year in the 6th Regt., and one year under Col. Morgan. On 7 April 1829, James, then aged 73, stated he served for two years. He was stricken from the Pension Roll. About thirty-three years earlier he purchased about 300 acres of land subject to the lien that the colleges have on it for the original price, He failed to pay the interest on the debt and now holds the same at the indulgence of the state. He has rents and profits of the land (which is not of good quality) worth $25.00, owns one negro man, and has various livestock, but is not able to work. His wife is about 60 years old, and his sister, aged 65, has long been insane.

Gideon (X) Crews, deposed on 4 June 1818.

John (X) Childers deposed on 31 July 1819 in Knox Co. that he was present when James Crews enlisted, and that he saw the brothers Gideon and James in service together.

Shadrack (X) Maxey deposed on 31 July 1819 in Knox Co.

James Crews of Knox Co., Tenn., private in the company of Capt. Patton in Col. Matthews' Regt. of the Va. Line for two years from 1776 to 1778 was placed on the East Tenn. Pension Roll at $8.00 per month from 4 June 1818 under the Acts of 1818 and 1820. Cert. no. 17107 was issued 24 May 1820. The executors of James Crews were paid arrears of pension to 6 March 1814.

CYRUS, BARTHOLOMEW, and wife PHEBE. Revolutionary Pension No. W. 25467. BLWt. 1475-100; BLWt. 9327-160-55. Bartholomew Cyrus deposed on 20 April 1818 in Buckingham Co., Va., that he enlisted in Sept. 1777 in Chesterfield Co., Va., in Capt. James Harris' company, and was later in the 15th Regt. of Col. Mason, of Gen. Woodford's Brigade. He also served under Col. Russell, Col. Richard Campbell, Capt. Kilpatrick, and Gen. Muhlenberg. He was at the Battles of Monmouth, Guilford, Eutaw, Ninety-Six, and Camden, and served to the end of the war. He was discharged near Winchester in July 1783. On 20 July 1818, Cyrus, now over 60, deposed in Buckingham Co., as to his service, and as to his property. His property is valued at $34.00. He is a farmer who lost the use of one hand when a gun burst. His wife Sally is very old and cannot work. The only other person in his family is Sally Tredwell, aged about 9.

Cyrus made depositions as to his service on 21 Nov. 1821, 19 Jan. 1829 (aged 73) in Buckingham Co., Va., and on 5 April 1855 in Appolattox Co., Va., aged 97.

His file contained a certificate granted 31 July 1783 by Virginia to Bartholomew Cyrus, drummer of infantry in the Continental Line, for £ 113.19.6 for the balance of full pay.

Bartholomew Cyrus married Mrs. Phebe Callaway on 2 January 1833 in Campbell Co., Va.

John H. Tanner deposed 6 Sept. 1855 in Appomattox Co., Va., that Bartholomew Cyrus and Phebe Galloway were married 22 January 1833, and that Cyrus died 11 July 1855.

Mrs. Phebe (X) Cyrus, aged 61, deposed on 6 Sept. 1855 that she was the widow of Bartholomew Cyrus, a musician who received Bounty Land Warrant No. 3839 for 160 acres. She was married to Cyrus on 22 Jan. 1833 by Mr. Burge, a minister of the Gospel. Her name was Galloway, formerly Durrum. Her husband died 11 July 1855. On 27 Dec. 1865 she swears to support the Constitution of the United States. On 29 Dec. 1865 in Appomattox Co., aged about 70, she declared her pension certificate was destroyed by the armies in the Battle of Appomattox Court House. She has been supported by her relatives and friends and by a small allowance from the pauper's fund of the Overseers of the Poor. She has no property. On 15 Dec. 1879 she gave power of attorney to receive a land warrant. She died 28 February 1883. Chas. W. Statham wrote of her death from Lynchburg, Va., and sent a newspaper clipping.

William W. C. Durrum deposed on 29 Dec. 1865 in Appomattox Co. that Mrs. Phebe Cyrus was a near neighbor of his and that her pension certificate was destroyed.

Jas. G. Patteson, Presiding Justice of the County Court of Appomattox County certifies the seal of the county court was stolen.

Bartholomew Cyrus of Buckingham Co., Va., private in the 2nd Va. Regt., for four years was placed on the Va. Pension Roll at $8.00 per month from 20 April 1818.

DAVIDSON, STEPHEN, Revolutionary Soldier. Pension S. 8306. Stephen Davidson of Buckingham Co., Va., aged 76 years, declared on 29 July 1833 that he enlisted in 1778 or 1779 under Capt. John Thomas, and later served under Capt. Garland Burley. He was at Albemarle Barracks where the officers were Col. Francis Taylor, Col. Fontaine, and Major Roberts. Later he was a private under Capt. Perkins. He was born in Cumberland Co., Va., about 1767. He now resides in Buckingham Co.

Josiah Giles deposed on 6 Aug. 1832 in Buckingham Co., Va.

Giles Davidson deposed on 7 June 1833 in Buckingham Co. that he has known Stephen Davidson since his earliest recollections and believes him to be 76 years old.

Stephen Davidson of Buckingham Co., Va., private in the company of Capt. Thomas in the Va. Line for fourteen months, was placed on the Virginia Pension Roll at $46.66 per annum under the Act of 1832. Certificate no. 23048 was issued 29 October 1833.

DAVIS, SAMUEL, Revolutionary Pensioner, Va. Service. Pension Claim No. S. 37878. When he applied he was 68 years old. Davis stated that in the fall of 1779 his father moved from Buckingham Co. to Kentucky and they settled in Bourbon Co., Ky., in October 1779. On 1 Jan. 1780 he volunteered

for a tour of six months, to serve under Capt. Isaac Riddle and Lieut. John
Davis, the applicant's brother. He was taken prisoner in June 1780 and held
by the British until June 1783. The pensioner was born in 1765 in Pennsylvania. After his release as a prisoner he went to Danville, Mercer Co., Ky.,
where he has lived with his children since the death of his wife. For the
last eighteen months he has lived in Henry Co. He states he has always been
a volunteer and has never been drafted or acted as a substitute. Kenard
Younger and Rev. Will Peck swore they were well acquainted with him.

    John Conway stated he was taken prisoner at the same time as the
pensioner.

    Samuel Davis of Henry Co., Ky., private in the company of Capt. Riddle
in the Va. Line for two years, was placed on the Kentucky Pension Roll at
$80.00 per annum, under the Act of 1832. Certificate no. 26781 was issued
27 May 1834.

    DEPP, WILLIAM, Revolutionary Pensioner, no. S. 2511. William (X) Depp,
aged 72, in Barren Co., Ky., stated on 15 July 1833 that he was born on 25
March 1761 in Powhatan Co., Va. He entered service the year before Cornwallis
surrendered and served in the Virginia Militia under Capt. Thomas Harris and
1st Lieut. George Smith. It was late in the year 1780 that he entered service
under Harris. In 1781 he enlisted under Capt. Robert Hughes at Powhatan Court
House, and later served in a regiment under Gen. Lawson, Maj. Tucker, and Col.
Randall. He was at the Battle of Guilford Court House. In May 1781 he enlis-
ted under Capt. Porter, 1st Lieut. George Smith, and Second Lieut. George
Smith, two brothers of different mothers with the same first name. Since the
war he has lived in Buckingham Co., Va., then in Chesterfield Co., then in
Powhatan Co. He came to Kentucky in 1795 and lived for seven years in Fayette
Co., near Lexington, and then served in Barren County.

    Benjamin Harbard of Powhatan Co. testified in Chesterfield Co., Va.,
on 1 January 1833 as to the service of William Depp. Harbard states he
has found Depp's age to be 76, according to the old church register.

    William Depp, of Barren Co., Ky., private in the company of Capt. Harris
in Col. Randall's Regt. in the Va. Line for six months and twelve days, was
placed on the Kentucky pension roll at $21.33 per annum under the Act of 1832.
Certificate no. 22106 was issued 26 Sept. 1833.

    DIBRELL, ANTHONY, and wife WILMOUTH or WILMUTH. Revolutionary Pension
no. 3398. Mrs. Wilmuth Dibrell, aged 71, on 25 December 1845 in Amherst
Co., Va., stated she was the widow of Anthony Dibrell who often spoke of
being in the United States service. They were married some eight or nine
years after the year, in 1790, in Amherst Co. Anthony Dibrell died in 1816.
The file contains a marriage bond dated Amherst Co., 3 Nov. 1790 for Anthony
Dibrell (signed "A. Dibrell), and Wilmoth Watson. James Watson was security
and Will Loving, Jr., was witness.

    David Patterson, 87 years, in Buckingham Co., Va., on 22 Jan. 1846
testified to Anthony Dibrell's service starting in February 1778
and ending with Cornwallis' surrender.

    John Patteson, 82 years old, on 22 Jan. 1846 in Buckingham Co., Va.,
testified to Dibrell's service.

    John Thomas, a pensioner, stated on 9 March 1846 in Buckingham Co.,
that Dibrell was in the service.

    Cha. L. Dibrell wrote from Richmond on 14 March 1846 concerning his
mother's application. He stated she was quite old and infirm, was very
needy and entirely dependent on her children (who are also needy) for
support.

    Wilmuth Dibrell, aged 74 in Nelson Co., Va., applied for continuance
of pension.

    Wilmouth Dibrell of Amherst Co., Va., widow of Anthony Dibrell who died
in 1816, private in Va. for nine months, was placed on the pension roll at
Richmond at $30.00 per annum. Certificate no. 9981 under the Act of 1838,
and no. 7708 under the Acts of 1843 and 1844 were issued 28 April 1846. Certificate no. 3627 under the Act of 1848 was issued 2 February 1849.

    DIBRELL (Dibbell, Ditrill, Debrill), CHARLES, Revolutionary Pension
No. 21160. Ditrell, aged 75, in White Co., Tenn., on 5 Sept. 1832, stated

that his first short tour of duty was in 1775. In 1776 he enlisted under Capt. Thomas Ballew, Lt. Edmund Peters, Ens. John Moss, and Col. Hains Morgan, and later Col. Nathaniel Gist. In 1777 he was commissioned ensign and served under Capt. John Bates and Lieut. Tandy Key. Charles May from Buckingham was his colonel. In 1781 he renlisted as an ensign under Capt. William Perkins. In the fall of 1781 he was at Yorktown and saw Cornwallis give up his sword. On this occasion Dibrell had gone to relieve an only brother who was in feeble health, but finding that the enemy was about to surrender they both remained. Dibrell was born on 24 October 1757 in Buckingham Co., Va., he moved to Kentucky in 1782 ehere he lived until about ten years ago when he moved to White Co., Tenn. In 1790 he was a captain in Harmar's campaign under Col. James Trotter from Lexington. Dibrell was in Madison Co., Ky.

Anthony Dibrell, Clerk of the Circuit Court of White Co., Tenn., sent a certificate.

John Catron, Chief Justice of the Supreme Court of Tennessee, certified at Sparta, Tenn., that he has known Col. Charles Dibrell since 1805.

Thomas Patteson declared in Davidson Co., Tenn., on 31 August 1833 that he has known Charles Dibrell for about 70 years, since they were boys in Buckingham Co., Va. He testified as to Dibrell's service.

Tandy Key of Fluvanna Co., Va., stated on 29 October 1833 he served with Tandy Key and Charles Dibrell.

Charles Dibrell testified on 12 Feb. 1834 in Davidson Co., Tenn., as to his service.

Charles Dibrill of White Co., Tenn., private in the company of Capt. Bates in the Virginia Line for eight months as a private and three months as ensign, was placed on the West Tennessee pension roll at $56.66 per annum under the Act of 1832. Certificate no. 29524 was issued 27 February 1834. Charles Dibrell died 16 July 1840.

DILLARD, JAMES, Rev. Pension Application no. W-7019. On 20 Jan. 1839 in Amherst Co., Va., Moses Wright of Buckingham Co., Va., stated he enlisted under Capt. James Dillard of Amherst Co., Va., and served out his time. When he first joined the army his company was put in the 10th Regt. of Volunteers under Col. Edward Stevens.

DIUGUID, GEORGE, Revolutionary Pension no. S-5348. George Duiguid, aged 70 next October, stated in September 1832 in Campbell Co., Va., that he was drafted in 1776 or 1777 in Capt. Robert Hew's Company under Col. Littleberry Mosby from Powhatan Co., Va., where he was a guard for two weeks; in 1780 he removed to Buckingham Co., Va., where he was drafted and ordered to Camden, S. C. He served furing the tour of Gates' defeat, part of the time in person, and part of the time paying a substitute, John Bassnaw, whom he paid in property in the amount of $100.00. His captain was Peter Guarrant. In the fall of 1780 he again removed to Powhatan Co., where he was drafted into Capt. William Poor's Company. He also served under Captain David Patterson and Capt. Mirock. In 1781 he volunteered in a troop of horse raised by Capt. Littleberry Mosby, son of Col. L. Mosby. Duiguid stated he was born in 1762 in Buckingham Co., and has a record taken from his father's register.

Duiguid deposed to his service again on 30 May 1833 in Campbell Co., Virginia.

George Duiguid of Campbell Co., Va., private of cavalry and infantry in Capt. Peterson's company, Col. Bowling's Regiment in the Va. Line for six months and five days was placed on the Virginia Pension Roll at $22.21 per annum under the Act of 1832. Certificate no. 16221 was issued on 18 July 1833. The administrator of George Duiguid was paid arrears of pension to 25 August 1838.

DOLAND, JOHN, and wife SUSANNA. Pension file no. 6040; BLWt. 26872-160-55. John Doland, aged 75 years, in Buckingham Co., Va., declared on 8 October 1832 that he was born in the said county, and that in one winter or spring (he cannot remeber the year) he was drafted as a militiaman and placed under Capt. Charles Patteson, marched to Guilford, N.C., then to Norfolk, Va., and then returned home. In a month or two he was recalled into service and served under Capt. John Couch, later under Col. Fleming, and was discharged a short time before the surrender of Cornwallis. He was called into service at the age of 18 or 19, and is entirely illiterate.

William Thornhill, on 8 October 1832, in Buckingham Co., testified as to Doland's service.

John (X) McFadden, Sr., declared 11 July 1853 in Buckingham Co., that he knew John Dolling and Suckey Wood and remebered their marriage, performed by Rev. Charles Maxey many years ago. John Doland died in Buckingham Co. about 1838.

Polly (X) Hardiman, declared 11 July 1853 in Buckingham Co., that she witnessed the marriage of John Dolling and Suckey Wood.

Susannah (X) Doland, aged 80, on 17 April 1855 declared in Cabell Co., Va., that she was the widow of John Doland, who was a private and a resident of Buckingham Co. They were married in the 1780's and her husband died in April 1838.

John (X) Doland, son of John and Susannah Doland, on 10 May 1855, in Cabell Co., Va., declared his mother has lived with him since the death of his father.

John (X) McFadden declared on 17 Nov. 1855 in Buckingham Co., Va., that he was between 12 and 16 when he witnessed the marriage of John Doland and Susannah Woody were married by Charles Maxey, a Methodist clergyman.

John Doland of Buckingham County, private in the company of Capt. Patteson in the regiment of Col. Fleming in the Virginia Line for six months, was placed on the Virginia pension roll at $20.00 per annum under the Act of 1832. Certificate no. 12505 was issued 4 May 1833.

Susanna Doland, widow of John Doland, private of the Virginia Line, was placed on the Richmond, Va., pension roll at $20.00 per annum. Certificate no. 5653 under the Act of 1853 was issued on the 9th of Feb. 1856. Bounty Land Warrant no. 26872 for 160 acres was issued on 26 Nov. 1856.

DOSS, JOHN, Revolutionary pensioner no. S-5350. John (X) Doss, aged 75, declared on 20 June 1833 in Buckingham Co., Va., that he entered service as a private under Capt. Cannon. He was drafted from Buckingham Co. a second time as a private under Capt. Chambers, and was at the Battle of Guilford. He was drafted a third time from Buckingham Co. in 1781 in Capt. Cary's company, under Col. Matthews, and was discharged 18 September 1781. He was born in Buckingham County in 1758, but has no record of his birth. He was a resident of Buckingham County during the Revolutionary War, and has lived there ever since. He lives nearly 30 miles from the courthouse.

John Doss of Buckingham Co., Va., private in Capt. Cary's company in the Virginia Line for six months and twelve days was placed on the Virginia pension roll at $21.32 per annum under the Act of 1832. Certificate no. 16198 was issued 17 July 1833. Arrears of pension was paid to the executor of John Doss to 2 December 1841.

DOSS, WILLIAM, and wife NANCY, Revolutionary pension application no. W-9404; BLWt. 80029-160-55. William (X) Doss, aged 69 in May 1832, in Fentress Co., Ky., on 23 April 1833 stated he had no record of his age, and entered service in Buckingham Co., Va., where he was born and raised, and lived until the end of the war. He was drafted as a private in the militia under Capt. Mosely. Later he was under Capt. John Chambers and Col. Holcum, was at the Battle of Guilford, and was discharged in the spring of 1781. He was called out again under Capt. Miller, and was at the Siege of York. Part of the time he was under Col. Skipper (or Skipwith?). He was discharged after the surrender of Cornwallis. After the war he lived in the following places: a few years in Franklin Co., Ga.; a short time in Buckingham Co., Va.; a few years in Wilkes Co., N. C.; a few years in Buncombe Co.; a few years in Wayne Co., Ky.; then to Overton Co., Tenn., to the part that is now Fentress County, where he has lived for about 12 years.

Thomas Butler, aged 70, of Anderson Co., Tenn., declared on 3 Sept. 1833 in Morgan Co., Tenn., that he was with William Doss after the Siege at York.

William (X) Doss, on 14 May 1838 in Wayne Co., Ky., declared he has lost his pension certificate. He resided in Fentress Co., Tenn., until eighteen months ago when he moved to Wayne Co., Ky. He asks for a transfer to the Lexington, Ky., agency.

Nancy (X) Doss, deposed on 3 October 1853 in Fentress Co., Tenn., that she was the widow of William Doss who died in said county on 15 September 1853, and that she and her husband were married in Haywood Co., N. C., by Squire McHenry about 40 years ago. She and her husband both lived in Buncombe Co., then moved from N. C. to near Jacksborough, Tenn., and from there to Fentress Co. Their oldest child is now about 38 years old. Most of her children live in Fentress County. On 10 April 1855 Nancy Doss gave her age as about 65 years old, and said she was married to William Doss about 25 or 26 years ago.

William Doss, aged 24, declared on 10 August 1857 in Clinton Co., Ky., that his father William Doss died on 15 September 1853. His oldest sister, Fanny Doss, if living would be about 15 or 16 years older than he.

Ennuiss Doss, aged 33, and Sally (X) Doss, aged 27, deposed on 14 October 1857 in Fentress Co., Tenn., that they were both children of William and Nancy Doss, and that their father died on 15 September 1853.

P. H. Smith of Albany, Clinton Co., Ky., deposed on 21 October 1857 that a year or two ago W. J. Dabney deposited $1.00 in a letter to the Clerk of Haywood Co., N. C., asking for recorded evidence of the marriage of William Doss and Nancy Brown. Smith is deputy postmaster.

William Doss of Morgan Co., Tenn., private in the company of Capt. Mosely in the Virginia Line for nine months, was placed on the East Tennessee Pension Roll at $30.00 per annum under the Act of 1832. Certificate no. 22323 was issued 25 October 1833, and later transferred to the Kentucky Pension Roll.

Nancy Doss, widow of William Doss, private in Virginia, was placed on the Nashville, Tenn., Pension Roll at $30.00 per annum from 15 September 1853. Certificate no. 6285 under the Act of 1853 was issued 11 November 1857. Bounty Land Warrant no. 80029 for 160 acres was issued 26 April 1858.

DUVAL, WILLIAM, Revolutionary Pension no. S-8362. William Duvall applied for a pension on 14 June 1832 in Buckingham Co., Va. He stated that he and others joined as volunteers in Henrico under Col. Patrick Henry. In June 1775 Duval was a lieutenant under Capt. Thomas Prosser in an independent company. In July 1775 William Duval was appointed Captain of a company, with Lt. Hodges and William Mosby as his subaltern officers. In January 1781 Duval and sundry volunteers from the upper part of Hanover marched to Richmond to assist in driving Arnold and his troops from Richmond. On 27 July 1832 William Duval made another deposition in which he stated that his parents told him he was born in King William Co., Va., on 4 Sept. 1748, and there was a record in his father's family Bible. His father died in February 1784 at "Mont Comfort" near Richmond. The deponent's brother, Claiborne Duvall, was executor of the estate. He took the Bible and the register in it to Kentucky about 1791, where he died many years ago. Duvall stated that some of the men who served under him included Joseph Selden; Samuel Selden, who was afterwards subaltern in the Continental service and lost his arm at the Siege of Ninety-Six under Gen. Greene; and Col. John Pope who enlisted with him as a sergeant.

Philip Duval, aged 75, deposed in Buckingham Co., on 14 June 1832 that William Duval, aged about 80, served in the Revolution as a captain.

Obadiah Gathright, aged 66, of Richmond, deposed on 16 July 1832 that Maj. William Duval and his brother Philip were raised in Henrico Co. The deponent's father, Miles Gathright, enlisted as a volunteer under Capt. William Duval.

J. Marshall, Chief Justice, declared on 23 July 1832 that he has known Willian Duval since the spring of 1782 when he first served with him in the Virginia House of Delegates.

P. V. Daniel, stated on 26 July 1832 that he has known Maj. William Duval since the early part of 1805.

William Duval of Buckingham Co., Va., captain in the regiment of Col. Elliot in the Virginia State Line for five months and fourteen days, for nine days as private, and for some months as lieutenant, was placed on the Virginia Pension Roll at $136.86 per annum under the Act of 1832. Certificate no. 139 was issued on 2 August 1832.

EDWARDS, THOMAS, and wife MARTHA. Revolutionary pensioner W-7076.
Martha (X) Edwards, aged 73 years, declared on 17 August 1841 in Buckingham
Co., Va., that she is the widow of Thomas Edwards, late of said county, who
was a private in the continental and militia service of Va. He was at the
Battle of Guilford and the Siege of Little York. She was married 23 July
1785 and her husband died 16 October 1794. On 18 April 1843, Martha Edwards,
aged 74, applied for continuance of the pension.
    Joseph Childers declared on 20 August 1841 that he knew Thomas and
Martha Edwards were married about 1785, and that Thomas died in 1793 or
1794. He also deposed to Thomas Edwards' service. He deposed again on
28 October 1841 as to Edwards' service. He stated that Thomas and Martha
were married in Buckingham Co. about 1785 at the church of Tillotson
Parish by Rev. James Saunders. Thomas Edwards left four children and
his widow now holds her dower right in a small piece of land. Thomas
Edwards served with the deponent's brother, John Childers. On 24
January 1842 Childers, aged 79 next 28 February, stated both of his
brothers served with Edwards, but have died several years ago.
    Armistead Garnett deposed on 21 August 1841 in Buckingham Co.
as to Edwards' marriage and service.
    Capt. Stephen Hooper, deposed on 11 October 1841 as to Edwards'
marriage, and that Edwards died when his children were very young, for
he was killed by accident.

Martha Edwards, widow of Thomas Edwards, who died 16 October 1794,
private in the Virginia Line for six months, was placed on the Richmond, Va.,
Pension Rolls at $20.00 per annum. Certificate no. 6699 under the Act of
1838 was issued 8 July 1842 and certificate no. 645 under the Act of 1843
was issued 20 June 1843.

FLOWERS, ROWLAND, and wife ANN. Revolutionary pension application no.
W-12. Rowland Flowers applied for a pension in July 1834 in Fentress Co.,
Tenn. He stated he was born in Buckingham Co., Va., in 1746, and was the son
of James Flowers. He enlisted in the spring of 1781 from Buckingham Co., and
served three months in the company of Capt. Silas Williams. Later he served
as a substitute for his father in Capt. Peter Gearin's Company under Major
Bois, and was at the Siege of Yorktown. After the war he lived in Virginia
until he was 22, then moved to Overton Co., Tenn., and drew pension while in
Fentress Co., Tenn.
    Ann or Anna Flowers applied for a pension in October 1838 in Fentress
Co., Tenn. She stated her husband died in Fentress Co., on 23 Sept. 1837;
that as Ann or Anna Jarot or Garrot, born 15 March 1762, she married Flowers
in Buckingham Co., Va. about 1 Dec. 1782. Ann or Anna Jarot Flowers died
29 May 1854. Rowland and Ann had twelve children: 1) William, the eldest,
born about August 1783; 2) Betsey; 3) James; 4) Rowland J.; 5) Arthur;
6) Rosanna; 7) Maggie; 8) Sally; 9) Polly; 10) Deliela; 11) Judy, the youngest,
aged 31 in 1838, married Rodney King and had eight children; 12) unnamed.
    In 1834 Anthony Flowers, younger brother of the soldier, aged 61, lived
in Fentress Co., Tenn.
    (Tim Huddleston, in Pioneer Families of Pickett Co., Tenn., states
there was a Rev. William Flowers, a Baptist preacher in Smith Co., Tenn.,
who may have been a brother of Rowland Flowers and who also came from Buckingham Co., Va. - ERW).

GEVIDAN (GEVERANN, GEVANDIN), JOHN, and wife Mary. Revolutionary pension
application no. W-8845, Va. service. Gevidan applied for a pension at the
age of 77 years. He was drafted in the militia in October 1776 and served
under Capt. Millen. In September 1777 he was drafted to serve for three months
under William Curd. In August 1779 he was drafted to serve under Capt.
Patterson for three months. Later he was under Col. Cooper. In July 1780 he
was drafted to serve under Capt. Mc. Perkins. In July 1781 he was drafted
under Capt. Moseby. The applicant was born in Buckingham Co., in 1756, and
lived there until 1823 until he moved to Shelby Co., Ky., where he lived for
three years; from there he moved to Henry Co., Ky., where he has lived ever
since.
    Stephen Powers and William McCrackin deposed that they knew him and
that he was reputed to have served in the Revolution.

Mary Gevedann, aged 74, the widow of John Gevedann, stated they were married in Jan. 1784 in Goochland Co., Va., and that her husband died 17 April 1835. Their oldest son was born 1785.

Shadrack M. Gevidan stated he was a son of John and Mary Gevidan.

George Clarke and Brazella Brown said that they were both acquainted with John and Mary and that John died at the time stated by the widow.

John Chilton, a Justice of the Peace, states he knew the widow Mary Gevidan.

A certified copy of the marriage bond bore the signatures of John Gevidan and Drury Mims.

John Gevidan was on the Kentucky Rolls at the rate of $50.00 per annum. His certificate for that amount was issued 9 October 1838, and was sent to the Hon. R. M. Johnson, of the House of Representatives.

Mary Gevidan, widow, was on the Kentucky Pension Roll at $50.00 per annum, and her certificate was issued on 22 April 1839. It was sent to S. Todd at Frankfort, Ky. Another certificate for $50.00 per annum was issued to Mary Gevidan on 30 Nov. 1843, and was sent to Thomas Robertson at New Castle, Ky.

GLOVER, SAMUEL, served in the Revolution as a private. He was born 2 June 1759 in Buckingham Co., Va., and died died there on 7 June 1820. (Roster of Virginia DAR, 1892-1936, p. 389).

HARRIS, WILLIAM, Revolutionary pension application no. W-8893. He was a private in the Revolutionary War. He was born 25 August 1755 in Cumberland Co., Va., entered service in May 1776 from Buckingham Co., Va., and after the war lived in Henry and Patrick Counties, Va. From there he moved to Barren Co., Ky. His pension began 4 March 1831, and certificate was issued 28 Nov. 1833.

HOWARD, SAMUEL, Sr. in 1834 applied for a pension from Harlan Co., Ky. He stated he was born in 1762 in Buckingham Co., Va. He spelled his name Hoard but others spelled it Howard. From 1778 to 1781 he served eighteen months in the Va. Line. In 1781 he moved to Greenbrier Co., Va., where he lived for seven years, then lived in Hawkins Co., Tenn., for a year. Then he moved to Powell's Valley, Russel Co., Va., and lived there for six or seven years. Since then he has lived in Harlan Co., Ky. About 1779 Samuel Howard, Sr., married Cloe Osborn in Buckingham Co., Va. She was born c.1760 or 1765 and died about 1841 in Harlan Co., Ky., and is said to have been a sister of Ephraim Osborn, Sr.

Samuel Howard is first found in Kentucky Records when he was granted land in Knox Co., Ky., on 24 April 1804. The 1810 Census of Knox Co. lists Adrian Howard, Benjamin Howard, Jas. Howard, James Howard, John Howard, Julius Howard, Thomas Howard, and William Howard. Benjamin, John, James, and Thomas Howard were brothers.

Harlan Co., Ky., was formed from Knox Co., Ky., in 1819, and the 1820 Census of Harlan Co. lists Benjamin and John Howard, and Andrew Hord, Adron Hord, John Hord, Samuel Hord, and Thomas Hord.

Samuel Howard died in Harlan Co., Ky., on 5 December 1840. His children were: 1) Andrew Howard, b. 1780, m. Miss Metcalf, and lived in Harlan Co.; 2) Adrain Howard, b. 1782, m. Hannah Lewis, and lived in Harland Co.; 3) Elizabeth Howard, b. 1783, m. James Napier, and lived in Clay Co., Ky.; 4) John N. Howard, b. 1785, m. Mary (Brock?) and went to Missouri; 5) Mary Howard, b. 1786, m. James Hensley, and lived in N. C.; 6) Nancy Howard, b. 1787, m. Lewis Hensley on 1 Sept. 1803 in Knox Co., Ky., and lived in N. C.; 7) Samuel Howard, Jr., b. c.1793, m. Elizabeth Brittain and lived in Harlan Co., Ky.; 8) Sarah Howard, b. 1794, m. Edmond Napier, and lived in Clay Co., Ky.; 9) Wilkerson Howard, b. 1798, m. Mary Jones and lived in Harlan Co., Ky.; 10) Dred Howard, b. 1804, m. Sarah Hensley, and lived in Owsley Co., Ky.

(A notice in the Virginia Gazette of 1772 and published in the William and Mary Quarterly, 1st ser., vol. 9, p. 239, stated that Mr. Benjamin Howard, clerk of Bedford, and one of the Burgesses of Buckingham Co., died.- ERW).

JENNINGS, JAMES, applied for a pension at aged 75 from Buncombe Co., N. C., on 18 October 1832. He was born 14 Feb. 1757 in Buckingham Co., and died 4 December 1837. In his application he stated he enlisted for service in the Revolution in Jan. 1777 in Prince Edward Co., Va., in Capt. John Morton's company, 4th Va. Regt. commmanded by Col. Adam Stephens. He was at the Battles of Brandywine, Germantown, Trenton, and Princeton. Later he moved to Surry Co., N.C., and served five months under Capt. James Shepherd. In 1808 he moved to Buncombe Co., N. C. He stated he was acquainted with John Anderson, Abner Jarvis, and Rev. James B. McMahan.

Daniel Carter of Buncombe Co. stated he has known James Jennings for many years.

John Lee of Cocke Co., Tenn., on 28 April 1831 deposed he served with James Jennings. John Lee has since died. His testimony mentioned Samuel Jennings, and William C. Roadman(?) postmaster of Newport, Cocke Co. Lloyd B. Young declared that John Lee had been a respectable member of the Baptist Church.

James Jennings married Hannah Martin in 1788 in Surry Co., N. C. A copy of his marriage intentions shows James Jennings and Andrew Martin posted bond of 50 pounds on 10 March 1788 for marriage license of Hanah (sic) Martin and James Jennings.

James Jennings was allowed a pension on his application, executed 18 October 1832. He died 4 December 1837 in Buncombe or Yancey Co., N. C. His wife was living in Buncombe Co. as late as 1843.

Hannah Jennings applied for a widow's pension on 16 December 1841. She declared that she was married to James Jennings by one William Meredith, Esq., in Surry Co., N. C., in the Spring of 1781 (sic).

(See Doughertie, Jennings and Allied Families - ERW).

JONES, ABRAHAM, lcaimed bounty land under the Act of Congress of 15 May 1828. On 17 September 1828 he write to the Bounty Land Office from Buckingham Co., Va., that he had sent his declaration and evidence to that department some time last winter or spring. His papers were enclosed with Capt. John Thomas' claim. Jones stated he served under Capt. John Thomas who should be able to attest to the evidence.

Charles Yancey wrote from Buckingham Co. on 17 Nov. 1829 in support of Abraham Jones' claim. He enclosed the muster roll of Capt. John Thomas, showing Abraham Jones as a soldier of his company. Yancey write again on 29 Dec. 1829 from Richmond.

Abraham Jones, aged 71, applied again at Buckingham Court House on 20 July 1832, stating he enlisted in 1779 under Capt. John Thomas, under Col. Francis Taylor. The declaration was sworn to before George Christian, J. P., of Buckingham Co., Va., and witnessed by Hardin Woodroff and Littleberry (?) who stated they knew Abraham Jones was a soldier in the manner stated.

KEY, TANDY, Revolutionary pension application S-18069, Va. service. He applied 14 March 1834 from Fluvanna Co., Va., and stated that he was born on 29 October 1754 in that part of Albemarle Co. called Fluvanna. In August or September 1777 while living in Buckingham Co., Va., he was commissioned a lieutenant and served three months in Capt. John Bates' company in the Va. Regt. of Cols. Cabell and May. In December 1779 he served five and one-half months as private in Capt. Jones' Virginia company, and in 1780 was a private for two months in Capt. Tilghman's company.

Charles Dibrell, on 23 Nov. 1833 in Davidson Co., Tenn., declared that in 1777 he was ensign and Tandy Key was a lieutenant in Capt. John Bates' company. Both were under Cols. Cabell and May, and both lived in Buckingham Co., Va.

Tandy Key drew pension from the Virginia Agency. Certificate no. 23829 for $65.00 per annum was issued 22 May 1834 under the Act of 7 June 1832. (See National Genealogical Society Quarterly, vol. 36, no. 3, p. 101 - ERW).

MANN, EBENEZER, pension application no. S-38927. He was born c.1759, and died 25 August 1832. He enlisted in Buckingham Co., Va., under Capt. Thomas Patterson in the 6th Va. Regt. under Col. Buckner. He was 74 in 1818 when he applied for pension. He mentioned but did not name his wife, who was born in 1762. They had at least one son, and had other children. In 1818 he was on the Pension List of Hawkins Co., Tenn.

MANN, ROBERT. Revolutionary pension S-38922. Robert Mann, probably a brother of Ebenezer Mann, was born in 1763, and enlisted 9 February 1776 under Capt. Thomas Patterson, Col. Buckner, 6th Regt., Va. Line, and was discharged at Valley Forge under General Wheeler. The pension list of 1818 gave his age as 71, living in Hawkins Co., Tenn. Papers show no children living in 1820. He was issued certificate no. 6826. He died after 1834.

McCORMICK, JOHN, aged 70 years, declared in Maury Co., Tenn., at the January 1824 Term of Court that he enlisted in Buckingham Co., Va., in the company commanded by Capt. Thomas Patterson, 1st Regt. of Col. Butler, Brigade Commander Gen. Muhlenberg. His family consisted of himself, his second wife, aged about 25 years, a son John, aged 4, and Sarah Butler, his mother-in-law, aged about 60 years. (Taken from Maury Co., Tenn., Minute Book No. 8, 1820-1824, pp. 185-186.)

McGLASSON, MATTHEW, served as a private in the Virginia Line during the Revolution. He was born 3 January 1756 in Buckingham Co., Va., and entered service October 1778 in Buckingham Co.; moved to Amelia Co., Va., about 1779 and then moved back to Buckingham Co. After the war he moved to Campbell Co., Va., and in 1813 moved to Cumberland Co., Ky. In 1830 he was in Adair Co., Ky. When he was drafted in Sept. 1781 he hired a substitute as his wife was sick. His pension began 3 March 1831. The certificate was issued 7 February 1834.

McGRAW, FRANCIS, aged 73, in Buckingham Co., Va., on 23 June 1833 declared that he served for three months as a private in Gen. Lawson's Brigade.

MILLER, FREDERICK, Revolutionary pension application no. 830589, Va. Service. Frederick Miller, aged 80, appeared in Wayne Co., Ky., on 25 September 1832 and stated he was drafted in Buckingham Co., Va., in Dec. 1780 and marched under Capt. Charles Patterson and Lieut. George Creacy. In July 1781 he was drafted again under Capt. John Mosely and Lieut. Charles Burke, and got to York and was discharged the day before Cornwallis surrendered. He was born in Pennsylvania and lived there until he was 10 years old. His father was killed by Indians, and then his mother and family moved to the Shenandoah River, then to Buckingham Co., Va., where he lived for about 20 years, then 18 years in Wilkes Co., N. C., then 1 year in Bedford Co., Tenn., and finally in 1810 he moved to Wayne Co., where he is still living.

MOORE, WILLIAM, Revolutionary pension application no. S-16982. Moore, aged 76, applied for a pension in Jackson Co., Missouri, stating he enlisted in Buckingham Co., in February 1776 under Capt. Thomas Patterson and Lieut. James Burret. Later Capt. Samuel Cabel and Lieut. Reuben J. Cabel took command of the company. He was at the Battles of Stillwater and Chestnut Hill. He was discharged on 14 February 1778.
He was placed on the Missouri Pension Roll for service as a private in Va., at $80.00 per annum from 4 March 1831, under the Act of 1832. Certificate no. 22349 was issued 17 October 1833.

PASLEY (Paslay), THOMAS, and widow WINFRED. Revolutionary pension application no. W-8506. Pasley applied for a pension on 5 Sept. 1826, aged 65, in Owen Co., Ky. He stated he enlisted in February 1779 in Buckingham Co., Va., and was in Capt. Ben. Taliaferro's company, Col. Richard Parker's Regiment, Gen. Scott's Brigade. He was at the Siege of Savannah and at Charleston, and was taken prisoner, detained in the West Indies for five years and returned home in 1784. In 1826 he stated he had a wife, Winifred, aged 57 years, and four children: Stephen aged 21, Thomas aged 19, Polly aged 15, and Pamelia aged 13.
    George Adcock stated on 1 Sept. 1826 in Shelby Co., Ky., that he enlisted Pasley in 1779, and that Pasley was sworn as a regular.

The file contains a Bible Record which reads: Thomas Pasley and his wife were married 5 Nov. 1785. Betsey Pasley, their first daughter, was married to John McGinnis on 5 June 1809. William Pasley, their first son, married Polly Collins on 14 May 1812. Elkhannah Pasley, their second son, married Polly Manary on 21 April 1812. Angelina Pasley, their second daughter, was married to William Scott on 4 April 1819. Their fourth son was married to Betsey Blunt on 22 August 1819. Anderson Pasley was married to Jane Scott on 3 July 1821. John Pasley, the third son, married Elizabeth Tinder (or Linder or Tinker) 14 November 1822. Dan Burgess (?) Pasley, sixth son, was married to Margaret Tinder on 16 September 1824. Thomas Pasley married Susannah Carter 12 December 1833. Polly Pasley married John Adcock 26 December 1833. John Pasiley died 10 July 1833. William Pasley died 22 July 1833. Susannah Pasley, wife of Thomas Pasley, died 6 July 1837. Pamelia Carter, wife of Joseph Carter, died 9 August 1837. John Adcock and Polley Adcock made affidavit on 30 April 1844 as to the identity of the handwriting of Charles Pasley. (See DAR Magazine, Dec. 1937, p. 1118).

PENDLETON, MICAJAH, Revolutionary pension application no. S-8951, Va. He applied for a pension on 26 August 1833 from Nelson Co., Va., and stated he was born in Buckingham Co., Va., in 1758. He entered service from Buckingham in the winter of 1778 or 1779, and served three months as a private under Capt. Wm. Duiguid. On 10 Jan. 1781 he enlisted in Capt. Charles Patterson's company. In June 1781 he was detailed to serve a tour of three months under Capt. Robert Cary.

Pendleton was placed on the pension roll on 9 January 1834 under the Act of 7 June 1832, at $30.00 per annum. Certificate no. 23352 was issued 9 Jan. 1834.

PIERCY (PEARCY), JAMES, Revolutionary pension application no. W-2849; Bounty Land Warrant no. 26547-160-55. Va. James Pierce, age 70 on 4 May 1832, stated in Wayne Co., Ky., that he was drafted in Bedford Co., Va., not long before the Battle of Guilford, and served under Capt. Daniel Beard, Lieut. Wm. Ewing, Ens. Samuel Beard, Col. Charles Lynch, and Maj. John Calloway. He was born in Buckingham Co., Va., in 1762. His parents moved to Bedford Co., Va., where he lived for 50 years, and then spent seven years in Franklin Co., Va., and finally arrived in Wayne Co., Ky., in March 1817.

Elizabeth (Betsy) Piercy, widow of the soldier, applied for a pension in Wayne Co., Ky., on 27 November 1843. She stated she and the soldier were married 1 May 1783 in Bedford Co., Va., and that her husband died on 23 June 1843 in Wayne Co., Ky. She was born in September 1760. Her name before she married was Betsy Snelser, and Preacher Nathaniel Shrewsbury performed the ceremony. She says Mrs. Jane Craig of Wayne Co. can prove she was married to the said James Piercy for about 10 years before 1 January 1794.

Jane Craig of Wayne Co., in 1844 stated she knew James and Betsey Piercy well in Bedford Co., Va., and in Wayne Co., Ky., and that she was married about one year after the Pierceys.

The papers contain a certificate of the marriage in Bedford County, minister's return of Nathaniel Shrewsbury, that James Pearcy and Betsy Smelser were married 25 April 1783.

SANDERS, JOHN, Revolutionary pension application no. 9189. Virginia Service. John Sanders, aged 79, states in Wayne Co., Ky., on 24 June 1833 that he was born in Lunenberg Co., Va., in 1754 and was drafted into the militia in June 1781. He served under Capt. Richard Cary, Lieut. James Barnett, Gen. Lawson, 1st Col. (?) Shepperd, and Col. Tucker. He entered the service from Buckingham Co., Va., and for the last 33 or 34 years has lived in Wayne Co., Ky. He married Mrs. Sally Buster, widow of Charles Buster, and daughter of Joshua Jones, (one of Wayne County's early settlers), on 9 June 1804. Rev. Nathaniel Shrewsbury performed the ceremony in Wayne Co.

STAPLES, ISAAC, served as a private in the Virginia Militia during the Revolution. He was born in 1762 and entered service in January 1780 from Buckingham County. His pension began 4 March 1831. His certificate was issued on 6 November 1832.

TYREE (TYRE), WILLIAM, and wife SARAH, Revolutionary pension application no. W-6331. Tyree applied for a pension in Smith Co., Tenn., on 28 August 1832, when he was 80 years of age. He stated he was born in Powhatan Co., Va., in December 1752 and was drafted in April or May 1780 in Prince Edward Co., under Capt. James Owen and Col. Stubblefield. He served six months as a wagon master.

Sarah Tyree, aged 81, applied for a pension on 19 January 1837, from Smith Co., Tenn. She stated that she was the widow of William Tyree who died 30 September 1833, and they were married in Buckingham County, Va., in 1773 or 1774. They had seven or eight children, the oldest was Flanders, born 19 March 1775.

William Tyree was pensioned at $30.00 per annum on the West Tennessee Pension Roll. Certificate no. 7523 was issued 20 April 1833 under the Act of 1832. Sarah Tyree was pensioned at $30.00 per annum. Certificate no. 311 was issued 1 May 1837. (See National Genealogical Society Quarterly, vol. 23, p. 88).

WHEELER, JAMES, and wife ELIZABETH, Revolutionary pension application no. W-9887, Va. Service. James Wheeler applied 28 July 1818 from Gibson Co., Indiana, stating he was born in March 1758 or 1760. He enlisted in Buckingham Co., Va., in Jan. or Feb. 1776 and served under Capt. Thomas Patterson in Col. Buckner's Va. Regt. He was at the Battles of Trenton, Princeton, and at the taking of Burgoyne. On 25 December 1777 he enlisted in Col. Lee's Legion of Light Dragoons and was at Guilford.

Elizabeth Wheeler, aged 80, applied for a pension on 6 September 1843 from Gibson Co., Indiana, and stated she was the widow of James Wheeler who died 2 July 1843. She married to him on 21 March or 21 June 1786 in Buckingham Co., Va. Her maiden name was Elizabeth Welch. She stated she assisted in providing soldiers with clothing and food.

John Wheeler and William R. King of Gibson Co., Ind., state on 1 Sept. 1843 that James Wheeler died 2 July 1843.

James Wheeler was pensioned at $100.00 per annum. Certificate no. 26713 was issued 2 May 1834, to take effect from 4 March 1831.

WINFREY, PHILIP, applied for a pension, stating that he was a private in the Virginia Line. He stated he was born in Powhatan Co., Va., in 1764, and was taken from there to Buckingham Co., Va., where he entered service. He was a substitute for his father, John Winfrey, for whom he served in the militia. He had a younger brother, Henry. In 1795 he moved to Lincoln Co., Ky., for two years, and then moved to Green River where he was living when he applied for a pension in 1832. He was living in Adair Co., Ky., at the time of the pension.

WOOTEN, TURNER, and wife NANCY (ROPER), Revolutionary pension application no. R-1160. Turner Wooten was born in Buckingham Co., Va., in 1757, and died in Dandridge, Jefferson Co., Tenn., on 22 November 1833. He lived in Buckingham Co. during the Revolutionary War. In 1781 he enlisted under Capt. Tabb, Col. Charles Dabney, in a Virginia Regiment, and was at the Siege of Yorktown. He was pensioned in 1832 while living in Jefferson Co., Tenn. He married Nancy Roper on 26 October 1794 in Chesterfield Co., Va. She was born 25 January 1775, and died 28 June 1851 in Bradley Co., Tenn.

The pension file contains the following list of children, born to Turner and Nancy (Roper) Wooten: 1) Nancy, born 6 August 1794, married Joseph Townsend; 2) Jack, born 1 September 1797, died young; 3) Sally, born 22 December 1803, married Thomas Davies; 4) Polly, born 6 October 1804, married Jonathan John Wood; 5) Rhoda, born 1805, married Alfred Costeller (or Costiller); 6) Josiah, born 18 March 1807, married Elizabeth Shelby; 7) John R., born 26 November 1808, married Anna Walker; 8) William H., born 6 October 1810, died 1 October 1823; 9)George W., born 27 October 1812, married Eliza Bryan; 10) Elizabeth, born 2 April 1815, married 1st James Gillett, and 2nd Rev. Henry Price; 11) James, born 2 April 1817, married in Jefferson Co., Tenn., Clarissa Hope; 12) Robert A., born 10 April 1819. (See Armstrong's Tennessee Pensioners).

WRIGHT, MOSES, was a Revolutionary soldier from Buckingham Co., Va. In the pension file of James Dillard (W-7019) is a statement made by Moses (X) Wright on 20 Jan. 1829 that he enlisted under Capt. James Dillard of Amherst Co., Va., for three years. His company was put in Col. Edward Stevens' 10th Regiment.

BUCKINGHAM COUNTY, VIRGINIA,

PENSION LIST OF 1883

No. 87,683: JAMES H. NOBLE, Post office, Buckingham Court House, Va., disability pension due to gunshot wound in the back. Placed on the pension roll Aug. 1879 at $4.00 per month.

No. 19,958: MARTHA A. OLIVER, Post office, Buckingham Court House, Virginia; widow of War of 1812. Placed on the roll March 1879 at $8.00 per month.

No. 5,179: JORDAN TAYLOR, Post office, Buckingham Court House, Va., a survivor of the War of 1812. Placed on the roll Sept. 1879 at $8.00 per month.

No. 9,320: MARTHA G. SHEPHERD, Post Office, Buckingham, widow of the War of 1812. Placed on rolls Sept. 1878 at $8.00 per month.

No. 100,710: NOAH WINEMILLER, Post office, Buckingham, disabled soldier, with shell wound in skull. Placed on roll Nov. 1869 at $8.00 per month.

No. 31,477: MARTHA GILLESPIE, Post office, Curdsville, Va., widow of the War of 1812. Placed on the rolls March 1881 at $8.00 per month.

No. 25,844: LOUISA HURT, Post office, Curdsville, Va., widow of the War of 1812. Placed on rolls July 1879 at $8.00 per month.

No. 23,515: SUSANNA ROBINSON, Post office, Gary's Store, Virginia, widow of War of 1812. Placed on the rolls May 1879 at $8.00 per month.

No. 13,050: NANCY HUBBARD, Post office, Gary's Store, Va., widow of the War of 1812. Placed on the rolls December 1878 at $8.00 per month.

No. 14,157: MARTHA M. ANDERSON, Post office, Gary's store, Va., widow of the War of 1812. Placed on the rolls January 1879 at $8.00 per month.

No. 20,199: FRANCES PERKINS, Post office, Gary's store, Va., widow of the War of 1812. Placed on the rolls, March 1879, at $8.00 per month.

No. 32,832: SARAH E. MORRIS, Post office, Gary's Store, Va., widow of the War of 1812. Placed on roll December 1882 at $8.00 per month.

No. 5,820: DELILA MILES, Post office, Glenmore, Va., widow of the War of 1812. Placed on the pension roll December 1873 at $8.00 per month.

No. 17,331: JUDITH JASMONTREE, Post office, Gold Hill, Va., widow of the War of 1812. Placed on roll February 1879 at $8.00 per month.

No. 12,944: FRANCES OSLIN, Post office, Gold Hill, Va., widow of the War of 1812. Placed on the pension roll February 1879 at $8.00 per month.

No. 21,313: MARY ANN THOMAS, Post office, Gravel Hill, Va., widow of the War of 1812. Placed on the roll March 1879 at $8.00 per month.

No. 11,661: DANIEL JIMERSON, Post office, Gravel Hill, Va., survivor of the War of 1812. Placed on the roll January 1872 at $8.00 per month.

No. 24,214: PETER HALE, Post office, New Store, Va., survivor of the War of 1812. Placed on rolls September 1878 at $8.00 per month.

No. 14,374: JUDITH B. JONES, Post office, New Store, Va., widow of the War of 1812. Placed on roll Jan. 1879 at $8.00 per month.

No. 23,520: LUCY W. ROUTON, Post office, New Store, Va., widow of the War of 1812. Placed on the roll May 1879 at $8.00 per month.

No. 15,880: FRANCIS E. STEGER, Post office, Well Water, Va., survivor of the War of 1812. Placed on roll Jan. 1879 at $8.00 per month.

CHAPTER FIVE

FAMILY SKETCHES

THE BLAKEY FAMILY

The Blakey Family Bible shows that some of them lived in Buckingham County, Virginia, and that some migrated to Logan County, Kentucky.

BLAKEY, CHURCHILL (1), son of Thomas and Susanna Blakey was born 30 March 1691, and died 8 May 1738. On 30 November 1710 he married Sarah George, daughter of Robert George. Churchill and Sarah Blakey had at least one son: a. THOMAS, born 20 March 1712.

BLAKEY, THOMAS (2), son of Churchill and Sarah (George) Blakey, was born on 20 March 1712 in Middlesex County, Virginia, and died 19 January 1791 in Buckingham County. On 12 January 1746 he married Ann Haden, daughter of Anthony Haden. Ann Haden was born 7 November 1724. Thomas and Ann (Haden) Blakey were the parents of: a. SARAH, born 20 February 1747; b. GEORGE, born 22 November 1749; c. THOMAS, born 7 April 1752; d. CATHERINE, born 24 November 1753; e. JOHN, born 30 December 1754; f. WILLIAM, born 16 October 1756; g. REUBEN, born 4 November 1758; h. CHURCHILL, born 11 April 1760; i. JOSEPH, born 28 August 1762; j. ANN, born 26 May 1765.

See: George H. S. King, "Blakey-George Bible Records," *Virginia Genealogist*, (April-June 1957), I, 89.

DR. BOCOCK

Dr. Bocock was a native of Buckingham County as it was before the setting off of Appomattox County. He was a brother of Thomas S. Bocock, Speaker of the Confederate House of Representatives, a graduate of Amherst College. He became a Presbyterian minister at Georgetown, D. C., and elsewhere. He was a man of very wide reading, and a contributor to many periodicals. Throughout his life he was much interested in political questions.

See: Alfred J. Morrison, "Extracts from John H. Bocock's Diary and Commonplace Books," *William and Mary Quarterly, 1st series* (April 1912), XX, 295-297.

THE BOLLING FAMILY

Robert Bolling of "Cellowe," Buckingham County, wrote, in French, about 1764, A Memoir of a Portion of the Bolling Family in England and Virginia. It remained in manuscript until 1868 when a handsome edition, containing a translation, was published by the well known Virginia Antiquary, the late Thomas H. Wynn.

Robert Bolling, of "Chellowe," was born at Varina, Henrico County, on 17 August 1738 and died in 1775. He married first Mary Burton, and second in 176 Susannah Watson. The second marriage took place in Amherst County. Robert was a member of the House of Burgesses for Buckingham at the sessions of November 1761 and January 1762, March 1762, November 1762, May 1763

January, 1764, October, 1764, May, 1765, and of the Convention of July 1775. His children are given in the book Descendants of Pocohantas.

Powhatan Bolling, born 1767, died 1802, served as a member of the House of Delegates from Buckingham County in 1798-1799.

Archibald Bolling of Buckingham County was born 20 March 1749/50. He married first, in 1770, Sarah, daughter of Archibald Cary of "Ampthell." She died in October 1773 and Bolling married second in February 1774 Jane, daughter of Richard Randolph of "Curles." Bolling's third wife was Mrs. Clarke, a widow.

See: "Bolling of Virginia," *Virginia Magazine of History and Biography* (1914), XXII, 332 ff.

Robert Bolling, *A Memoir of a Portion of the Bolling Family in England and Virginia* (Richmond: W. H. Wade and Co., 1868).

Wyndham Robertson, *Pocahontas, Alias Matoaka, and Her Descendants Through Her Marriage at Jamestown, Virginia, in April 1614, with John Rolfe, Gentleman* (Richmond: J. W. Randolph and English, 1887).

THE BRANCH FAMILY

BRANCH, CHRISTOPHER (1), of Kingland, Chesterfield County, Virginia, was the first of the name in Virginia. He died at an advanced age.

BRANCH, SAMUEL, I (2), probably a grandson of Christopher (1), made a will in Chesterfield County dated 11 December 1789. In it he named the following children: CHARLES, SAMUEL, HANNAH, HOPKINS, MARY MARSHALL, ELIZABETH, HARRIS, and ARTHUR.

BRANCH, SAMUEL II (3), son of Samuel (2), died about 1788 in Chesterfield. In September 1784 he married Jane Martin. He was an officer in the Revolutionary War. His known children were: SAMUEL, and SARAH, m. C. A. Jennings.

BRANCH, SAMUEL, III (4), son of Samuel (3), married first Winnifred Jones Guerrant, and second, Mrs. Watkins. He was a trustee of Hampden-Sydney College of Virginia from 1820 to 1847. He was a lawyer and planter of Buckingham County, and was an attorney. He was an ensign in Capt. John P. Dickardson's Company, Fourth (Greenhill's) Regiment of Virginia Militia in the War of 1812. His Virginia homestead was called "Woodlawn." By his first wife Samuel Branch was the father of: MARY JANE, SARAH ELIZABETH, ROBERT GUERRANT, HARRIET EVELINE, Dr. JOHN, SAMUEL, WILLIAM DANIEL, ANTHONY MARTIN, JAMES HEATH, and MARTHA WINNIFRED.

Other members of this branch family included Matthew Branch (who was appointed Justice of Buckingham County in 1793), and Samuel Branch who was appointed Justice of Buckingham in 1841. A Col. Branch of Buckingham is mentioned in 1828. Henry Branch, and Susannah C., daughter of the late Col. Henry Bell, all of Buckingham, were married in 1885. Winifred, wife of Capt. Samuel Branch of "Woodlawn," died in 1828 aged 38 years.

The will of Matthew Branch, Sr., about 1766, named sons Matthew, Samuel, Edward, Thomas, and a brother John. The will of John Branch in 1768 named only his brother Matthew Branch. The will of Matthew Branch who died about 1772 named wife Midley, sons Matthew and Peter, and daughters Elizabeth and Mary. The will of John Branch who died about 1772 named daughter Johanna Sandiber and sons Samuel and Matthew.

Thomas Branch of the fifth generation called himself Thomas Branch of Hannah Spring. Deeds show that on 8 September 1786 Thomas Branch and his wife Mary conveyed a tract of land on Pokershook Creek to William Fowler. On 25 May 1788 Thomas and Mary Branch conveyed to William Fowler land on the north side of Pokershook Creek. On 3 November 1791 Thomas Branch, Sr., of "Hannah Springs" and wife Mary conveyed to Reuben Winfree 700 acres which the said Branch had purchased from William Byrd. Another deed, dated 1 November 1792 shows Thomas and Mary again conveying land, 235 acres on Pokershook Creek to Reuben Winfree, which land Branch had purchased from Wm. Byrd.

On 13 October 1794 Thomas Branch, Sr., of Hannah Springs conveyed 4 acres of land to Thomas Burton. He conveyed 24 more acres to Burton on 11 February 1799.

The will of Thomas Branch has not been found. He married Mary, daughter of Thomas Eldredge, and had issue (among others): Bolling Branch of Buckingham County, who married Rebecca Graves, and in turn had issue: Mary Susan who married John F. Wiley, William, and Sarah who married Edward Gregg. Matthew Branch, brother of Bolling, married Martha Cox and had issue: Polly who married Thomas May. Thomas Branch, son of Matthew, is mentioned in the <u>William and Mary Quarterly</u>, 1st series, XXV, 116.

Olive Branch purchased 94 acres of land on the east side of Powhite Creek from William Byrd on 13 February 1764, and is mentioned in another deed of 6 April 1764. On 9 March 1756 he patented 200 acres of land, presumably in Lunenberg County. The patent was recorded in Land Book 18, p. 713, according to the index, but the page is missing. The last portion of the patent is on p. 714. The following patent, dated 10 March 1756, shows Olive Branch patenting 365 acres in Lunenberg County, on the south side of Morton's Creek, adjoining the land of Lewis Franklin. Branch was a member of the Buckingham County militia in the early years of the Revolution, but according to his father's will, must have died by October 1779. He seems to have left no issue.

John Harris married Elizabeth Branch of Buckingham County, and their children were: Phoebe, born 1796, married William McReynolds; Matilda, born 1799, married Elbert Harris; and Rosanna, born 1803, married Francis Harris.

See: James Branch Cabell, "Thomas and William Branch of Henrico and Some of Their Descendants," <u>William and Mary Quarterly</u>, 1st series, XXV, 116, and XXVI, 111-121.

<u>Historical Collections of the Joseph Habersham Chapter, D. A. R.</u>, ed. by Mrs. William L. Peel, vol. for 1901, p. 312.

THE BRANSFORD FAMILY

John Bransford of Richmond, Virginia, was the first of the name recorded in America. He was a member of the Old St. John's Church in Richmond, and died in 1768, leaving five children and a large estate. His eldest son, John, married Judith Ammonett, and removed to Buckingham County, where he built and supported a Methodist Church until his death in 1809. He was one of the Virginia farmers who rallied to Washington's call in 1781, and was present as a soldier at the surrender of Cornwallis at Yorktown. He had eight sons. The eldest, Thomas, married Ann Lee Snoddy. They had eight children, and thirty-eight grandchildren, all living to maturity and rearing large families. Their descendants reside throughout the south and west.

Two other children of John Bransford, Sr., were Elizabeth and James. James married Sarah Owen and lived in Buckingham County. Elizabeth Bransford married Francis West, a wealthy farmer of Chesterfield County. John Bransford, Jr. (another son of John, Sr.) married first Sarah Easter, and in 1765 he married second Judith Ammette, a Huguenot. They lived in Buckingham. John, Jr., had five children by Sarah Easter, and ten by Judith. (Her name is found spelled Amnett, Amet, Ammonette, etc.)

Thomas Bransford, born 1767 in Goochland County, son of John Bransford, Jr., and Judith, married Ann Lee Snoddy on 3 November 1789. Ann Lee Snoddy was born in 1773. Thomas moved to Buckingham County with his father in 1779, was educated in Buckingham, and settled on a plantation given him by his father. In 1817 he and his family migrated to Barren County, Kentucky, where he continued as a planter.

See: Edward S. Lewis, "Bransford Family," <u>William and Mary Quarterly</u>, 2nd series, VIII, 34.

THE BROOKE FAMILY

Robin Brooke (Robert Brooke IV) was a son of Robert Brooke, III, and a grandson of Robert Brooke, Jr., a "Knight of the Golden Horseshoe." The will of Robin Brooke, dated 30 September 1778 was proved in Essex County, Virginia in 1778. He names his father Mr. Robert Brooke, mother Mrs. Mary Brooke, brother Humphrey Brooke, brother Edmund Brooke, and sisters Mary, Catherine, Susannah, Sarah, and Elizabeth Brooke. The executors were the testator's wife, Mrs. Lydia Bushrod Brooke, his father Robert Brooke, Robert Beverly, Esq., and Dr. John Breckenridge.

The sister Catherine Brooke mentioned in the will married Peter Francisco of Revolutionary fame, of Buckingham County. Sarah Brooke married Jesse Michaeux.

The will of Robert Brooke, oldest son of Robert Brooke, Jr., the "Knight of the Golden Horseshoe, dated 28 January 1785, describes him as gentleman, of St. Ann's Parish, Essex County. The will was brought to court by Humphrey Brooke and Edmund Brooke, who were named in the will as executors. Robert Brooke's wife, Mary, daughter of William Fauntleroy, was not named in the will.

Catherine Brooke, born 14 February 1762, died 23 October 1821, married Peter Francisco, died 16 January 1831.

See: Prof. St. George Tucker Brooke, "The Brooke Family of Virginia," Virginia Magazine of History and Biography, XIII, 103, 224.

THE CABELL FAMILY

WILLIAM CABELL (1), progenitor of the family, was in Goochland County, Virginia, when he executed a power of attorney on 27 August 1735 appointing his wife Elizabeth Cabell and friends William Mayo and George Carrington his attorneys. Joseph Scott and John Brown were witnesses. William and Mary Cabell were the parents of: MARY, WILLIAM, JOSEPH, JOHN, GEORGE, and NICHOLAS.

Col. JOSEPH CABELL (2), son of William (1), born 19 September 1732, probably at his father's home on Licking-Hole Creek, near Dover, in what is now Goochland County. In 1737 he began to go to school; by 1739 he "could read well;" in 1740 at his request his mother wrote to his father to bring him a Bible from England; in 1741 he went to school to Mr. William Ward. Some time after his father's return from England in 1741, he moved with his parents to their Swan Creek estate in present Nelson County. On 20 September 1751 he was entered in the sheriff's office as one of the deputy sheriffs "on the north side of the Fluvanna in the County of Albemarle during Capt. Daniel's cheriffsom." The appointment expired in 1753 but he continued to act as deputy under Capt. Daniel's successor, Col. Samuel Jordan until 1755, and may have continued even later under Col. John Reid. He was married in 1752 at the age of 20 years and 1 month to Mary Hopkins. The marriage bond, read: "I, William Cabell do hereby signifie to Henry Wood, clerk of Goochland County, that I do consent to the marriage of my son Joseph with Mary Hopkins. Given under my hand and seal this XCii day of October MDCCLI. Signed, Wm. Cabell."

Mary Hopkins was a daughter of Dr. Arthur Hopkins of Goochland County. Dr. Hopkins was probably born in New Kent County, Virginia, about 1690. About 1710-15 he married Elizabeth Pettus of New Kent. He bought land on "Ye Byrd Creek" in Goochland County in 1731 (in the deed he is styled "Arthur Hopkins of St. Paul's Parish, Hanover County, physician.") He was appointed a justice of the peace for Goochland County in 1737, was high sheriff in 1739-1741, and was a member of the vestry of St. James Northam Parish. Between 1731 and 1750 he acquired much land in Albemarle, Fluvanna, and Goochland Counties. In 1751 he bought lots in the new town of Beverly at Westlawn. He was a Colonel in 1752 and a citizen of Albemarle in 1762. His will, 31 May 1765 - 12 March 1767, named his wife Elizabeth, sons Samuel, John, Arthur, William, and James, daughter Isabella, and son-in-law Col. Joseph Cabell, and he mentioned his married daughters but did not name them.

Joseph Cabell was a Justice in Albemarle County by 1760 and probably as early as 1755. When Albemarle County was divided in 1761 into Albemarle, Amherst and Buckingham Counties, he owned land in each of the three counties, and at various times lived in each of them. He served as Burgess from Buckingham County. A public ferry from his land in Buckingham , "Sion Hill," to his father's land in Amherst was established by an act of the November, 1766, Session of the House of Burgesses.

In 1768 he was Burgess from Buckingham County and continued to represent that county until 1771. He was active throughout the Revolutionary War. After the War Col. Cabell again was a delegate to the General Assembly of Virginia. He was the Senator from this district in the State Senate, probably continually from 1781 to 1785, and was the delegate from Buckingham County in the House of Delegates from 1788 to 1790.

At some point in time he moved from "Sion Hill" (later called "Yellow Gravel" and lived at "Variety Shades." He died 1 March 1798 and he and his wife are buried at "Sion Hill." Their tombstones are inscribed "Sacred to the memory of Joseph Cabell, Born Sept. 8, 1732, died March 1, 1798, age 65 years 7 months. Mary, his wife, was born Jan'y 1735 and died July 12, 1811, age 76 years. Erected by Eliza Lewis, their daughter."

The will of Joseph Cabell of Buckingham County, made 19 December 1794 and proved 12 March 1798, named the following heirs: grandson Joseph Cabell Megginson; Nancy Burks; daughter Mary Hopkins Breckenridge and her husband John Breckenridge; granddaughter Lettecia Preston Breckenridge; granddaughter Mary Hopkins Breckenridge; grandson Joseph Cabell Breckenridge; daughter Ann Harrison and son-in-law Robert Carter Harrison; granddaughter Susanna Randolph Harrison; granddaughter Mary Hopkins Harrison; grandson Joseph Cabell Harrison; daughter Elizabeth Lewis; son Joseph Cabell; granddaughter Sophonisba Cabell; granddaughter Sarah Bolling Cabell; grandson Robert Bolling Cabell; grandson Edward Blair Cabell; grandson Benjamin Cabell; grandson Archibald Bolling Cabell; Mrs. Rachel Townsend; wife Mary Cabell; kinsman William Burks; deceased son Benjamin Cabell. The executors were testator's son Joseph Cabell and son-in-law Robert Carter Harrison, and sons-in-law John Breckenridge and William Lewis. Witnesses to the will were: Rachel Townsend, Abraham Jones, Jr., Thomas Sanders, Thomas Matthews, Samuel Ferguson, Flemsted Jones, Willis Wills, and John Garrott.

JOHN CABELL (3), probably son of WILLIAM CABELL (1) (and not son of Joseph Cabell - ED), married Pauline, daughter of Col. Samuel Jordan on 20 May 1762. On 13 Sept. 1763 he is referred to as Capt. John Cabell at the fall session of the House of Burgesses. In 1764 a public ferry was established between the lands of John Cabell near Bowman's Warehouse in Amherst, across the Fluvanna to his lands in Buckingham. The ferry ran between his "Green Hill" and "Fork Field" estates, which had recently been deeded him by his father.

In 1775 John Cabell was chairman of the Buckingham commission, and one of the deputies from that commission to the district commission which first met on 8 September 1775 at the house of James Woods in Amherst. Cabell also served as County Lieutenant. On 23 November 1775 the commissions for the militia officers of Buckingham County were delivered to Col. John Cabell. On 29 January 1776 he was paid £ 72, the recruiting money for that county. He was one of the delegates from Buckingham County to the convention which met at Williamsburg on 6 May 1776.

The will of John Cabell (which was not included in Brown's The Cabells And Their Kin) was signed 22 April 1815 and proved 12 June 1815. It named the following heirs: son Robert Jones Cabell son of Elizabeth B. Jones; grandson Samuel Jones Cabell; natural born daughter Elizabeth Burke Cabell; natural born sons Napoleon Bonaparte Cabell and Alexander Cabell; son Frederick Cabell; Frances Johnson named as the mother of the three last named natural born children; lawful children George Cabell, Frederick Cabell, John Cabell, Samuel Cabell, and Pauline J. Cabell; natural born children Elizabeth Burks Cabell, Napoleon Bonaparte Cabell and Alexander Cabell. Sons Frederick and John Cabell were named executors. The will was witnessed by Charles Burks, Reuben D. Palmer, and George Burks.

JOSEPH CABELL (4), son of Col. Joseph Cabell (2), was born 6 January 1762, went with his father to Kentucky in 1811, settled in Henderson County, and died there on 31 August 1831. He married Pocahontas Rebecca Bolling, daughter of Robert Bolling of "Chellowe," Buckingham County.

At first he was taught by tutors, and was at Hampton-Sydney in 1778 and 1779, and at William and Mary College from 4 May 1779 to 1781. He belonged to the company of students attached to the regiment of Col. Joseph Cabell, the elder. By 1787 he was captain of a militia company. He was the subject of a deed in Hanover County, Virginia, dated 12 June 1789. (See "Records of Hanover County," William and Mary Quarterly, 1st series, XXI, 145).

The will of Joseph Cabell of Madison County, Kentucky, signed 16 June 1827, was proved in Henderson County, Kentucky at the October 1831 Court. A copy was furnished to the author by Mrs. Mary Lillian Eubank Sullivan of Nashville, Tennessee. Joseph Cabell named the following heirs: wife Ann E. Cabell; daughter Jane R. Allen; sons John B., Robert B., George W., and Richard R. Cabell; son Benjamin W. S. Cabell of Virginia and his wife Sarah E. Cabell; daughter Sophonisba E. Grayson; son Edward B. Cabell; grandson Joseph Cabell Meredith; daughters Mary Ann H. Cabell, Jane R. Allen, and Elizabeth R. Pollett; children by former marriages have already been provided for but are remembered with paternal affection. Executors were to be his wife Ann E. Cabell and son John B. Cabell. The witnesses were: F. E. Walker, Tandy K. Perry, and Gabriel Lilly, Jr.

See: Alexander Brown, The Cabells and Their Kin (Boston: Houghton Mifflin and Co., 1895).
Will of Joseph Cabell (2) is in the Archives Division, Virginia State Library, Richmond.

THE CANNON FAMILY

WILLIAM CANNON of Buckingham County married first Sarah Mosby, daughter of Col. Littleberry Mosby by his Netherland marriage. Cannon married second to Martha Cocke, fourth child of James Cocke. Her marriage was recorded in Amelia County on 24 June 1790.

William Cannon of Buckingham is mentioned several times in Hening's Statutes at Large, and seems to have been a man of influence. Towards the close of his life he lost his home, "Mount Ida," in Buckingham County, probably around 1804 or 1805, and in 1807 migrated to Nashville, Davidson County, Tennessee with his sons John, James, and William (by his second marriage). In 1820 or about that time he moved to Caldwell County, Kentucky, and settled near the "Big Spring on Indian Camp Creek." He died that year and is buried in the Catlett or Bennett graveyard on a farm near Princeton, Kentucky, in an unmarked grave.

William's daughter by his first wife was Martha, who married Silas Flournoy (See The Flournoy Family, below).

See: Flournoy Rivers, "Littleberry Mosby—William Cannon," Virginia Magazine of History and Biography, X, 100.
"Cocke Family of Virginia," in Virginia Magazine of History and Biography, IV, 438.
"The Flournoy Family," Virginia Magazine of History and Biography, I, 469.

THE CHASTAIN FAMILY

Rev. RENE CHASTAIN, a Baptist minister of French extraction, was born in Powhatan County, Virginia, on 28 June 1741. While he was still young the family moved to Buckingham County, where they lived for the rest of their lives. When Rene was 19 years old he married Ann Ford, daughter of James Ford, Sr., and granddaughter of Pierre Faure who emigrated to Virginia.

On 28 February 1761 James Ford of Tillotson Parish, Albemarle County (later Buckingham County) conveyed 100 acres of land on the Slate River to Ann Chastain. (Albemarle County Records).

Soon after his marriage Rene Chastain was awakened "to the exercise of a pungent conviction of sin," by the preaching of Elder C. Clark. In August 1770 he rejoiced in Christ, was baptized and immediately began to preach. He was ordained in Buckingham Church in April 1772, was at once chosen pastor and continued for 53 years, as long as he lived. At different times he supplied Cumberland, Providence, and Mulberry Churches.

Reverend JOHN CHASTAIN (known as "Ten Shilling Bill") and Mary O'Bryan (or O'Brien) were married about 1765 in Buckingham County, Virginia, and moved to Pickens County, South Carolina.

See: Genealogy of the Chastain Family, published by the Huguenot Society.
James S. Taylor, Lives of Virginia Baptist Ministers, 2nd ed., 1838.
B. J. Kincaid, "Chastain, O'Brien, Green, Braselton," William and Mary Quarterly, 2nd series, IV, 190.

THE CHRISTIAN FAMILY

THOMAS CHRISTIAN (1), the progenitor, was in Virginia by 21 October 1687 when as "Mr. Thomas Christian" he patented 1080 acres of land in Charles City County. In 1694 he was called "Thomas Christian, Sr.," when he patented 193 acres in Chickahominy Swamp. The word "Sr." may indicate that he had a son Thomas who was already of age. Thomas Christian, Sr., may have been the father of: THOMAS; CHARLES; JAMES; JOHN.

THOMAS CHRISTIAN (2), probably son of Thomas (1), patented land in 1712 and 1727 in the forks of Beaver Dam Creek in that part of Henrico County that was Goochland. His will was proved in Goochland County in 1736. He married Rebecca (perhaps a daughter of Drury Stith). He patented 1320 acres of land on 16 December 1714. His children were: THOMAS; ROBERT; WILLIAM (of Albemarle County); JAMES; CONSTANT; REBECCA; ANN; and MOURNING, who married Mr. Coleman.

CHARLES CHRISTIAN (3), probably son of Thomas (1) of Charles City County also located on land in Goochland County in 1714 and 1727.

JAMES CHRISTIAN (4), probably son of Thomas (1), located on land adjacent to Thomas Christian in 1719.

JOHN CHRISTIAN (5), probably son of Thomas (1), was on land in the same vicinity in 1724.

JAMES CHRISTIAN (6), son of Thomas (2), died in Goochland County leaving a will dated 18 May 1752 and proved 15 June 1759. He named his wife Susannah and James Christian as executors. His heirs were named in a lawsuit (Christian's devisees vs. Christian and others, in Munford's Reports, 6:534); his children were: CHARLES, died 1761 without surviving issue; JAMES, died 1794 without issue; JOHN, of Buckingham County, married Joyce (---) and was living in 1805; GEORGE, died c.1784/5.

Captain Henry Christian, whose will was proved in Amherst County on 17 June 1805, married Martha Patteson. He was captain of a company of Minute Men of Buckingham District (which was made up of Amherst, Buckingham, Albemarle, and East Augusta Counties); he was also captain of a company in the Revolutionary War, and was in active service under Col. Daniel Gaines and Major General Lafayette. (H. H. Hardesty, Geographical Historical Encyclopedia, Special Amherst County, Virginia Edition (1884), pp. 409-411).

George Christian, son of John, grandson of William, lived at "Mountain View," in Appomattox County, formerly a part of Buckingham County. He married Joyce Duiguid, sister of the wife of William Christian, and had Dr. William Duiguid, and a daughter Mildred Collier who died in infancy.

See: "Christian Family," William and Mary Quarterly, 1st series, V, 262, and VIII, 269.

THE CLOPTON FAMILY

ANTHONY CLOPTON (1), of the fourth generation of Cloptons in Virginia, was a son of Benjamin, of Walter, of William. He was born 20 November 1750 and died 28 July 1824 in Tennessee. He married on 24 May 1804 in Tennessee Rhoda Hoggett, born 23 December 1785 in Buckingham County, Virginia, died 23 November 1831 in Tipton County, West Tennessee. She was the daughter of John Hoggatt and his first wife, Agnes Watkins. John Hoggatt married as his second wife Diana Sandifer. Anthony and Rhoda (Hoggatt) Clopton were the parents of: JOHN HOGGATT; BENJAMIN MICHAUX; WILLIAM ANTHONY; JAMES WILFORD; AGNES WATKINS, married a Mr. Morgan; EVELINA, married Mr. Whitlock; ELIZA HOGGATT; VIRGINIA; MARY.

JOHN HOGGATT CLOPTON (2), son of Anthony (1) and Rhoda, was born in Virginia on 23 April 1805, died 31 August 1855. On 17 March 1830 he married Matilda Caroline Drake, born 10 February 1813, daughter of John Briton Drake of Tennessee. She died 6 June 1865. John Hoggatt and Matilda Caroline had ten children, the youngest of whom was: Col. WILLIAM C. CLOPTON, who lived in New York.

See: "Clopton Family," William and Mary Quarterly, 1st series, XI, 70.

THE COBB FAMILY

Robert Cobb, son of Robert, and grandson of Ambrose Cobb, lived in York County, Virginia. His first wife was Rebecca, daughter of William Pinketham. She died in 1715 leaving two children. Robert Cobb married second Elizabeth, daughter of Daniel Allen. After Robert's death his widow married Samuel Weldon of Henrico County. Robert had two children by his second wife also. His children were: (by the first wife) Elizabeth, born 1704, married James Shields in 1719, and Rebecca; (by the second wife) Sarah, married Robert Jones, Jr., of Sussex County (by whom she was the mother of Allen and Willies Jones of Revolutionary War fame), and Martha, married Major Dudley Richardson.

Augustus Cobb or Cobbs married Elizabeth Abram or Abrums. He raised his family in Buckingham County. Augustus and Elizabeth (Abram) Cobb were the parents of: James Napoleon, born in Buckingham County and went to Georgia; Jacob Levi, born in Buckingham and went to Georgia; Pleasant Augustus, born in Buckingham and died in Lynchburg; Richard, married Miss Harvey; John Anderson, married Elizabeth Ann Pullin of Highland County; Frances, married Willie P. Bowman and went to Ohio (had two sons, John Anderson and Delifaiette Bowman).

Thomas Cobb, brother of Augustus, went to one of the Carolinas or to Georgia. Norvel Cobb, a nephew of Augustus, was a Colonel in the Confederate Army and lived in Richmond after the war.

See: "Cobb or Cobbs Family," William and Mary Quarterly, 1st series, XIX, 56.
"Armistead Family," William and Mary Quarterly, 1st series, VII, 21.
Fanny B. Hunter, "Cocke, Gray, Bowie, Robb &c.," Virginia Magazine of History and Biography, X, 101.
Virginia Cobb, "Cobbs--Abrams--Henry," Virginia Magazine of History and Biography, XXXIII, 201.

THE COUPLAND FAMILY

David Coupland is stated in the Family Bible of Elizabeth Bassett (Coupland) Trent (the Bible was in the possession of Stephen W. Trent of "Bell Branch," Buckingham County) to have been the second son of William and Alice (Apsley), and to have been born at the seat of his grandfather, David O'Sheal, in Nansemond County on 3 August 1749. David Coupland was a Justice of Cumberland County, appointed 24 October 1778 (Cumberland County Order Book, 1774-1778, p. 508), and vestryman of Littleon Parish. He died in 1821. He married Ann Harrison, who died in 1821. Their home was at "Springfield, " lying in both Cumberland and Buckingham Counties, on the west side of Willis' river and opposite (north) side of Great Buffalo Creek, from "Clay Bank," an old Randolph and Trent home which was standing as late as 1926 (See Deed from Archibald Cary to David Coupland in Deed Book 5, p. 25).

There is no record of administration of estates for either David or Ann Coupland in Cumberland County, and the records of Buckingham County were burned in the nineteenth century.

See: "Harrison of James River," in Virginia Magazine of History and Biography, XXXIV, 90-91.

THE CURD FAMILY

EDWARD CURD (1) was in Henrico County as early as 1704 when on 2 October he purchased from John Woodson 600 acres of land on the north side of James River, adjoining land formerly belonging to James Blair, and part of a greater tract granted to John Woodson, Jr., by patent dated 23 October 1690. Edward's first wife is not known, although she was the mother of his children. He married secondly Elizabeth Branch, daughter of Thomas and Elizabeth Archer Branch. Elizabeth had married first in 1710 Robert Goode (died 1718), and second Page Punch (who died c.1726-7). Elizabeth Branch Curd died 30 November 1766.

Edward Curd patented 531 acres on the west side of the north branch of Beaver Dam Creek in Goochland County on 1 October 1716. On 17 August 1725 he patented 400 acres on the same creek. On 16 July 1733 he deeded land in Goochland County to his daughters Mary Richardson and Elizabeth Williams.

Edward Curd was elected to the vestry of Old St. John's Church in Richmond, on 17 June 1735. On 2 September 1735 he and Richard Randolph were appointed to view the chapel and report what "reparation and addition thereunto are wanting." He was chosen vestryman again on 2 October 1745, but died soon after as Beverly Randolph took the oath as Vestryman in place of Edward Curd, deceased, on 26 July 1745 (sic).

The will of Edward Curd, dated 4 February 1739/40, was proved on the 1st Monday in December 1742. In it he named his wife Elizabeth, sons Edward, Richard, and John, Mary Mackbride and her son Edward Mackbride, daughter-in-law (i.e., stepdaughter) Mary Punch, grandson John Curd, granddaughter Jane Mackbride, daughter Mary Richardson, and daughter Elizabeth Williams. His wife Elizabeth and son Edward were executors.

Each of his children were given land in Goochland County before Edward's death, and his sons John and Richard and daughter Mary Mackbride went there to live. The daughter Mary Richardson and her husband John went to Cumberland County, Virginia.

Edward Curd was the father of: EDWARD, called Edward Curd, Sr., in 1768, and living in 1771, not traced; JOHN, married Elizabeth; RICHARD, died in Goochland County, leaving a will, 22 June 1778 - 19 October 1778, which named wife Sarah and nine children; MARY, married first John McBride (by whom she had Jane, born 29 September 1726, Edward who married Elizabeth Williamson, and possibly other children), and second John Richardson (who died in Cumberland County in 1753 leaving a will proved 4 September which named children: Isham, John, Elizabeth, Mary, Martha who married a Dawson, Ann who married a Harvey, Sarah, Frances who married Lewis Jackson, Susannah who married a Gilliam, and Agnes who married a Vaughter. Mary Curd Richardson died in Charlotte County, Virginia leaving a will proved 3 October 1791 which named some of her children, and a granddaughter Martha Lumkin or Sumkin.); ELIZABETH, married Mr. Williams.

JOHN CURD (2), son of Edward (1), died in Goochland County in 1752 having married Elizabeth (probably Price). The division of his estate, dated 16 January 1759, named his wife Elizabeth and these children: JOHN, WILLIAM, JOSEPH, MARY, CHARLES, JAMES, ELIZABETH, and ANN. Elizabeth Curd, the widow, married second, on 29 August 1758, Richard Oglesby.

JOHN CURD (2), son of John (2), married Lucy Brent on 7 April 1758 in Lancaster County, Virginia, and about 1780 moved to Kentucky.

WILLIAM CURD (4), son of John (2), married first, about 1763, Mary (probably Watkins), and second, Ann (surname unknown). They moved to Buckingham County, where he died about 1798.

JOSEPH CURD (5), son of John (2), married first, on 28 September 1762 Mary Warren, and second, on 2 October 1772, Mary Truehart, daughter or granddaughter of Aaron Bartholomew Truehart, who came from England about 1740. Joseph died about 1811 in Buckingham County.

Joseph Curd moved to the southern part of Buckingham County on property now the site of the town of Curdsville. In 1782 he owned 408 acres of land and later purchases increased his property to 1200 acres. He was a First Lieutenant in the Sixth Virginia Regiment in the Revolutionary War, and like his brother John, was given large grants of land in Kentucky for services rendered to the State of Virginia in that struggle for independence. Joseph deeded this land to all his children, all of whom except John eventually settled in Kentucky.

Buckingham County Tax Records show that after 1811 property assessed to Joseph Curd was assessed to his widow Mary Curd, who later moved to Kentucky.

Joseph Curd had four children by Mary Warren, and the rest of his children were by Mary Truehart. He was the father of: ELIZABETH, born 24 July 1762, married William Johns; DANIEL, born 1768, married first, in 1793 Nancy Bowles (born 7 May 1770, died 1794), and second, Jane (---) (born 1773, died 1814); MARY (ANN), born 1770, married Michael Neyfong or Niphong on 18 October 1809, and died 1854; MARTHA, born 5 September 1771, probably died young; (by second wife); ANNE TRUEHART, born 1773; JOHN, born 21 March 1774; JOSEPH, Jr., born 13 June 1775, died 1860 in Kentucky, married first, Sarah Coghill, and second, Mildred Slaughter, daughter of Col. John Slaughter; MARTHA, born 1776, married a Small; BENJAMIN, born 24 December 1778, married Susan Belcher; PLEASANT, born 1781, died unmarried in the fall of 1817 in Mercer County, Kentucky, leaving a will, 15 September 1817 - December 1817 (Mercer County Will Book No. 6, p. 66); AARON BARTHOLOMEW, born 1784, married Nancy Woolridge; STEPHEN, born 1786, married Porter Curd, daughter of Newton Curd; SUSAN, born 1788, married Robert Higgins; NANCY, born 1790, married Philip Johnson; SARAH, born 1792, married R. O. Steenbergen; JAMES, born 15 April 1795, married Deliah Ward.

MARY CURD (6), daughter of John (2), married on 18 March 1764 her first cousin Edmund Curd, son of Richard Curd of Edward and Sarah Downer. He died in Goochland County.

CHARLES CURD (7), son of John (2), received a grant of land of 800 acres in Kentucky in 1780, and is said to have been an early settler at Louisville.

JAMES CURD (8), son of John (2), married Mary Graves on 20 February 1766 and died in Goochland County leaving an inventory dated 1792.

ELIZABETH CURD (9), daughter of John (2), married John Bowles on 2 December 1764.

ANN CURD (10), daughter of John (2), married Richard Sampson on 24 November 1771.

JOHN CURD (11), son of Joseph (5), was born 21 March 1774, and died 4 September 1822 in Wilson County, Tennessee, having married either in Buckingham or Cumberland County, Virginia, Elizabeth Lumpkin, born 12 May 1775, died 5 March 1840. Elizabeth was a descendant of Captain Jacob Lumpkin who came from England to Virginia prior to 1677.

John Curd moved to Tennessee in the late fall of 1817 or early spring of 1818 with his wife and eleven children. On 27 March 1818 he purchased from

Daniel Small a tract of 334 acres of land in the first district of Wilson County, part of a larger tract granted by the State of North Carolina to John Donelson on 20 May 1793, Grant no. 2167. John and Elizabeth are buried in the family burial ground on his estate, with tombstones inscribed with their dates of birth and death.

John and Elizabeth (Lumpkin) Curd were the parents of: MARY (or POLLY), born abouy 1801, married Ozburn Thompson, and had issue: Martha, born 12 May 1831, married E. T. Griggs, Margaret, born 17 May 1838, married 12 January 1859 James M. Riggan, Mary (or Mollie), married Jack Clemmons, John Thompson, and James K. P. Thompson; SARAH, born 10 November 1802, died 11 August 1887, married Isham F. Davis, born 19 January 1800, died 20 January 1880, son of Nathaniel Davis, an early settler in Wilson County; MARTHA, born 22 November 1803, died 22 November 1886, married Colonel Jonas Swingley, born 30 October 1800, died 25 September 1854; NANCY, born 10 December 1804, died 25 January 1872, married on 4 March 1823 William Lanius, born in Fincastle, Botetourt County, Virginia, 22 January 1802, died 26 February 1874, having moved to Missouri in 1820 and in 1823 to Wilson County; WILLIAM M., born 25 November 1805, died 17 August 1842, married Susan Davis (half-sister of Isham Davis who married Sarah Curd, above), born 29 September 1813, died 11 June 1871; JOHN, born 3 April 1807, died unmarried 29 September 1837; PRICE, born 6 May 1808, died 19 August 1883, married first Martha Cherry, and second Elizabeth A. Hall, and third, Mrs. Minerva Bonner, a widow; JAMES, born 25 September 1809, died 13 January 1876, married Susan Everett (born 4 July 1810, died 22 Seotember 1896, daughter of John Everett) on 18 November 1833; ELIZABETH, died 13 November 1887, having married John G. Gleaves on 18 December 1828, and residing in Davidson County, Tennessee; RICHARD, living March 1841 when his mother'e estate was divided, married Emily E. Hall, daughter of John Hall; THOMAS, living in 1823, died before 1841.

See: Frank D. Fuller and Thomas H. S. Curd, The Curd Family in America (Rutland: Tuttle Publishing Company, Inc., 1938).
The Edward Pleasants Valentine Papers, 4 vols. (Richmond: The Valentine Museum, 1927).
"Virginia Quit Rent Rolls, 1704 (Henrico County)," Virginia Magazine of History and Biography, XXVIII, 210.
"Notes from Records of Goochland County," Virginia Magazine of History and Biography, XXII, 314-315.
William Clayton Torrence, "Thomas and William Branch of Henrico County, and Some of Their Descendants," William and Mary Quarterly, 1st series, XXV, 66-67.
Chamberlayne, Douglas Parish Register (perhaps William Douglas, The Douglas Register, orig. pub. 1928, and repr. Baltimore: Genealogical Publishing Company, 1973).
Francis B. Heitman, Historical Register of Officers of the Continental Army During the War of the Revolution, April 1775 to December 1783 (repr.: Baltimore: Genealogical Publishing Company, 1973).
Goodspeed's History of Tennessee: Wilson County volume.
Edythe R. Whitley, Marriages of Wilson County, Tennessee, 1802-1850 (Baltimore: Genealogical Publishing Company, 1981).

THE DUNCAN FAMILY

Joseph C. Duncan of Buckingham County, Virginia, was of Scottish descent. He married Nancy Maddox and settles in Christian County, Kentucky in 1817. In 1829 he went to Missouri and settled in Callaway County, where he died in 1870. His wife died in 1860. They had none children: Joel, died young; Richard, died young; Elizabeth A., married John McMahan; Frederick W., went to Oregon; Ouslaw G., married Julie A. Broadeater and lived in Audrain County Missouri; Jerome B., married Mary George; Articinica, married Col. Marshall Coats of Coat's Praire; Metter B., married Mary E. Berkett, and was a banker in Mexico, Missouri; Edward, married Martha Mhan (sic) and lived in Monroe County, Missouri.

See: William S. Bryan and R. Rose, <u>A History of the Pioneer Families of Missouri, 1876,</u> (Repr.: Columbia, Mo., 1935), p. 325.

THE ELDRIDGE FAMILY

Rolfe Eldridge, son of Thomas, of Thomas, was Clerk of Buckingham County, Virginia, from 1770 to 1806. He married Susanna Everard Walker, daughter of Col. George Walker of Elizabeth City County, in 1773.

At the time of his appointment as county clerk, Eldridge was in the chancery clerk's office at Williamsburg. After his appointment he located at a place about eight miles east of the court house, and established the clerk's office at his home, which he named "Subpoena," and there all of the business of the clerkship was transacted except that which appertained to the sessions of the courts. Mr. Eldridge had a body-servant called Mars who would transport the necessary records from "Subpoena" to the court house on horseback.

Rolfe and Susanna (Walker Eldridge were the parents of: Rolfe (see below); Mary Meade, unmarried; Susan Meade, married Mr. Webber; Nancy Meade, unmarried; David Walker, unmarried; Thomas Kidder, married Mary Ayres; Jane Pocohantas, married Mr. McDonald; George Wythe, unmarried; Courtney Tucker, married John Williams; Martha Bolling, unmarried.

Rolfe Eldridge, Jr., son of Rolfe and Susanna, was clerk of Buckingham County from 1806 to 1859. He married Mary Moseley, daughter of Benjamin Moseley and Mary Branch who were married 25 December 1783 in Chesterfield County. Benjamin was a First Lieutenant of the First Battaliion of Artillery in the Virginia Continental Line from 2 May 1779 to 4 March 1783. He was given a grant of land in Ohio for his service, and died in Buckingham County on 26 July 1799.

Rolfe Eldridge, Jr., entered his father's office in 1795 at the age of 15, and in 1797 qualified as deputy clerk. He was appointed to succeed his father and immediately moved nearer the court house as a convenience for attending to the business which was rapidly increasing. He was clerk from 1806 to 1858. He died in the spring of 1861. Attending to the preparation of the most important entries himself, he was possessed of a wonderful facility in laying out ordered to meet special cases under new laws. He gave his personal attention to every detail of his office and to the presentation of the work of the courts. He had great influence in the county as well as among his contemporaries. He declined reelection in 1858 and was succeeded by his son-in-law Robert K. Irving. Eldridge was devoted to his family, friends, and church, and was an earnest member of the old school Presbyterian Church.

See "Eldridge Family," <u>William and Mary Quarterly, 1st series</u>, XX, 207.

THE FEARN FAMILY

JOHN FEARN (1), born 1665 in England, settled in Gloucester County, and married Mary Lee in 1687. Family tradition states that the family had a coat of arms blazoned: Per bend Or and Gules, two lions' heads erased Counterchanged; Crest: A talbot's head Argent, collared Gules, garnished and ringed Or, issuing out of a fern proper. John and Mary (Lee) Fearn were the parents of: JOHN, born c. 1692.

JOHN FEARN (2), son of John (1), born c.1692, died 1720, married Sarah Worthem, and had issue: JOHN, born in 1717.

JOHN FEARN (3), son of John (2), born 1717, died 1782 in Buckingham County. About 1744 he married Mrs. Leanna Lee, and was a captain during the Revolutionary War.

84

The will of John Fearn was proved in Buckingham County on 8 April 1782 and 11 November 1782, and registered in Campbell County, Kentucky on 27 August 1827.   It named his children Thomas, John, Samuel (last two not yet 21), Fanny Putney, Jane, and Mary. William Cannon was one of the executors. Craddock Blanks and William Webb, Sr., were witnesses.

John and Leanna had (perhaps among others: THOMAS; JOHN; SAMUEL; FANNY, married Mr. Putney, JANE; MARY.

THOMAS FEARN (4), son of John (3), was born in 1745, and about 1785 went to Danville, Virginia. In the same year he married Mary Burton, born 1751, died 1845, daughter of Colonel Robert Burton of Caswell County, North Carolina. Col. Burton was one of those who aided in the settling and founding of Kentucky, and was the agent for the Transylvania Company. Thomas and Mary (Burton) Fearn had: ROBERT.

ROBERT FEARN (5), son of Thomas, was born 1795 and died 1856. In 1818 he married Eliza Maria Henderson, and they were the parents of: Col. ROBERT FEARN, born 1830, died 1873, lawyer and graduate of Harvard University.

See Hugh S. Watson's article in the Newport News-Hampton, Va., _Daily Press_, Sunday, 24 April 1966.

THE FLOURNOY FAMILY

SILAS FLOURNOY married Martha, daughter of William and Sarah (Mosby) Cannon. On 25 April 1799 Silas and Martha sold to Jordan Flournoy 400 acres in Powhatan County on Jones' Creek, adjoining the land of Jordan and David Flournoy. By 4 March 1807 the Flournoys were in Davidson County, Tennessee, when they purchased from one Williams $599\frac{1}{2}$ acres of land on the south side of the Cumberland, near the mouth of Stone's River, for $3,071,56. In the deed Flournoy was described as "of Buckingham County, Virginia." (Davidson County, Tennessee, Deed Book G, p. 328). Flournoy was still in Davidson County on 20 May 1817 when he sold his first purchase to Mr. Sims for $9,000.00 cash. On 13 August 1817 he styled himself in a deed as of Giles County, Tennessee. The remaining Giles County records show that in 1818 and 1819 he purchased several tracts of land, one of which was a plateau, "Locust Hill," two miles northeast of Pulaski, on the Cornersville Pike. Flournoy was an ardent Jackson supporter, and lived for a while at the Hermitage. He belonged to the Episcopal Church. He died 18 May 1822 and is buried in Giles County with several of his family. His wife is buried on the farm in Davidson County. (Davidson County, Tennessee, Deed Book I, p. 18, L, p. 235, and H, p. 292; Giles County, Tennessee, Deed Book E, pp. 72-75.)

Silas and Martha had two children: Eliza, married Judge Harris, and Alfred, married twice.

ELIZA FLOURNOY, daughter of Silas and Martha, was born 18 November 1794 and died 16 April 1829. She married Judge Alfred M. Harris, of the Pulaski Bar in Giles County, Tennessee, and first judge of the 6th circuit when it was created in 1817. Judge Harris died 21 February 1828. Alfred and Eliza (Flournoy) Harris had three children: Martha, married Jerome Pillow; Alfred H., married Martha Jones; and Eliza, who went to Shreveport with her uncle, and there married a Mr. Watson, by whom she had children.

ALFRED FLOURNOY, son of Silas and Martha, married first Martha Moore, who died childless in 1834 at Pulaski, and second, Mrs. Maria Ward, daughter of John Hamlin Camp of Giles County, Speaker of the Tennessee House of Representatives, who died in 1829.

THE FORD FAMILY

Samuel Ford, son of Boaz and Hannah Ford, was born 30 October 1790 and died 2 April 1846. His will, signed 14 March 1846, was proved in Buckingham County on 14 April 1846.   In it he named his sister Magdalene Maupin, her son Benjamin, her daughters Martha S., Jane, and Mildred Maupin, his deceased sister Maria Ayers and her children, Elizabeth Ayers, John W. Ayers, and Mariah Chambers, Albert B. Ayers (relationship not stated), Addison J. Ford (no relationship stated), brother Ambrose Ford and his son Ambrose, friend Miller Woodson, friend Capt. William Mosley, and appointed George W. Kyle, William Branch, Thomas M. Bondurant executors. John Hill and N. H. Thornton were witnesses. (See The Huguenot, Publication no. 10, p. 96).

Peter Ford left Bucnkingham County, and went to Kentucky. His will, signed 4 March 1779, was proved in Madison County, Kentucky, on 5 October 1801. In it he named his son Daniel, his four daughters Ruth, Ann, Judith, and Sally, son Joel, son Jack, son Salon, step-daughter Polly Slone, step-son Samuel Slone, wife Sarah, daughter Polly (if she is ever recivered from the Indians), son John, and appointed his wife Sarah and sons Daniel and Joel as executors. John Manier, Christopher (X) Coy, Hutchins (X) Burton, and Elisha (X) Coy were witnesses. (See The Huguenot, Publication no. 16, p. 145).

THE FRANCISCO FAMILY

Peter Francisco came to Virginia in 1765 as the victim of a kidnapping. On his arrival in City Point, Virginia, he told his story to Judge Anthony Winston of Buckingham County, who secured permission to take the boy home, known as "Hunting Towers." The Judge was an uncle of the noted orator, Patrick Henry.

A few years later, with the start of the Revolutionary War, Peter obtained permission from the Judge to enlist, and became a private in the Tenth Virginia Regiment, Continental Line, under Col. Hugh Woodson. During his military career Peter was wounded several times, but always returned to the army. He was at Gates' defeat at Camden, and at Guilford Court House. Francisco was a friend of General Nathaniel Greene, who gave him a razor case inscribed "Ptere Francisco, New Store, Buckingham County, Virginia, a tribute to his moral worth and valor. From his Comrade in Arms Nathaniel Greene." Francisco was also friends with George Washington and General Lafayette.

Peter Francisco served in the Revolutionary Army from 1777 to 1779. In 1819 he applied for a pension, but his application was denied. His pension application contained affidavits from Captain Hezekiah Morton, Lieutenant William Evans, Philemon Holcombe, and John Woodson. After the United States Givernment turned down his application, Peter Francisco wrote to the General Assembly of Virginia on 11 November 1820 detailing his military service. After his death in 1831, Peter's widow, Mary B. Francisco, again applied for a pension, which she received.

After the War Francisco kept a tavern at New Store, Buckingham County, and for many years was Sergeant at Arms of the Virginia House of Delegates. Although he was illiterate when he entered the army, he taught himself to read and write.

He died in Richmond, Virginia, on 16 January 1831, having been married three times. He married first Polly Anderson of Cumberland County, second Catherine Fauntleroy Brooke of Essex County, and third Mary B. Grymes, who at age 68 was living in Botetourt County when she applied for a pension on 27 February 1854. She stated she and Francisco were married 3 July 1823.

By his first wife Peter Francisco was the father of: Peter, died young; James Anderson; Eva, married John Thomas, but had no issue; and Robert L., who married Keziah, daughter of Charles Black of Blacksburg, Virginia.

By his second wife, daughter of Robert Brooke of Brooksby, Essex County, Peter was the father of: Peter, died unmarried; Benjamin Morris (married first

Mary Jane Lawrence, and second Frances Annie Goodwin, both of Louisa County, Virginia); Catherine Fauntleroy (married Dandridge Spotswood); and Susan Brooke (married Edward Pescud).

Peter Francisco had no issue by his third wife, Mary B. Grymes (Widow West).

See: Nannie F. Porter, <u>The Romantic Record of Peter Francisco</u> (Staunton, Va.: The McClure Co., 1929).

"Letters Regarding Peter Francisco," <u>William and Mary Quarterly, 1st series</u>, XIV, 6-8.

"Peter Francisco and His Descendants," <u>William and Mary Quarterly, 1st series</u>, XIV, 107-112.

"Peter Francisco, the American Soldier," <u>William and Mary Quarterly, 1st series</u>, XIII, 213-219.

THE GANNAWAY FAMILY

According to Harrison's <u>Surnames of the United Kingdom</u>, the name comes from the Old English words "gegn" and "weg" and means "dweller at the straight road."

JOHN GANNAWAY (1), and his brother MARMADUKE were in America about 1700, living in New Kent County, Virginia. John had at least two sons: JOHN, Jr.; and WILLIAM, born 31 August 1723 in St. Peter's Parish, New Kent County, Virginia. (St. Peter's Parish Register, p. 85)

MARMADUKE GANNAWAY (2), brother of John (1), also lived in New Kent County, where he married Hannah (?) and had issue (births recorded in St. Peter's Parish Register): HANNAH, born 22 July 1736; SARAH, born 22 February 1738 (St. Peter's Parish Register, p. 123).

JOHN GANNAWAY (3), son of John (1), died in Buckingham County, Va., probably c.1770, and definitely by 1781 when there were twelve claimants for parts of his estate. The claimants were: Mary Gannaway, Thomas Gannaway, Gregory Gannaway, Robert Gannaway, Meney (probably nickname for Edmund) Gannaway, John Gannaway (who was also guardian of his sisters Betty Gannaway and Susannah Gannaway), Robert Sanders for his wife, James Johns for his wife, and John Woodson for his wife. In 1793 documents relating to the same estate named Robert Sanders, John Woodson, John Gannaway, James Johns, Gregory Gannaway, Money Gannaway, Charles Walker (probably married one of the daughters), Reuben Sca...(married one of the daughters), Robert Gannaway, William Gannaway, and Thomas Gannaway.

John Gannaway's children were found listed in an old Hymn Book, made available to the author by Mrs. W. B. Spratt of Richlands, Virginia. The children were: WILLIAM, born 26 April 1747; JOHN, born 4 September 1748; CATHERINE, born 4 January 1749; THOMAS, born 8 May 1751; GREGORY, born 8 December 1753; MARY, born 18 May 1754; ROBERT, born 7 September 1756; FRANCES, born 6 March 1759; SALLY, born 19 July 1761; BETSY, born 24 September 1764; SUSANNAH, born 9 February 1768; EDMUND, born 1763.

WILLIAM GANNAWAY (4), son of John (3), was born 26 April 1747 and married Elizabeth Wright.

JOHN GANNAWAY (5), son of John (3), was born 4 September 1748, died in Goochland County in 1798, and married Martha Woodson on 11 April 1773 in Cumberland County, Virginia. Martha Woodson, daughter of John and Elizabeth (Anderson) Woodson, was born about 1753. Her father was a Burgess from Goochland County.

John Gannaway's Revolutionary service is found in Rev. War Aud. Accts., xxxi, 88, in the Virginia State Library.

John and Martha were the parents of: JOHN E., born 1778, married Catherine Evans; MARMADUKE, married Drusilla Woodson; BURRELL, died about 1855 in Murfreesboro, Rutherford County, Tenn., married Sally; THOMAS, married Judith Woodson, c.1810; THEODORICK, married Mrs. Judith Lancaster Gills; FRANCES, married Gilliam Molloy; WARREN, married Miss Snell; WILLIAM G., born 17 August 1780; WOODSON, born 11 September 1782, married Judith Jane Woodson.

THOMAS GANNAWAY (6), son of John (3), was born 8 May 1751, and married Sally (?).

GREGORY GANNAWAY (7), son of John (3), was born 8 May 1753 and died 24 August 1804, married Rhoda Robertson, daughter of Jeffrey Robertson.

FRANCES GANNAWAY (8), daughter of John (3), was born 6 March 1759, and married Edward (?) Morgan of New Kent County. She left at least one child: GANNAWAY MORGAN who was named in the 1793 documents pertaining to John Gannaway's estate.

EDMUND GANNAWAY (9), son of John (3), was born 6 June 1760, and called "Money," married Drusilla Walker.

BETSEY GANNAWAY (10), daughter of John (3), was born 24 September 1764, probably married Reuben Seay.

SUSANNA GANNAWAY (11), daughter of John (3), was born 9 February 1768, and probably married Charles Walker.

BURRELL GANNAWAY (12), son of John (5), died about 1855 in Murfreesboro, Rutherford County, Tennessee. He married Sally (?). On 27 February 1836 he wrote from Murfreesboro to his brother Marmaduke. He mentioned cousins: John Gannaway who has laid on his bed for 14 weeks and is just able to go about. His oldest son William is unhealthy. The children are smart but needy. When William Gilliam was in your country we sent a power of attorney by him to get some money due from some of his wife's relations in Chesterfield (who are dead), but the power of attorney was not properly filled out and the money could not come. I then wrote a letter to Lawson Fosee and Thomas Purdy, execs., and admr., to inform me what names to insert, but instead they wrote to Purdy Robinson in North Carolina, and Purdy write to me...all this and no money to the proper owner who needs everything calculated to make life desirable. Will you go to Chesterfield County and see Thomas Purdy and Lawson Fosee and tell them to make a proper form for signatures.

THEODORICK GANNAWAY (13), son of John (5), lived for a while in Murfreesboro, Rutherford County, Tennessee, about 1810, but returned to Virginia. He served in the War of 1812 as Sergeant in a detachment of Infantry, 24th Regiment, Virginia Militia, Buckingham County. His service was from 31 December 1813 to 11 April 1814. On his return to Buckingham County he married Mrs. Judith Lancaster Gills. He took care of Richard and William Gannaway, sons of his brother John E. Gannaway, who had died. The boys attended Washington and Lee College at Lexington, Virginia.

FRANCES GANNAWAY (14), daughter of John (5), married Gilliam Molloy. He died in Murfreesboro, Tennessee about 1812, and Burrell Gannaway administered the estate. Gilliam and Frances were the parents of: WILLIAM, living in 1846 with his mother in Murfreesboro; JOHN, died by 1846 in Murfreesboro, married and had four sons, one of whom, Robert H., was in Natchez, Mississippi in 1846; JUDITH; FANNIE M.; DAVID B., married 1834 Miss Harrison, and lived in Holly Springs, Mississippi, in 1836, had a son Ferdinand, born 1830 in Murfreesboro; ELIZABETH, married John Jones; MARTHA WOODSON, married Gilliam Giller in Tenn.

John Molloy, nephew of Theodorick C. Gannaway, wrote from Rutherford County, Tennessee, in October 1838 stating he had four children, all sons.

A. Gannaway wrote from Lynchburg, 11 August 1837: "Inform me of the prospects of a sale of land in Buckingham on which subject I have expected a letter...Our family is quite well at present; our relatives are generally well; William's family much better than when you were with us."

Sarah Jane Gannaway who married Miller Shepard, was descended from John Gannaway who served in the French and Indian War. She was (probably-ED.) the daughter of John Gannaway who married Catherine Evans, having served in the War of 1812 as captain of a company in the Eighth (Wall's) Regiment, Virginia Militia, from 29 August 1814 to 24 February 1815.

See: Catherine Adams, Adams Family MSS., 1925, in Tennessee State Library.

Old Letters of the Gannaway Family.

Register of St. Peter's Parish, New Kent County.

Letters in possession of Mrs. John Trent of Dillwyn, Virginia.

Virginia War of 1812 Records, Virginia State Archives, Richmond.

William Shepard, "Shepard and Other Buckingham Families," William and Mary Quarterly, 2nd series, VI, 151-153; ("Part II,"), Ibid., VII, 177-178.

THE GIST FAMILY

Nathaniel Gist, son of Christopher Gist of Maryland, is said to have been with his father and brother at Braddock's Defeat. During the Revolutionary War he was a Colonel in the Virginia Continental Line, and was captured at Charleston, 12 May 1780. He retired on 1 January 1781. He married Judith Cary Bell, daughter of David Bell of Buckingham County, and niece of Archibald Cary of Ampthill. Nathaniel and Judith were the parents of: Henry Cary; Thomas Cecil; Sarah Howard, married Jesse Bledsoe, U. S. Senator from Kentucky; Ann, married Col. Nathaniel Hart of Kentucky, brother of Mrs. Henry Clay; a dau., married Dr. Boswell of Lexington, Kentucky; Elizabeth V. H., married Francis P. Blair, brother of Montgomery Blair; a daughter, married Benjamin Gratz, of Lexington, Kentucky.

See: Jean M. Dorsey, Christopher Gist of Maryland and Some of His Descendants, 1679 - 1957 (Chicago: J. S. Swift, 1969).

THE GLOVER FAMILY

Samuel Glover of Albemarle County, on the "xvij day of May, MDCCXLVII," for the sum of five shillings deeded to Phineas Glover of Goochland County one tract or parcel of land containing nine hundred and fifty acres of land, being the tract where the said Phineas Glover now dwells, the greater part whereof lies in Goochland County, the rest in Albemarle, and bounded Eastwardly by George Carrington, Southwardly by the South branch of Cattail Creek, Westwardly by Joseph Price's. Valentine Martin, and Northwardly by Isaac Bates, and is part of one thousand acres granted to Samuel Glover, deceased, by Patent dated 10 September 1735 which said nine hundred and fifty acres were devised to said Phineas by the last will and testament of Samuel Glover, and by the said Phineas sold to the Samuel first mentioned above by deed dated 17 May 1748. Samuel Glover acknowledged the deed in court on 17 May 1748 (Goochland County Deed Book # 5, pp. 407-408).

Phineas Glover on Goochland County, on "xvij day of May, MDCCXLVII," for Ten pounds fifteen shillings current money, sold to Joseph Price of the same county eighty acres of land in Goochland County, being part of one thousand acres granted to Samuel Glover, deceased, by patent dated 10 September 1735. Phineas Glover acknowledged in court on 17 May 1748. (Goochland County Deed Book # 5, pp. 402-403.)

THE GRAY FAMILY

John Taylor Gray, son of James Gray and Harriet Ann Wherry, his wife, married Julia Randolph Trent on 1 May 1867 in Buckingham County. He died 24 August 1876. For several years he was an apothecary in Richmond, but after his marriage, moved to his wife's parents' home, "Clay Bank," where he died. Julia Randolph Trent was the daughter of Alexander Trent by his second wife, Elizabeth Randolph. Julia was born at "Clay Bank" on 10 November 1841. John Taylor and Julia Randolph (Trent) Gray were the parents of: James, born 23 January 1868, died 19 April 1868; Alexander Trent, born 18 May 1869 at "Clay

Bank;" John Taylor, born 16 December 1870, also at "Clay Bank;" Julian, born 9 October 1872; Elizabeth Randolph, born 4 March 1874; and Harriet Wherry, born 30 August 1875 at "Clay Bank."

Mildred W. Gray, daughter of William and Susannah Gray, was born on 30 April 1785 in Amelia County, Virginia, and died 17 February 1852, aged 66 years, 10 months, and 3 days in Buckingham County. William Gray, Sr., of Prince Edward County, Virginia, was born on 20 February 1745 in Surry County, Virginia, and died in Prince Edward County in 1826, aged 81 years, 3 months, and 24 days. Susannah Crenshaw Gray of Prince Edward County, was born in Amelia County on 17 October 1756, and died on 11 June 1847 in Charlotte County, Virginia. (Gray Family Bible)

See: Edward Pleasants Valentine, The Edward P. Valentine Papers, 4 vols. (Richmond: 1927), pp. 2259 and 2266.

THE HUBARD FAMILY

JAMES HUBARD (1), of Gloucester County, bought a book in London in 1735, and placed his bookplate in it. He is believed to have married Ann Todd, aunt of Judge Todd of Kentucky, and had the following children (listed in the handwriting of Col. William Hubard of the Revolutionary War): MATTHEW, born 11 March 1736; ANN, born 26 March 1738; ELIZABETH, born 6 September 1739; MARY, died in infancy; JAMES, born 6 February 1743; WILLIAM, born 19 December 1744; JOHN, born 2 November 1747; MARGARET, born 24 October 1749; MARY, born 12 June 1752; ELIZABETH, born 15 December 1754.

Col. WILLIAM HUBARD (2), son of James (1), was born 19 December 1744, and died about 1805. He married Frances Thruston, daughter of Col. Charles Mynn Thruston, on 25 May 1768.

Col. William Hubard was a physician who studied at William and Mary and later graduated from the University of Edinburgh. He was the first Senator from the district composed of Halifax, Charlotte, and Prince Edward Counties after the Republic was formed. At the July 1774 Court of Charlotte County he produced a commission from the governor, appointing him to be a captain of a company of foot. When the Revolutionary War broke out he took the side of the colonists and marched with a battalion to Fort Moultrie. He was ay the battle of Guilford Court House, where his horse was killed underneath him.

After the Revolution he was a Senator in 1785, a colonel of Charlotte County Militia in 1787, Sheriff of the County, and County Lieutenant in 1787. He was a man of extensive learning, and a friend of Patrick H nry. He was wealthy, but lost much money because of British debts that had to be paid after the war.

Col. William and Frances (Thruston) Hubard were the parents of: JAMES THRUSTON, born January 1776.

JAMES THRUSTON HUBARD (3), son of Col. William (2), was born in January 1776, married Susan Wilcox of Buckingham County, and moved there to live. He and his wife were the parents of: EDWARD WILCOX, born 20 February 1806; ROBERT THRUSTON, born 26 September 1808; daughter who married a Burwell (and had a son William Burrell who moved to Vicksburg, Mississippi).

EDWARD WILCOX HUBARD (4), son of James Thruston (3) and Susan, was born 20 February 1806 and died 9 December 1872. He was a member of Congress for six years. He married Sarah Eppes on 26 November 1846, and they were the parents of: Dr. JOHN E., born 27 September 1847, died 1892, married Lucy Moseley and had three children; EDMUND WILCOX, Jr., born 5 April 1853, became Commonwealth Attorney; WILLIE I., born 27 July 1855, was a Representative from Buckingham and Cumberland Counties; SUSAN W., born 25 May 1851, married Mr. Crow of Baltimore, Md.

ROBERT THRUSTON HUBARD (5), son of James Thruston (3) and Susan, was born 26 September 1808, and died 19 October 1891 in Buckingham County. He married

Susan Boling in 1834, and twice served in the Legislature. The children of
Robert Thruston and Susan (Boling) Hubard were: Col. JAMES L., born 27 February 1835, was a Lieut.-Col. in the Forty-Fourth Regiment, Virginia Volunteers,
C. S. A., married Miss Isaetta C. Randolph on 13 November 1860, and eleven
children; WILLIAM BOLLING, born 24 December 1836, married Eliza Galloway and
had six children; Col. ROBERT THRUSTON, born 1839, member of the Legislature
and on the staff of Governor Cameron, married Sarah Edmundson; EDMUND WILCOX,
born 27 February 1841, became an Episcopal minister, and married Julia Taylor
of Louisa County, Virginia; EUGENE, died aged eight years; LOUISA, married
Dr. L. C. Randolph; BOLLING, married Julia Chapman; PHILIP A., married Mary
Wilson and lived in Cumberland County, Virginia.

See: "Hubard Family," in Genealogies of Virginia Families from the
William and Mary Quarterly Historical Magazine, Volume III (Baltimore:
Genealogical Publishing Co., Inc., 1982), 73 - 85.

THE JENNINGS FAMILY

William Jennings, Jr., seems to have resided in Buckingham County, and
was probably the father of the following children: Samuel, Phoebe, Agnes,
Fanny, Rhoda, and Nancy Jennings.

Samuel Jennings had 248 acres in Buckingham County, on a branch of the
Appomattox River beginning at pointers and running to William Jennings' line,
Samuel Watkins' old line, thence to William Jennings' old line near the
river, (patented?) 29 March 1792 (Virginia Land Patents, Book 26, 1792, p.
123).

Samuel Jennings of Prince Edward County deeded to "Little John" Baldwin
on 16 September 1799 200 acres of land adjoining Chapman and Dabney land.
(Prince Edward County Deeds Book 11, p. 360).

Samuel Jennings moved to Tennessee, where in Cocke County, on 5 August
1818 he gave a power of attorney to Wm. Stephens of Buckingham County, to sell
all of his (Jennings') land in Prince Edward County lying on the south side of
Appomattox River, adjoining land of Samuel Watkins, John Land, and John Sears,
containing 122 1/3 acres, for whatever price Stephens should think fit.
William Jennings and Richard Kelly witnessed the instrument which was proved
and recorded on 21 September 1818 (Prince Edward County Deeds, Book 16, p.
374).

Samuel Jennings was a Justice of the Peace in Cocke County on 28 April
1831, and went to Missouri by 3 May 1833 (Revolutionary Pension Claim W-7897
at National Archives). Samuel Jennings was probably the father of: James,
William, and Thomas J.

James Jennings was in the Tennessee Militia as a Lieutenant in the 8th
Regiment, 9 April 1811. James Jennings was a 1st Lieutenant under Capt.
Branch Jones, Col. Bayless, Tennessee Militia, in the War of 1812.
He applied for a pension under the Pension Act of 1855, but his claim was
rejected. (Pension no. 223970).

Thomas J. Jennings, aged 32, residing in Bates County, Missouri, on 6
November 1855 was made guardian for Samuel Jennings, minor child of James
Jennings, dec. He filed an application for bounty land due James Jennings
under the Act of 1855. Thos. J. Jennings declared that James Jennings served
as a 1st Lieutenant in Capt. Branch Jones' company, Col. Bayless' regiment
of Tennessee Militia in the War of 1812, and that he was drafted at Newport,
Tennessee on or about 1 November 1814 for six months, and continued in actual
service for 14 days, being honorably discharged.

Thomas Jennings, ensign, Cocke County, was in the Tennessee Militia in
1808 (Tenn. State Archives).

Phoebe Jennings, born 1773, married William Kelly and went to Newport,
Cocke County, Tennessee. William Kelly of Newport stated that he married
Phoebe (aged 73 at the time of his declaration), daughter of William Jennings

of Buckingham County, Virginia, and sister of Samuel Jennings, Agnes Jennings, Fanny Jennings, Rhoda Jennings, and Nancy Jennings.

THE JOHNS FAMILY

The Maryland Family of Johns, from whom Johns Hopkins descends, has descendants in Virginia, but most of the Johns in Virginia trace their roots to Johns of King William County, Virginia, who came from Wales. The Johns of Buckingham County are closely related to the Johns of Charlotte and Pittsylvania Counties. They are also related to the Glovers and other prominent families of the area.

An old Johns Bible, owned in 1927 by a descendant living in Roanoke, Virginia, stated that Col. John Johns lived at New Store, Buckingham County, and that Edmund Winston Johns was a noted divine.

Using several early Bible records and other sources, the author has been able to construct the following Johns pedigree.

Col. John Johns was born 14 October 1746 and died about 1821. On 28 February 1766 he married Elizabeth (surname not known), born 30 October 1749, died between 1784 and 1788. They were the parents of: William M., born 10 January 1766 (sic); Edmund Winston, born 24 May 1767; Judith, born 2 May 1768; Glover, born 25 December 1769, married in 1803 Martha Jones, daughter of Joel Jones, born 1780 in Buckingham, died 1828 (Glover died in 1834 in Mississippi); Anthony Benning, born 11 March 1771; Martha, born 27 October 1772; Mary, born 4 January 1775; Samuel, born 28 September 1777; Elizabeth, born 24 March 1779; Sarah, born 12 March 1780; Ann, born 6 March 1781; John, born 3 June 1784.

Glover Johns, son of Col. John and Elizabeth, was born 25 December 1769, and died 1834 in Mississippi. He married in 1803 Martha, born 1780 in Buckingham County, died 1828, daughter of Joel Jones. Glover and Martha (Jones) Johns were the parents of: John Jay, born 27 June 1818 in Buckingham, died 3 April 1899 at St. Charles, Missouri, married Amanda Jane Durfee; and Mary, married William Cowan.

Thomas Johns, born about 1758, died 30 December 1794, married in 1775 Gartie Hood Flover, possibly a daughter of Samuel Glover, Sr., of Buckingham County. She married 2nd on 16 November 1799 in Pittsylvania County Charles Lewis of "The Bird" in Caswell County, N. C., near Milton, where she is buried. She had several children by her first husband, and none by her second. Most of the children by the first marriage migrated to Rutherford County, Tennessee. ("Johns Family Bible Record," in Virginia Magazine of History and Biography, XXXV, 78-79).

THE PETER JONES FAMILY

Peter Jones, born 1599 in Wales, died 1662 in Henrico County, Virginia. He came to Virginia in 1623 and was Deputy Clerk of Henrico County. In 1676 he commanded fifty-seven men from Elizabeth City County, and served as a major and colonel in the colonial wars in Virginia. He married Margaret, daughter of General Abram Wood. They had at least one son: Peter, Jr.

Peter Jones, Jr., son of Peter and Margaret (Wood) Jones, was born 1651 and died in 1726. He was a founder of Petersburg, Va. He married his cousin, Mary Wood, who died in Prince George County. They had at least one son: John.

John Jones, son of Peter and Mary (Wood) Jones, was born in 1710, and married Elizabeth Walker, born 1719. They had at least one son, William, born 1745, lived in Buckingham County.

William Jones, son of John and Elizabeth (Walker) Jones, was born 1745, died 15 March 1781, having married Agnes Walker, born 1749, died 1819. William served in Capt. Robert Powell's company, Col. William Hethlos (Hetlis?) 3rd Virginia Regiment, and was killed at the Battle of Guilford Court House on 15 March 1781. William and Agnes (Walker) Jones had at least one son: James.

James Jones, son of William and Agnes (Walker) Jones, was born 2 January 1772, and died 12 August 1830. He married Katherine Stith, born 28 May 1773, died 2 April 1858. They had at least one son: Richard Stith, born 10 August 1793, died 4 October 1853, married Lucy Gibson, born 20 August 1795, died 10 January 1870.

See "Jones Family Lines," National Genealogical Society Quarterly, (Dec. 1938), XXVI, 133-134.

THE ARTHUR JONES FAMILY

Arthur Jones was born 24 October 1769, and on 8 January 1795 married Sarah Baker, born 4 January 1779. They moved from Buckingham County to the vicinity of Huntsville, Alabama, where many descendants still live. Caleb Baker, Jr., married Catherine Hodnett of Buckingham County.

See: Johnson, Baker and Buford Families, p. 14.

THE ABRAHAM JONES FAMILY

Abraham Jones' Bible was handed down to P. R. Jones, by P. R. Jones to James Seborn Jones, by him to Vie E. Jones, and by him to his son William Jones. On 16 September 1964 the Bible was photostated in the presence of Robert Randolph Jones, who made a notarized statement that they were true photostatic pictures taken from Abraham Jones' Bible.

The entries given below were copied just as they were found, with no rearrangement.

New Testament, Published and Sold by Daniel D. Smith, New York, 1821.

Nancy M. Jones was born 15 August 1810.

Abraham Jones was born 5 March 1761.

Nancy Jones, his wife, was born 23 February 1770.

Abraham Jones was married to Nancy his wife on 28 January 1796.

Peter R. Jones, was born 21 December 1796.

Robert G. Jones was born 23 April 1801.

Elizabeth G. Jones was born 23 April 1801.

Nancy Jones was born died 7 April 1803.

Abraham G. Jones was born 17 September 1805.

William M. Jones was born 15 November 1807.

Nancy Jones died 24 July 1836.

William M. Jones died 23 May 1838.

Abraham Jones died 2 December 1851.

Dr. Robert C. Jones died 8 May 1862.

Charles R. Jones died 3 July 1862.

William E. Jones was killed in battle at Gettysburg on 3 July 1863.

Saml. B. Jones died from wounds received in battle at Chapins farm in Hospital at Richmond, 1 May 1865.

Ann H. Jones, died 4 November 1878.

James S. Jones died 7 September 1909.

Uphm. S. Jones died 23 July 1906

Ila K. Jones died 23 July 1906.

James S. Jones died 7 September 1909.

C. J. Jones died 7 January 1919.

Abraham Jones died 30 May 1919.

Vivan DeViver Ethridge Jones died 24 September 1966.

Births of children of J. S. and Annie H. Jones

Ila Jones was born 4 August 1868.

Peter R. Jones was born 14 April 1870.

Ellis W. Jones was born 31 December 1871.

St. George Sidney Jones was born 14 April 1873.

Uphuleon Syler Jones was born 8 September 1874.

Robert E. L. Jones was born 30 January 1876.

Eppa Seaborn Jones was born 2 April 1877.

Ann Hasllatine Jones, daughter of Ann H. and J. S. Jones, was born 22 October 1878.

Howard Lewis Jones was born 19 October 1915.

William Hervey Jones was born 12 October 1916.

James Jones and Annie H. Putney were married 10 October 1867.

Lavonia L. Jones and James C. Locknane was (sic) married 28 June 1906.

Lucy M. Jones and Lee B. Staton was married 30 December 1908.

James C. Jones and Ethel Allen was married 25 December 1912.

Mary M. Jones and Harvie L. Baird was married 5 February 1913.

Jas. S. Jones and Margaret was married 18 March 1886.

Chloe J. Jones and J. H. Slanton was married 31 January 1913.

Vivian E. Jones and Mary E. Nukles was married 27 October 1914.

Lou Jones and Henry Harris was married 26 September 1921.

William Henry Jones and Nancy Elizabeth Baber was married 29 October 1940.

Howard Lewis Jones and Mildred Johnson were married 14 October 1953.

Mary Willis Chambers was born 6 March 1859.

Abraham B. Jones was born 12 (?) September 1805.

Lavonia Levenworth Jones was born 7 May 1887.

Vivan De Viver Ethridge Jones was born 25 July 1889.

Lucy Malinda Jones was born 14 January 1891.

Cyallone (?) James Jones was born 4 August 1892.

(Illegible entry)

Jas. L. Jones was born 19 June 1834.

Annie H. Jones was born 19 October 1850.

Margaret A. Jones was born 2 October 1862.

Mary Magdelin Jones...(illegible)...1846.

Abraham Joshua Jones...(illegible).

Elizabeth...(illegible)...12 May 1900.

(Loda?) Lenwood Jones was born 20 February 1909.

One of the most distinguished families of early Buckingham County was the Jones family.

ABRAHAM JONES (1), born 5 March 1761 in Buckingham County, and died 2 December 1851. He served in the Revolutionary War. He married Margaret or Cloey or Nancy Garrott, and was the father of: PETER RANDOLPH, born 21 December 1796; Dr. CLAIBORNE, born 31 December 1798, died 3 May 1862 or 1863; ROBIA; ELIZABETH (or BETSY), born 23 April 1801, married Mr. Gough; NANCY, born 7 April 1803, married James LeSuer; ABRAHAM B., born 17 September 1805, died 1878, married Sarah (?), and moved to Henry Co., Tennessee, in 1823; WILLIAM M., born 15 November 1807, died 23 May 1838.

PETER RANDOLPH JONES (2), son of Abraham (1), was born 21 December 1796, died 22 June 1883, and married Lucy Garrott or Garrett on 31 October 1822. She was born 25 February 1804, died 19 April 1879, and was the daughter of Charles and Chloe Agee Garrott (whose married bond was dated 11 December 1785 and is at the Virginia Historical Society, Richmond). Chloe Agee was the daughter of James and Mary (Faure) Agee. Peter Randolph and Lucy were the parents of the following children: ANN ELIZABETH, born 12 October 1824; SARAH FRANCES, born 25 October 1826; CHARLES ROBERT, born 7 December 1829; ELIZABETH MARGARET, born 16 May 1832; JAMES SEABORNE, born 19 May 1834; JOHN PETER, born 9 June 1838; WILLIAM EDWARD, born 1 November 1840, killed at Gettysburg 3 July 1863, first lieutenant in his brother John Peter's company; SAMUEL BENTON (known as Benny), born 24 May 1843, died 1 May 1865 in the Hospital at Richmond from wounds received in the battle at Chapin's Farm.

ANN ELIZABETH JONES (3), daughter of Peter Randolph (2) and Lucy, was born 12 October 1824, married John R. Agee, and was the mother of: ROBERT; FRANK; MOODY; BUSHROD; VAN LEW; and a daughter, died young.

SARAH FRANCES JONES (4), daughter of Peter Randolph (2) and Lucy, was born 25 October 1826, married Charles Nuchols, and was the mother of: ROBERT; LUCY; ANN; CLARA; VICTORIA; and HUSTON NUCHOLS.

ELIZABETH MARGARET JONES (5), daughter of Peter Randolph (2) and Lucy, was born 16 May 1832, died 2 February 1916, and married Robert Baber. They were the parents of: CORNELIS ELIZA; THOMAS HOWARD; EVELINA ELIZABETH; ALICE CORA; McDORA LAMBKIN; ROBERT JONES; JULIUS CAESAR; JEFFERSON DAVIS; WILLIAM PETER; JAMES EDWARD; HENRY LEE; AMYNTAS ROSSE; ATTICUS BEADLES; FRANK WALKER; and GRANVILLE RUSSELL.

JAMES SEABORNE JONES (6), son of Peter Randolph (2) and Lucy, was born 19 May 1834, and died 7 September 1909. He married Lucy Ann Haseltine Putney, born 19 October 1850, died 4 November 1878, on 10 October 1867. Lucy Ann was the daughter of Ellis W. and Mary Ann (Glover) Putney. James Seaborne and Ann Haseltine (Putney) Jones were the parents of: ILLA, born 4 August 1868, married William Edward Hanner; PETER RANDOLPH, born 14 April 1870, died 5 July 1961, married 30 June 1905 Mary Daniel, born 11 September 1875, died 26 May 1962; ELLIS WASHINGTON PUTNEY JONES, born 31 December 1871, married Mary Carter; ST. GEORGE SIDNEY, born 14 April 1873; EUPHOR S., born 8 September 1874, died 23 July 1904; ROBERT EDWARD, born 30 January 1876, married first Blanche Locknane, and second, her sister, Marie Locknane; EPPA SEABORNE, born 23 April 1877, died 12 February 1949, married 12 September 1900 Ethel Miner of Washington, D. C.; ANNIE ELIZABETH, born 22 October 1878, died 18 December 1966 in Richmond, Va., married Eldon Miner, born 4 July 1871 in New York, died 16 October 1949 in Richmond.

(Edna Miner, Ethel Miner, and Eldon Miner were children of Elon Galusha and Margaret (Begley) Miner.)

JOHN PETER JONES (7), son of Peter Randolph (2) and Lucy, was born 9 June 1838, died 17 January 1910, married 1st Mary Elizabeth (Mollie) Putney on 19 December 1861. She was born 1841, died 1878, daughter of Ellis W. and Mary (Glover) Putney. John Peter Jones married 2nd on 4 June 1879 Mary Goodman.

John Peter Jones and Camm Patterson organized a company on the Civil War, called Buckingham Yancey Guards (Virginia Volunteers). Camm Patterson was the captain and John Peter was the lieutenant. This company subsequently became Company D, 56th Regt., Virginia Infantry. John Peter Jones was appointed captain on 3 May 1862. He was wounded at the Battle of Gaines' Mill on 27 June 1862. On 3 July 1863 he was captured at Gettysburg and imprisoned at Johnson's Island near Lake Erie. He was parolled and forwarded for exchange at Point Lookout, Maryland on 14 March 1865, and was received at Cox Wharf, James River, Virginia on 22 March. During the war he married Mary Elizabeth Putney, better known as "Mollie."

John Peter Jones was the father of the following children: (by his first wife) ARIUS CONRAD, b. 1866, d. 2 July 1919 having married on 25 June 1906 Effie Owens (born 1868, died 15 November 1935) and having no children; PETER WAVERLY, born 10 January 1868; M. ADELICIA, born 12 December 1870; JOHN HERVEY, born 1872; WILLIAM OTTO, born 1874, went to Oregon, and was killed by a falling tree, December 1906, died unmarried; RICHARD JETER, born 1876; (by his second wife): FLORENCE; RIVES; GROVER; RUTH; STUART, born 1890, married Reba Harris, had no children.

PETER RANDOLPH JONES (8), son of James Seaborne Jones (6), was born 14 April 1870, died 5 July 1961, married Mary Daniel on 30 June 1903. She was born 11 September 1875, died 26 May 1962. They were the parents of: ROBERT RANDOLPH, born 4 June 1904; RIVES J., born 2 July 1905; IRVING CARLYLE, born 8 January 1908, died 15 June 1963; ANGELOE BURNETTE, born 13 September 1910, married a Bunks; ESTELLE ELIZABETH, born 2 April 1914, died 10 September 1937, married a Dawson; MARVIN S., born 10 April 1918.

ST. GEORGE SIDNEY JONES (9), son of James Seaborne Jones (6), was born 14 April 1873, died 2 July 1936, married 4 December 1895 in Richmond, Edna Miner, born 11 November 1874 in Henrico County, and died 5 July 1960 at Rockwood, Roane County, Tenn., buried in Murfreesboro, Rutherford County, Tennessee, Evergreen Cemetery, where St. George Sidney Jones is also buried.

PETER WAVERLY JONES (10), son of John Peter Jones (7), was born 10 January 1868, died 12 April 1940; married on 19 October 1893 Harriett (Hattie) Belle Owens, born 28 September 1864, died 16 July 1949, daughter of Theodore Evans Owens (born 1 October 1829, died 27 June 1891) and Willie Virginia Gossett (born 20 November 1838, died 14 June 1922). Peter Waverly and Harriett had issue: WAVERLY GOSSETT, born 30 June 1895, died 15 December 1968, married Edith Ellis on 24 October 1922, and had two children: Ellis, born and died 23 November 1924, and Sue, born 22 May 1933; HARRIETT (HATTIE) TURPIN; VIRGINIA ELIZABETH; AGNES BROADDUS; ALFRED OWENS, married Virginia Lee on 10 January 1931 and had issue: Virginia Lee, born 22 December 1931 in Richmond, and Alfred Owens, Jr., born 29 September 1933 in Richmond; HELEN MARTHA, married first on 12 January 1935 Joseph Travers Chiott, and second David E. Black, had issue by her first husband: Martha Travers, born 13 September 1938 in Asheville, North Carolina, and Joseph Travers, Jr., born 11 April 1940 in Asheville.

M. ADELICIA JONES (11), daughter of John Peter Jones (7), was born 12 December 1870, died 17 March 1957; married Benjamin B. Dawson on 23 February 1893. They had issue: MARY, married Oscar Middlebrook; ROY, married Marguerite (?); FLORENCE, married Ben Black; GLADYS, married G. Robert Fiest; JOHN STANLEY, married Georgia Mann; WILLIAM OTTO, married Edith Cocke; DOROTHY, married L. B. Thomas; ARIUS WAVERLY, married Helen Smith; JACKSON.

JOHN HERVEY JONES (12), son of John Peter Jones (7), was born in 1872 and died in the 1940's. By his wife, Mamie Mayo, he was the father of: MABEL, born 1901, died January 1971.

RICHARD JETER JONES (13), son of John Peter Jones (7), was born in 1876 and died in 1915. He married Betsy Lee and had issue: ELIZABETH, married Mr. Rodman; RICHARD JETER, married Ruth Cox and had issue: Richard Putney; Lucian; and Anne Byrd; FRANCES LEE.

FLORENCE JONES (14), daughter of John Peter Jones (7) by his second wife, married Otto Feutchenberger, and had issue: MARY LEE, married Stonewall Jackson Wingfield, Jr., and had a son: Charles Jackson Wingfield.

RIVES JONES (15), son of John Peter Jones (7), married Rosa Feutchenberger, and had issue: RIVES, Jr., married Mary Jane (?) and had a son: Rives Jones, III; WILSON; GOODMAN.

GROVER JONES (16), son of John Peter Jones (7), married Gertrude Powell and issue: WATSON; and RANDOLPH.

RUTH JONES (17), daughter of John Peter Jones (7), married Theodore C. Harrell on 35 June 1913, and had issue: DORIS; and ELIZABETH, married Dr. William Bennett Lowe on 11 February 1955, and issue: Anne Lowe.

ST. GEORGE SIDNEY JONES, Jr. (18), son of St. George Sidney Jones (9) and wife Edna Miner, married 24 June 1939 in Fountain City, Tennessee, Mary Evelyn Allen, born 20 March 1913. St. George Sidney was a retired Insurance agent, and his wife was a teacher. They had issue: EDGAR SIDNEY, born 21 May 1940; VIRGINIA ANN; and DANIEL ST. GEORGE.

EARL CLAIBORNE JONES (19), son of St. George Sidney Jones (9) and Edna (Miner), was born 8 November 1915 at Richmond, married May 1942 Margaret Witmer. Earl C. Jones was an engineer with the TVA, and his wife was a public health nurse. A graduate of Oklahoma A. & M., Earl C. Jones was a master sergeant in the United States Marine Corps. Earl and Margaret had issue: EARL CLAIBORNE, born May 1945, married July 1967 in Nashville Betty Howard of Florissant, Missouri. They were divorced in 1979 in Texas. Mr. Jones is a safety engineer residing in Houston Texas. He and his wife had one son: Andrew Clayborn, born 4 April 1974, in Houston.

ELIA HASALTINE JONES (20), daughter of St. George Sidney Jones (9) and Edna (Miner) Jones, was born 6 August 1918 in Richmond. She married Asa Scobey Rogers, Jr., on 23 December 1950 at the Church of the Advent, in Nashville. Mr. Rogers, a professional engineer, was born 5 March 1918 in Nashville. Asa and Elia (Jones) Rogers had issue: ASA SCOBEY ROGERS, III, born 3 October 1954. (The author expresses her appreciation to Mrs. Rogers for this sketch of the Jones family).

EDGAR SIDNEY JONES (21), son of St. George Sidney Jones, Jr. (18), was born 21 May 1940 in Murfreesboro, and married on 6 June 1967 in Washington, D. C., at Walter Reed Chapel, Suzanne Scanlan, born 2 April 1942. Sidney was a first lieutenant, and Sue was a captain. They live in Dumfries, Va., and have issue: MICHAEL EDWARD, born 13 July 1968; THOMAS DAVID, born 16 November 1969; SUELLEN MARIE, born 2 May 1971; BENJAMIN CHARLES EDGAR, born 24 January 1976, and ANDREW SAMUEL, born 5 July 1977.

VIRGINIA ANN JONES (22), daughter of St. George Sidney Jones, Jr. (18), was born at Maryville, Tennessee, on 20 August 1942, and married 4 August 1961 at First Church, Rockwood, Tennessee, Frederick Herbert Crough, Jr., born 25 July 1941. They have issue: PAMELIA ANITA, born 25 August 1962, and PATRICIA ELAIN, born 15 January 1964 (The family now resides in Fredericksburg, Va.).

DANIEL ST. GEORGE JONES (23), son of St. George Sidney Jones, Jr. (18), was born 29 March 1948 at Rockwood, Tennessee, and married on 2 August 1968 at the First Church in Rockwood, Belinda Diane Nelson, born 20 February 1948. The family now resides in Dickson, Tennessee, and have issue: DEANNA VIRGINIA, born 2 April 1969; DEBORAH ELAINE, born 6 July 1970; DAVID DANIEL, born 12 October 1974.

THE LOUIS DIBRELL LEGRANDE JONES FAMILY

Louis Dibrell LeGrande Jones, with a name reminiscent of his French Huguenot ancestry, lived and died at historic New Store in Buckingham County. He was descended from Huguenot forebears who founded Manakin, Virginia, on both sides of his family. His mother was Judith Baker LeGrande, and a direct descendant of Pierre LeGrande who came over in the Peter and Anthony with his wife and children in 1700 and settled at Manakin. She was also a descendant of Abraham Michaux and his wife Suzanne Rochet, "the Little Night Cap," whose daughter Jane Michaux married Peter LeGrande, son of Pierre.

Louis D. L. Jones' father was William Dibrell Jones, a soldier in the War of 1812. His grandfather was Michael Jones who served in the American Revolution, and who married Leanne Dibrell, daughter of Anthony Dibrell (born Jean Antoine Du Breuille, son of Dr. Christoffe DuBreuille and his wife Marianne Dutoi). Jean Antoine changed his name to Anthony. He married Elizabeth Lee, daughter of Thomas Lee, granddaughter of Charles Lee and Elizabeth Medshand, and great-granddaughter of Col. Richard Lee, first attorney general of America.

Mr. and Mrs. Jones took up their residence in New Store, Buckingham County, and lived to celebrate their golden anniversary. They were parents of fifteen children, twelve of whom lived until such time as the youngest among them had children of his own.

See: The Huguenot, Publication no. 10, p. 87.

THE JORDAN FAMILY

Samuel Jordan was born 15th day, 2nd mo., 1679, married 8th day, 8th mo., 1703, Elizabeth Fleming. Samuel Jordan, the elder, was a son of Thomas Jordan of Chuckatuck, Nansemond County, Virginia. Thomas was born 1634, and died 1699. A member of the Society of Friends, he married c.1658/9 Margaret Brashier (Brashere), daughter of Robert Brashier of Nansemond County.

Samuel Jordan and Elizabeth Fleming were the parents of Samuel Jordan, born c.1710, died 1789, of Buckingham County, Virginia. Samuel, the younger, was a magistrate in Albemarle County, and served as a captain of militia, as sheriff, as presiding magistrate, and as county lieutenant of Buckingham County, and was a member of the House of Burgesses. Although he was an old man when the Revolutionary War started, he was colonel of Buckingham County militia, and was a member of the County Committee of Safety. After June 1776 he was State Commissioner for the foundry of casting cannon in Buckingham County.

See: Edward P. Valentine, The Edward P. Valentine Papers, 4 vols. (Richmond, 1927), p. 2270.

Fairfax Harrison, ed., Aris Sonis Focisque: Being a Memoir of an American Family, the Harrisons of Skimino (New York: DeVinne Press, 1910), p. 24.

Alexander Brown, The Cabells and Their Kin (Boston: Houghton Mifflin and Co., 1895), pp. 127-128.

Brashier Family Notes, vol. 1.

Robert Jordone of Powhatan County, Va., was conveyed 280 acres in said county by Robert Moseley of Buckingham County, 2 February 1782. The land was on Jones Creek and adjoined lands of Anthony Martin, Thomas Smith, David Patterson, and Isaac Porter. (Powhatan Co. Deed Book 1, p. 165).

Benjamin Jordan of Buckingham County, on 1 June 1799, conveyed to James Loving of Amherst County, Virginia, for £ 50, conveyed an equal and undivided moiety of one certain one-half acre with its appurtenances lying in the town of Warminster on the south side of the Main Street, being no. 6, and being the same lot which the said Benjamin Jordan lately purchased from Joseph Harton and his wife Tabitha. (Amherst Co. Deed Book H, p. 556).

Benjamin Jordan of Buckingham County on 21 August 1798 was conveyed 200 acres in Amherst County by Philip Ryan of that county, for £ 130.9.5 current money (Amherst C. Deed Book H, p. 501).

Benjamin Jordan of Buckingham County on 20 June 1795 or July 1795, conveyed to Matthew Harris, Sr., of Amherst Co. 108 acres in Albemarle County, being part of a larger tract formerly belonging to the estate of Holdin. (Albemarle County Deed Book 11, p. 422).

Benjamin Jordan sold to Wm. Elsom of Albemarle County, on 30 June 1795, 103 acres in Albemarle County on Hog Creek, purchased by Jordan at a Sheriff's Sale. (Albemarle County Deed Book 11, p. 423).

Matthew Jordan of Albemarle County, in his will referred to land in Buckingham County, which he left to his sons: Reuben, William, and Benjamin (Albemarle County Will Book 2, p. 246).

THE KYLE FAMILY

There seems to have been two Robert Kyles in Buckingham County. One does not appear in the records after June 1774, and the other is mentioned as late as 1789. One Robert Kyle went from Buckingham to Hawkins County, Tennessee.

There was a Robert Kyle living in Albemarle County as early as 1746, believed to have been the father of Margaret Kyle, who married James Rowland. Other children of this Robert Kyle were: William, Joseph, and probably Robert. They lived in that part of Albemarle County that became Buckingham County in 1761. William and Joseph are listed as Revolutionary soldiers of Southwest Virginia (Summers, pp. 11, 396). Joseph, listed in an issue of the D.A.R. Magazine as having Revolutionary service, was born in Augusta County, and had a son Robert who died in Botetourt County in 1808 (D.A.R. Records, Washington, D. C.).

William Kyle is said to have married Sarah Ann Stephens. His will filed (probably in Botetourt County, Ky.) in 1821, names his wife Sarah. William and Sarah had twelve children, one of whom was Robert who died 28 October 1813. He was captain of a company of riflemen in the Flying Camp (McDowell's) Virginia Militia, 48th Regt., from Botetourt County. His father was granted administration on his estate.

These Kyles moved from Buckingham County to Botetourt County: Margaret Kyle Rowland in 1770, William Kyle in 1772, and Joseph Kyle in 1773. According to tradition the (Robert) Kyle who went from Buckingham County to Hawkins County, Tennessee, was a brother of Margaret Rowland and William and Joseph Kyle. Robert Kyle who died 1820 lived at Walnut Hill, Hawkins County, and married Leah Brooks (1747 - 1832).

See: Nashville Banner, 6 May 1949.

THE LESUEUR FAMILY

Peter Lesueuer of Halifax County, married S w a n Williams of Port Republic. Susan's mother was a Miss Kemper. This family moved to Buckingham before 1807, when Samuel Lesueur wrote from Elbert County, Georgia, to Col. Henry Bell of Buckingham County, directing him to sell certain land which Samuel's brother Peter has not been "fortunate enough to dispose of." The tax receipts of George K. Evans refer to the land of the "Estate Peter Lesueur."

Peter Lesueur had a daughter Susan Williams Lesueur who married Mr. Evans in Buckingham County, and whose sons George Kemper Evans and John Henry Evans died unmarried. George Kemper Evans served in the Fourth Virginia Cavalry and died in 1863 after a short confinement at Fort Delaware, after his capture at Gettysburg. His brother John Henry Evans died at Pine Forest, home of Burwell Shepard, on 4 December 1866.

See: William Shepard, "Shepard and Some Other Buckingham Families, Part II," William and Mary Quarterly, 2nd series, VII, 178-180.

THE LINDSAY FAMILY

Jacob Lindsay died in Henry County, Virginia, prior to October 1776, when his estate was administered by John Lindsay, administrator. Payments were made for or to: Jacob Stallings, Thomas Miller, Edmd. Winston, Col. Henry Bell, William Powel, Rolfe Eldridge (Clerk of Buckingham County), Edmd. Wilcox, John Staples, Rachel Gouge, William Hugins (dancing master), Henry France (for board at dancing school) for board of Reuben and William Lindsay, William Taylor, Spencer's orpn., Mrs. Sarah Lindsay, Mr. Marr's store,

Jno. Lankister, William Gray, Jno. Patterson, Christopher Owen, German Baker, Maj. John Dillard (sheriff of Amherst County), John Salmon, Jarrott Patterson, and James Lindsay (two of the legatees of James Lindsay, dec.. of Caroline), Col. George Hairston, Mr. Golloday (for teaching Caroline and Reuben Lindsay dancing). Also noted in the record were: receipts from: Thomas Smith (under-sheriff to Jacob Lindsay), Stephen and Bird Smith (execs. of Guy Smith), Jacob Cox (exec. of William Powel), James Shelton, Mr. John Marr. Buckingham and Caroline Counties are mentioned many times. Sarah and John Lindsay were administrators. Approved 1 October 1785 by A. Hughes, John Dillard, and John Marr, and returned to court 27 October 1785 (Henry County Will Book 1, p. 107).

THE LOCKETT/LUCKETT FAMILY

The Locketts were early seated along the James River, with the Osbournes. The name has been spelled various ways, but the spelling Lockett is used in this accout.

THOMAS LOCKETT (1), of Bristol Parish, Henrico County, died in 1686, having married Margaret (?), who died by 22 May 1708. The will of Thomas Lockett, 27 March 1686 - 1 June 1686, named wife Margaret, eld. son Benjamin, sons Thomas and James, and eld. daughter Susan. He referred to his residence near the River. The will of Margaret Lockett of Henrico County, 22 May 1708, named all six children and gave the married names of the daughters. (Henrico County Records, 1677-1692, Book 1, p. 367, and vol. V, p. 213).

Benjamin Lockett, aged about 23 on 1 August 1692. James Lockett was then about 16 years of age.

Thomas and Margaret were the parents of; BENJAMIN, age about 23 on 1 August 1692, married Winifred Pride; THOMAS, died c.1745/6; JAMES, died in Henrico County leaving a will, 4 December 1708 - 1 February 1709, in which he left property to his brothers and sisters; SUSAN (SUSANNAH), married William Grigg and had a son William who died in Prince George County c. 1713-28, leaving a will which named his parents; ELIZABETH, married (?) Standley; MARY, married (2) Mitchell.

THOMAS LOCKETT (2), son of Thomas Lockett (1), died in Goochland County, leaving a will proved 18 March 1745. He married 1st Martha Osborne, and 2nd Elizabeth (?). Martha was the daughter of Thomas Osborne, whose sister Margaret married Thomas Lockett (1). Martha was born c.1662 and her age was 26 years on 1 December 1688 (Henrico County Records, 5, p. 26).

Thomas Lockett patented 900 acres of land in Goochland County on the north side of the Appomattox River on 28 September 1730. The land adjoined Samuel Hancock and Arthur Moseley (State Land Office, Patent Book 14, p. 61). Thomas moved to Goochland before 1733 for on 19 September of that year he conveyed to Thomas Lockett, Jr., 200 acres on Butterwood Creek. He sold 300 acres to Benjamin Moseley on 13 September 1739. This was part of a patent he had dated 18 September 1730 and 29 March 1730 (Goochland County Deed Book 3, pp. 169 and 242). Thomas Lockett patented other lands in Amelia (later Prince Edward County) on the north side of the north fork of Falling River (Land Office, Patent Book 21, p. 370).

The will of Thomas Lockett of Goochland County, 13 November 1745 - 18 March 1745/6, named the following children: THOMAS (to have 2000 acres in Amelia County and 200 acres purchased from Edward Harris; Thomas d. c. 1775); JOEL (to have residue of testator's land on the north side of Butterwood Creek except 4 acres below the bridge. Joel died c.1769. His will, 1 Sept. 1767 - 27 Feb. 1769, named Mary his wife and children: Royal, Pleasant, Daniel, Benjamin, Fanny Hanksley, Mary, and Elizabeth); GIDEON (to have the "Manor Plantation" on which the testator lived and 4 acres on north side of Butterwood Creek below the bridge. Gideon died c.1808); HANNAH (born 22 December 1722, to have rest of land in or near Skinquarter Creek, two cows, and one horse and saddle); LUCY (to have a cow and calf). (Goochland County Deed Book 5, p. 90).

THOMAS LOCKETT (3), son of Thomas Lockett (2), married Judith Townes and died by 22 January 1775 in Cumberland County, Virginia.

Thomas Lockett had land transactions in Chesterfield and Cumberland Counties, and at a later date some of this land fell in Buckingham County. Two of his sons, David and Jacob, went from Virginia to Georgia after the Revolutionary War, and today many of their descendants are to be found in Hancock, Monroe, Baldwin, Jones, and Warren Counties, Georgia.

The will of Thomas Lockett, 28 September 1770 - 22 January 1775, named his wife Judith Townes, and these children: STEPHEN (born 14 November 1733, died 14 September 1791, married 2 November 1760 Mary Clay, born 22 September 1742, died 5 September 1823, daughter of Charles and Mary (Green) Clay); ABNER; JACOB; MARTHA; LUCEY; ELIZABETH; MARY (married William Gipson or Gibson); JAMES; DAVID; and probably OSBORNE.

ABNER LOCKETT (4), son of Thomas (3) and Judith married Ann Phoebe Marshall, daughter of William Marshall of Cumberland County. He moved to Mecklenburg County, Va., c.1777-89, selling his home on Butterwood Creek to Arthur Moseley. His will, 26 November 1789 - 8 February 1790, named his wife Anne, and these children: FRANCIS; THOMAS; PHILIP; PHOEBE; NANCY; and LUCY.

JACOB LOCKETT (5), son of Thomas (3), was born 1754 and died 1820. After the Revolutionary War he moved to Baldwin County, Georgia, but his estate was settled in Jones County, Georgia. He married Lucy Waddell or Waddill, daughter of Richard Waddell of Prince Edward County, on 17 March 1791 in that county.

MARTHA LOCKETT (6), daughter of Thomas (3), married Alexander Bass. They were the parents of: WILLIAM; ALEXANDER; THOMAS; POLLY; PATSEY; BETSY; NANCY; and LUCY BASS (Prince Edward County Deed Book 5, p. 432).

LUCEY LOCKETT (7), daughter of Thomas Lockett (3), married William Stone in 1767. She died 27 February 1769, and had issue: WILLIAM; DANIEL; OSBORNE; ELIZABETH (BETSY); MARTHA (PATSY); and NANCY.

JAMES LOCKETT (8), son of Thomas (3), married Hannah Hawkins Llewellen, and had issue: JOHN; BRITTIN; JAMES; DAVID; and perhaps others.

DAVID LOCKETT (9), son of Thomas (3), was born 1730 in Virginia and died 1796 in Georgia, having married Sally Lucy Winfrey in 1759. She died 1787.

David Lockett was in Buckingham County, Virginia, in k775, when he joined his brothers and sisters in a deed to his brother Jacob Lockett. In 1785 he moved with his family to Wilkes County, Georgia, where he bought 250 acres of land from Richard Fretwell and wife Frances, and from William Fretwell of Cumberland County, Virginia. The deed was dated 28 September 1784 and was witnessed by William Byram, Leonard Fretwell, James Wootten, James Alexander, and William Hamilton. (Wilkes County, Georgia, Deed Book, 1784-1785, p. 36).

When Warren County, Georgia, was established in 1793 it was found that David Lockett's land was in the new county. The Tax List for Warren County for 1794 showed David Lockett living on the Ogeechee River with his family and seven slaves.

David's will, 7 January 1796 - 12 March 1796, was proved in Warren County. His will mentioned his wife (unnamed), 50 acres of land where his sister Gipson was living, and left his bounty warrant land to his two youngest sons, Reubin and Doctor. His four youngest children were Winfrey, Reubin, Doctor (not yet of age), and Sally.

During the Revolutionary War David Lockett served in the First Company of Captain Nathaniel Gist's Virginia Regiment. Elsewhere he is referred to as a corporal, sergeant, and lieutenant.

David Lockett was the father of: WINFREY; REUBIN (married Sarah Hill on 27 June 1800 and moved to Morgan County, Georgia); DOCTOR (youngest son, not of age at father's death; married Mary Hill on 20 February 1800 in Warren County); SALLY, married John Patterson on 26 February 1803 in Warren County; SOLOMON (born 1760, married Patsy or Martha Alvord, born c. 1762;

in the lottery of 1806 he drew a lot in Wilkinson County. He also drew in the lottery of 1827 as a Revolutionary soldier. He left a will, 1829 - 1852, pp. 62-63); THOMAS; ABNER; and DAVID (said to have moved to Mississippi).

THOMAS LOCKETT (10), son of David (9), was the third child of his parents. He married 1st Betsy Sims (born 22 June 1794), and 2nd, on 4 September 1810 in Warren County, Tempy Rogers (born 21 October 1780, daughter of Reuben and Temperance (James) Rogers). Thomas died in Warren County, where his will was proved 8 July 1844. In his will he named his wife Temperance, and two sons: CULLEN R.; and THOMAS.

ABNER LOCKETT (11), son of David Lockett (9), married Patsey (?) and removed to Monroe County, Georgia. In the lottery for the distribution of the Ockmulgee lands, in 1806, he drew from Hancock County. He died in Monroe County leaving a will, July 1827 - January 1828 (Will Book A, p. 9). In his will he named these children: DAVID; ABNER; SOLOMON; HUGH (who drew in the 1821 lottery from Jones County, Georgia); POLLY BARRON, and MARTHA.

See Jewel Davis Scarborough, Southern Kith and Kin, 4 vols. (Abilene: Abilene Print Co., 1951 - 1953), vol. 1, for the Lockett family.
For David Lockett's Revolutionary service, see: John H. Gwathmey, Historical Register of Virginians in the Revolution: Soldiers, Sailors, Marines, 1775 - 1783, 1938 (Repr.: Baltimore: Gen. Pub. Co., 1973); also William T. R. Saffell, Records of the Revolutionary War, 3rd ed., 1894, 1913 (Repr.: Baltimore: Gen. Pub. Co., 1969), p. 285.

THE MOLLOY/MALLOY FAMILY

The name is found spelled Malloy, Molloy, and O'Molloy in various places.

JAMES DUNNE MOLLOY (1), son of Terrence and Miss Dunne of Offaly, Ireland, grandson of Arthur, great-grandson of Arthur O'Molloy, of Rathleen Castle, and a descendant in the male line of King Niall who ruled Ireland in 371 A. D. About 1771 James Dunne Molloy took part in an uprising, and to escape prosecution by the English officials, came to Virginia, with his wife, Elizabeth Hilliard, and several children.

During the Revolutionary War, James Malloy or Molloy served as a private Peter Bryan Bruin's Company, 11th Virginia Regt. (also designated as 11th and 15th Virginia Regiments, and 7th Virginia Regt., commanded by Col. Daniel Morgan. Molloy enlisted 3 December 1776 for the duration of the war; in June 1778 was transferred to Capt. William Johnson's company, same regiment, and his name last appears on the company muster roll for November 1779 with the notation under Remarks: "with General Scott."

The children of James Dunne Molloy were: NIALL (who died in infancy); WILLIAM; DAVID; JUDITH; THOMAS; DANIEL TERRENCE; and a daughter, who married Anderson Woodson.

DAVID MOLLOY (2), son of James Dunne Molloy (1), married a Miss Gilliam of Buckingham County. They were the ancestors of a long line of Molloys in Tennessee. One of their descendants, David Brownlow Molloy, married a granddaughter of Thomas Shepard of Tennessee.

DANIEL TERRENCE MOLLOY (3), son of James Dunne Molloy (1), married Mary Knight of Buckingham County, and had issue: DANIEL (died unmarried); NANCY, married Mr. Wright; MARY, married Christian Saunders; LUCY, married Goodrich Saunders; SARAH, married William Charlton; DAVID ARTHUR, married Jane Baugh Stratton, daughter of Peter Stratton by his wife Mary Netherland Steger.

DAVID MOLLOY (4), son of Daniel Terrence Molloy (3), married Jane Baugh Stratton. He was a private in Captain William Jackson's company, War of 1812. His service began 28 August 1814; he was promoted to corporal on 2 September; to sergeant on 16 October 1814, and his service ended 20 February 1815. He was Deputy Sheriff of Cumberland County where he moved shortly after his marriage. Jane Baugh Stratton was born 15 June 1797 and died 29

August 1880. David Molloy was born in 1795, and died 29 April 1826, after a short illness. He left two young children: MARY, married Richard Woodson Gannaway; and SARAH KNIGHT, who married the Rev. Archibald Clark.

See: William Shepard, "Shepard and Some Other Buckingham Families," Part I," in William and Mary Quarterly, 2nd series, VI, 152-153; also, "Part II," op. cit., VII, 178.

THE MOSBY FAMILY

Benjamin Mosby of the Parish of Southam, Cumberland County, left a will, 18 March 1771 - 26 September 1774. In it he named his wife Mary, son Littleberry, son Poindexter, daughter Mary Ann Netherland, daughter Theodosia Carrington, granddaughters Mary and Elizabeth Netherland and their father John Netherland, and Seth Burton. Sons Littleberry and Poindexter, and sons-in-law John Netherland and Joseph Carrington as executors. (Cumberland County, Va., Will Book 2, p. 145).

Littleberry Mosby of Powhatan County left a will dated 6 January 1809. In it he named the children by his first wife: Sarah Cannon, John Mosby, Littleberry Mosby, Mary Hughes, Wade Mosby, and Richard Mosby. He mentioned his daughters, Betsy Ann Carrington, Martha Nichols, and Judith M. Smith as having received property. He also named son Benjamin, dec. son Jacob Mosby and his son Jacob G. Mosby (grandson of the testator), daughter Narcissa Binford, and the following slaves: Tom, Sarah, Tim, Polly, and Dilly.

See: Edward P. Valentine, The Edward P. Valentine Papers, 4 vols. (Richmond, Va., 1927), pp. 885, 886, 887.

THE MOSELEY FAMILY

The will of Robert Moseley of Buckingham County, 7 July 1814 - 12 May 1817, named his wife Elizabeth, and his children: John Moseley, Evelina Moseley, Edward Moseley, Mary Ann Moseley, Robert Moseley, and Alexander Moseley. He mentions a negro man, Travis, who is to keep a blacksmith's shop, and if any of the testator's children have blacksmith work to be done they are to have it done at the shop of the said Travis. He appoints as executors his wife, son John, and brothers Arthur Moseley, William Moseley, and Daniel Moseley, and friends Dr. James Walker, Arch'd Austin, and James Austin. The witnesses were: Archd. Austin, R. M. Bondurant, Stephen Guerrant, and David Jones.

THE OGLESBY FAMILY

David Oglesby was born in 1744, lived the early part of his life in Buckingham County, and later lived in nearby Bedford and Campbell Counties. He died in the latter county on 26 July 1821, aged 77 years. His obituary in The Lynchburg Press of 27 July 1821 stated he left a widow and six children. He married Sarah (?) by 1773 as their daughter Constance was born in 1774. Sarah was born in 1750 and died in Campbell County in October 1828. Her obituary in The Lynchburg Virginian of 23 October 1828 stated she died Monday last, aged 78. Sarah may have been a Sanderson as two daughters of David and Sarah, Constance and Jinney, named their daughters Sarah Sanderson, and these daughters were always called Sallie. Six of the children of David and Sarah named one of their daughters Sarah.

The name of David Oglesby's father cannot be proven, but it may have been William, as David named his youngest son William Oglesby, Jr., but he also named one of his sons Jacob. There was a Jacob Oglesby, Sr., who also had a son William.

Jacob Oglesby, Sr., conveyed land in Albemarle County, which he had patented in 1761, to his son Shadrack Oglesby on 31 July 1770. David Oglesby and William Oglesby both witnessed the deed.

In 1773 David Oglesby, white male, was listed as a tithable in the household of Hardin Perkins (Robert F. and Isabel B. Woodson, Virginia Tithables from Burned Record Counties (Richmond: The Compilers, 1970).).

David Oglesby also appeared in a 1782 tax list for Buckingham County.

In 1818 a lawsuit was filed in Lynchburg Superior Court of Law & Chancery, Oglesby VS. Oglesby, a suit to clear title to land. The heirs of David Oglesby were named, and the file of more than one hundred pages contains depositions of all of the then living children of David Oglesby. Two of his married daughters died before he did. Also mentioned in the bill are 75 acres of land and three slaves in Campbell County. (From Lois Whitesell, Nashville, Tennessee).

Thomas Oglesby, born c.1750, died c.1832, married Martha Bradley and served as a private in Georgia during the Revolutionary War.

On 3 December 1796 Elizabeth Cunningham of Elbert County, Georgia, sold Thomas Oglesby of Buckingham County 250 acres of land on Pennington's Fork, otherwise called Dove's Creek, originally granted to Joshua Pickins. Allen Jones was a witness.

Drury, George, Leroy, Robert, Thomas, and William Oglesby were in Elbert County in 1820. (1820 Census of Elbert County, Georgia; Elbert County Deed Book D, p. 16; and Frances Wynd, They Were Here: Georgia Genealogical Records, vol. V, p. 893).

THE PANNILL FAMILY

David Pannill, son of William son of William, was born in January 1772 and died in Pittsylvania County, Virginia in November 1803, in his 32nd year, of typhoid fever. He married in Pittsylvania County Bethenia Letcher, daughter of Col. William and Elizabeth (Perkins) Letcher.

Col. William Letcher was in the Revolutionart army. In the spring of 1781, when his only child, Bethenia, was an infant in the cradle, he returned to his home in what is now Patrick County, Virginia, to see his family, and to collect recruits for General Greene's army. A British loyalist named Nichols, who was at that time collecting beef for Cornwallis' army encamped near the border in North Carolina, hearing of Col. Letcher's arrival and the object of his visit, entered Letcher's house, and shot him dead before the eyes of his wife and daughter. Nichols was pursued by enraged patriots, captured and hanged. Elizabeth Perkins Letcher, whose family had settled in Buckingham County, married as her second husband Major George Hariston of Henry County, Virginia. The Haristons of Virginia, North Carolina, and Mississippi descend from this second marriage.

In early life David Pannill and his brother Samuel emigrated to Kentucky, where they had been given valuable lands in the Blue Grass Region by their father, but a bout of malarial fever caused them to sell their lands and return to Virginia, where David settled in Pittsylvania County, and married.

The will of David Pannill, recorded in the clerk's office in Pittsylvania County, directed that his sword was to be given to his youngest brother, George, with teh injunction that it never be drawn in behalf of any "rebellious or Jacobinical party."

David and Bethenia had issue: WILLIAM LETCHER; and ELIZABETH LETCHER (who married the Hon. Archibald Stuart, who for many years represented his county in the Legislature, and was also a delegate to the Constitutional Convention of 1850, and was also a member of Congress for one term.

See: David H. Pannill, "The Genealogy of Gen. J. E. B. Stuart, and of His Collateral Relations on His Mother's Side—Pannill, Strother, Banks, Bruce, etc.," William and Mary Quarterly, 2nd series, VI, 115.

THE PAYNE FAMILY

The Payne Family Bible was once the property of George B. Payne who lived near Buckingham County Court House. When he moved to Micanopy, Florida, several years ago, he left it in the possession of Caroline Tiedeman Moore, of Charleston, South Carolina.

MARRIAGES

George B. Payne and Catharine G. Penn were married on the 9th of October 1839 by Revd. Nelson Sale.

Married at Salts Springs, Fla., Marion L., son of the same, to Jane Dupuis, Dec....

Married in Savannah, Georgia, Sallie (Sara) Penn, daughter of same, to J. C. Rembert, 28th October 1870, by Revd. King.

Married in Svannah, Ga., Rosaline, daughter of same, to D. Elwood McCuen, 8th June 1881 by Rev. C. H. Strong.

BIRTHS

George B. Payne, son of Geo. M. and Susan M. Payne, born on the 24th September 1816.

Catherine G. Penn, daughter of Edmond and Jane Penn, born on the 19th June 1819.

Ella Susan, daughter of G. B. & Catherine Payne, born on the 13th October 1840.

Ida, daughter of same, born on the 6th September 1843.

Rosalie Payne, daughter of the same, born on the 8th July 1850 at 4 o'clock P. M.

Sallie (Sara) Penn, daughter of same, born on 4th July 1852 at 9 o'clock A. M.

Virginia Morton, daughter of same, born on 17th September 1855.

George Elwood McCuen, son of D. E. & Rosaline McCuen, born 23rd July 1:30 P. M., Sunday, in Savannah, Ga., 1882.

Edwin G. Burke, son of D. E. & Rosaline McCuen, born in Savannah, Ga., 22 Nov. 1889, 20 minutes to 4 P. M.

DEATHS

Ella Susan Payne died on 9th November 1846, 20 minutes before 12 o;clock P. M., aged six years & 27 days.

Catherine G. Payne, wife of George B. Payne, died in Micanopy, Fla., 6th day of July 1859, at 6 P. M.

George B. Payne, died in Micanopy, Fla., Nov. 22 1859 at 8 o'clock P. M.

Virginia Morton Payne died in Savannah, Ga., 19 Nov. 1880.

D. E. McCuen died in Savannah, Ga., 20 day of January 1893, at 20 min. past 1 o'clock.

NEWSPAPER CLIPPINGS

McCuen – Payne: Married in this city, June 8, 1881, at the residence of J. B. G. O'Neill, by the Rev. C. H. Strong, Mr. D. E. McCuen, of Florida, to Miss Rosa L. Payne. (newspaper not identified).

Died in Buckingham, on the morning of the 14th inst., in the 24th year of her age, Mrs. Susan M. Payne, consort of George M. Payne, Esq., after an illness of many weeks which she sustained with an unyielding fortitude. To this event so afflicting to her husband and child, her relatives and friends, she looked as the consummation of hopes, founded on the promises of a Savior. She was not disappointed; for in the hour of desolation, she was enabled to rejoice in assurance that therw was in reserve for her "a building of God, an house not made with hands, eternal in the Heavens." (The Richmond Enquirer, 24 April 1821.

See: Carolyn Tiedeman Moore, "Payne Family Bible, Buckingham County, Virginia, and Icanopy, Florida," The Virginia Genealogist, XVIII, 304-305.

THE PLUNKETT FAMILY

John Plunkett of Orange County, Virginia, married Mildred Hawkins, who later married Isaac Rucker and moved to Amherst County, Virginia. The children of John and Mildred (Hawkins) Plunkett were: SALLY (married John Rucker, son of John, son of John, son of Peter Rucker, the immigrant); BENJAMIN.

Benjamin Plunkett, son of John and Mildred, married 1st Winifred Rucker, daughter of Ambrose, son of John, son of Peter the immigrant. Winifred married as her second husband Francis Ham, son of Stephen and Mildred (Rucker) Ham. Mildred Rucker Ham was a daughter of John, son of Peter. Benjamin Plunkett had by his first wife: AMBROSE; SALLY. By his second wife Benjamin had: JONATHAN; WILLIS RUCKER; NELLY RUCKER; and WILLIAM RUCKER PLUNKETT.

Ambrose Plunkett, son of Benjamin of John, was born 21 February 1782, lived in Campbell County, Virginia, and died in Buckingham County. He married Tabitha Hill, born 28 October 1781, daughter of James Hill of Amherst County. Ambrose and Tabitha had fifteen children: CYRENA, born 21 May 1802; JOHN HILL, born 9 September 1803; FRANCES, born 14 February 1805; WINIFRED, born 13 April 1806; TALIAFERRO, born 23 September 1807; SARAH, born 28 June 1809; NANCY, born 6 November 1810; NANCY ANN, born 13 April 1812; ELIZABETH, born 14 March 1814; WILLIS, born 13 October 1815; ADELINE, born 14 March 1817; JAMES, born 4 October 1818; WILLIAM, born 16 March 1820; NAPOLEON, born 29 November 1821; WASHINGTON, born 3 January 1824.

See: Edythe Johns Rucker Whitley, History of the Rucker Family and Their Descendants (Nashville: Hermitage Printing Co., 1927).

THE PRYOR FAMILY

DAVID PRYOR (1), of Buckingham County, married a Miss Susan Ballow or Ballou. He died the fourth Monday in September 1804, in Buckingham County, where he had lived for many years. He and his wife were the parents of: Dr. WILLIAM S., lived Hanover County, Va., and died 1840; Judge JOHN C.; ZANE, died 1854; LANGSTON, died in 1854; LEONARD, died 1830; NICHOLAS BALLOW, born 1789; BAYNTON; ZACHARIAH B., died in 1837, aged 55; MITCHIE B.

Susan Pryor, wife of David, died in Nashville, Tennessee, in 1831, aged 94 years.

Judge JOHN C. PRYOR (2), son of David Pryor (1), lived in Herman, De Soto County, Mississippi, and later in Tampa, Florida. He married a Miss Bullock, and they had five sons and one daughter: MEDORA, educated at Bardstown, Ky., in a Catholic School, and married Mr. Taylor; FRANK; JOHN; DANIEL; a son who drowned in the Mississippi on his return from California, with a large sum of money around his body, and a son who died in Tampa, Florida.

ZANE PRYOR (3), son of David Pryor (1), died in 1854; married a Miss Patterson of Buckingham County, and lived at a place called Zanesville, near Mt. Vinco Post Office, now in Buckingham. He had two children: Capt. WILLIAM, lived at White Hall, Dillwen, and kept the White House Hotel, married a Miss Cobb, but had no children; DAUGHTER who married Edmondson Nicolas Davis, lived at Lynchburg, Va., and had several children: Edward T. Davis, conductor on the Norfolk and Western Railroad; David Conway Davis; John Bernard Davis; Jonnie Davis; and Aurelia Davis.

NICHOLAS BALLOW PRYOR (4), son of David, was born in Buckingham County in 1789, and died in Nashville in 1833. He married Sallie Thomas of Amherst County, Virginia, and moved to Tennessee. He had two daughters, both of whom married Dr. James A. Dibrell of Van Buren, Arkansas; the first daughter, Ann Eliza had issue: Dr. James A. Dibrell of Little Rock, Arkansas, and Medora, married a Dr. DuVal.

MITCHIE B. PRYOR (5), daughter of David (1), married Randolph Jefferson, died 7 August 1815, brother of President Thomas Jefferson. Mitchie and Randolph had: John Jefferson, raised by his uncle Nicholas B. Pryor and his wife.

See: "The Pryor Family," Virginia Magazine of History and Biography, VII, 325.

THE PUTNEY FAMILY

Richard Putney died in 1778. He married before 15 January 1742/3 Sarah Eklis, daughter of Edward Ellis, whose will of that date named two grandsons Benjamin and James Putney. The will of Edward Ellis was presented to court on 20 December 1748 and proved 19 February 1754 (Surry County, Va., Deeds and Wills, 1738-1754, pp. 863-865).

The will of Richard Putney, 2 July 1773 - 22 December 1778, named the following children: Benjamin, James, Rebecca, Ellis (settled in Albemarle County by 1777 and owned land), Lewis, David, and Richard Putney. Richard's will also named one granddaughter, Rebecca Putney, daughter of his son Benjamin. There is no mention of a wife.

Ellis Putney, son of Richard and Sarah (Ellis) Putney, died about 1822, having married Frances Fearn, daughter of John and Leanna (Lee) Fearn. Ellis Putney's name appears in the Buckingham County Land Books between 1782 and 1821. In 1822 the estate of Ellis Putney is mentioned. At the time of his death, Ellis Putney owned 898 acres of land on Randolph's Creek. His estate was mentioned in the Land Books for 1823, 1824, 1825, 1826, 1827, and 1828. Ellis and his wife were the parents of: SAMUEL, born about 1789, died about 1830; RICHARD ELLIS, born 13 March 1793, died 22 May 1862, married Anne E. Ruffner on 10 October 1815; FRANCES, married William Glenn; MARY, married William Guerrant, descendant of a Huguenot family; REBECCA ANN, married Robert Bondurant, also of a Huguenot family; ELIZABETH, married 1st Robert Moseley, and 2nd Capt. Daniel Guerrant.

Samuel Putney, son of Ellis and Frances (Fearn) Putney, was born about 1789, and died about 1830. On 14 December 1810 he married Sally Bryant, daughter of Isaac and Mary or Molly (Ferrow) Bryant. Mary or Molly Ferrow was the daughter of Charles and Frances (Guerrant) Ferrow. In 1829 Samuel Putney's name appears on the Buckingham County Land Books as owning 204 acres of land on the Randolph Creek. Samuel and Sally (Sarah) (Bryant) Putney were the parents of: ELLIS W., born c.1812; ISAAC B., born c.1815; SAMUEL FEARN.

Ellis Washington Putney, son of Samuel and Sally (Bryant) Putney, was born c.1812, and died June 1880, having married Mary Ann Glover, born c.1812, died 6 June 1877, daughter of William (of Robert) and Susan Glover. Ellis and Mary Ann were the parents of: SUSAN, born c.1833, married James Dunkum; WILLIAM, born 1834; Ellis, born c.1836; SAMUEL, born c.1838; SARAH, born c. 1840; MARY ELIZABETH, born 1841/2, married John Peter Jones (See p. 95 above); RICHARD; JOHN, born 1848, married Ella Miner; ANN HASELTINE, born 19 October 1850, married James Seaborne Jones (See p. 95 above); VIRGINIA ALICE, born a.1858, married Walker Putney, sor of Samuel.

Isaac B. Putney, son of Samuel and Sally (Bryant) Putney, born c.1815, married 10 December 1835 Nancy Wilson. In 1850 he was listed in the Buckingham County Census with his children: SAMUEL; SARAH; ROBERT; ISAAC; FULTON; DAVID; and ANN.

Samuel Fearn Putney, son of Samuel and Sally (Bryant) Putney, was born in 1816, and died 15 October 1885. He married on 22 November 1848 at Enon Baptist Church, Buckingham County, Elizabeth Ann (Betty) Taylor, daughter of Rev. William Harris and Mary (Furgensen) Taylor. Elizabeth Ann Taylor Putney died 24 March 1892. Samuel and Elizabeth were the parents of: WILLIAM WITT; MARY ALICE; WESLEY TAYLOR; ELLIS WALKER (married his cousin Virginia Alice Putney); and JAMES LEE PUTNEY.

Susan Putney, daughter of Ellis Washington and Mary Ann (Glover) Putney, was born c.1833, and married James Dunkum. They were the parents of: MARY ARCHIE, 1850 - 1881, teacher in a private school, and the first teacher that Peter Waverly Jones (1868 - 1940) ever had; VIRGINIA, 1853 - 1914, married John Bersch; SUSAN, 1855 - 1913, married a Mr. Agee; WILLIE, 1857 -1883; GRATZ E., 1872 - , married Lula Warriner; OLNEY, 1876 - , married Minnie Acheson; ELLIS, married Samanthia Daniel; IRENE, married Frank Agee.

William Putney, son of Ellis Washington and Mary Ann (Glover) Putney, married Lucy Burruss. He was a doctor and served in the Civil War. He and his wife had issue: ZENOBIA, married A. Jack Bryant; WILLIE, died un- married of typhoid fever at age 26; JULIAN E., married Maude Goode.

Ellis Putney, son of Ellis Washington and Mary Ann (Glover) Putney, born c.1836, and married Rosa Wilkinson. He served in the Civil War. He and his wife had issue: LELIA, married Charles Reynolds; MARY, married Eustice Lawford; FANNY, married James Sneed of Fluvanna County; DUKE, married Nannie Scott; and KEMPER, married Miss Cobb.

Samuel Putney, son of Ellis Washington and Mary Ann (Glover) Putney, married Miss Brown, and served in the Civil War.

Sarah Putney, daughter of Ellis Washington and Mary Ann (Glover) Putney, was born c. 1840, and married George Wilkinson. They had two children: WILLIE D., married Mary Haines; HUNTER, married Essie Johnson.

Richard Putney, son of Ellis Washington and Mary Ann (Glover) Putney, was in the Civil War. He married Elizabeth Woodfin, and they were the parents of: THORNTON, married Edna Phillips and had two children; and J. NORMAN, married Etta Stinson and had two daughters.

Peter Waverly Jones, 1868 - 1940, said that the line between Cumberland and Buckingham Counties passed through the plantation of his grandather, Ellis W. Putney, near New Canton. The home place was built in the 1830's and is owned and occupied by grandson J. Norman Putney, son of Richard, and his wife. Jones described his grandfather, Ellis Washington Putney, as about 5'9", stout, pious, and very amiable. His grandmother, Mary Ann Glover Putney, was about 5'6", fat and very amiable.

This sketch of the Putney family of Buckingham County was contributed by Miss Agnes B. Jones of Richmond, Va., and Mrs. Elia H. Jones Rogers of Nashville, Tennessee.

THE RADFORD FAMILY

Thomas Radford was born in 1790 in Buckingham County, and moved to Cum- berland County, Kentucky, about 1819. He married 1st Anna Maxey, and 2nd Mrs. Mary Eliza Hopkins on 10 April 1853 in Cumberland County. He is shown in the 1850 and 1860 Censuses of Cumberland County, Kentucky.

THE REAGAN FAMILY

The family record of Erasmus Reagan of Sweetwater, Tennessee, is given in the Family Bible.

Erasmus Reagan, son of Jeremiah and Racheal Reagan, born 15 January 1818, in Buckingham County; married Nancy Amner Mize of Alabama and moved to Monroe County, Tennessee. He served in the Confederate Army from 1862 to 1863.

BIRTHS

Athalonia Reagan, born 11 February 1849.

Laura Amner Reagan, born 6 December 1851.

LaUna Reagan, born 4 January 1854.

Pan Dora Reagan, born 7 March 1857.

Dixie Reagan, born 10 August 1860.

John Fletcher Reagan, born 6 April 1864.

Mary Lee Reagan, born 6 June 1868.

Landon Carter Reagan, born 14 August 1871.

MARRIAGES

Laura Amner Reagan to Isaac Carroll Lee, 3 July 1870.

LaUna Reagan to Robert Thompson, February 1893.

Pan Dora (Reagan) to Andy K. Harper, no date.

Dixie Reagan to Samuel L. Crandal, no date.

John Fletcher Reagan to Mallie Cobb, no date.

Mary Lee Reagan to R. A. Aytry, no date.

Athalonia Reagan to William Lee, January 1868.

DEATHS

Erasmus Reagan, 8 March 1899.

Nancy Mize Reagan, 3 December 1886.

Athalonia Reagan Lee, 30 June 1919.

LaUna Reagan Thompson, April 1926.

Dixie Reagan Crandal, 24 April 1931.

Landon Carter Reagan, 21 January 1884.

THE RHODES FAMILY

John Rhodes of Albemarle County, Virginia, of the 3rd generation in America, was born 2 June 1766, died 1 March 1841. His will was proved on that date. He married May 1793 in Albemarle County, Francisco, daughter of Bernard Brown. John and Francisco had issue: SIDNEY, born 27 January 1794, died 23 July 1855, married 13 December 1811, Powhatan Jones, born 9 October 1792, died 13 September 1880; of "Breman," Buckingham County; RYLAND; JOHN D., married Mrs. Morris of Albemarle, and died without issue; WILLIAM; SARAH, married Samuel Woods of Nelson County, Virginia, and emigrated to Missouri; TYREE; VIRGINIA, married W. C. Smith of Nelson County, and died in 1854 or 1855; JACINTHA, married 1st J. Smith of Nelson County, and 2nd James Harris of Nelson County; FANNIE, married Garland Brown of Nelson County, and moved to Mississippi, where she died; LUCY ANN, married 1st James A. Payne of Warrenton, Va., and 2nd Mr. Newlands of Ralls County, Missouri.

Tyree Rhodes, brother of John, was born 24 December 1770, and died 17 July 1827. He settled in Giles County, Tennessee. His descendants have not been traced.

See: "The Rodes Family," Virginia Magazine of History and Biography, (July 1899), VII, 82-87.

THE SCOTT FAMILY

John Scott and Margaret his wife, of Albemarle County, Virginia, and John Nicholas and Martha his wife of Buckingham County on 24 December 1779 conveyed to John Christian of Amherst County for £ 145 current money, 1160 acres in Amherst County, being a tract of land granted by an Inclusive Patent to Martha Fry (now wife of John Nicholas) and Margaret Fry (now wife of John Scott), crossing Rocky Run of Buffalo River and adjoining land of James Warren; also 400 acres granted unto the said Martha and Margaret; the patents were dated 3 November 1752, and 400 acres the residue patented 27 June 1764, now in possession of John Christian.

See: Edward P. Valentine, The Edward P. Valentine Papers, 4 vols. (Richmond, 1927), p. 1498.

Brunswick County Deeds, Book (?), pages 230 and 371.

THE SCRUGGS FAMILY

Finch Scruggs, son of William and grandson of Thomas Scruggs, was born in Buckingham County on 13 July 1772. He married in November 1789 Nancy Thomas, born in Cumberland County, Virginia, on 27 October 1773. They were the parents of: MARY STEVENSON, born 3 November 1794; WILLIAM A., born 5 February 1797 in Buckingham County, died 25 July 1862 in Mississippi, having married Elizabeth (?): JESSE THOMAS, born 17 February 1799 in Buckingham County, and died 26 November 1882 in Texas, having married Susanna Thornton on 4 June 1823 in Tennessee; FINCH PHILLIPS, born 19 May 1801 in Buckingham County, and died 21 September 1882 in Mississippi having married 1st Martha Kittrell and 2nd S. (Boyce) Murphy; ALLEN FRANKLIN, born 8 November 1803; PHINEAS THOMAS, born 29 March 1806 in Davidson County, Tennessee, died 18 October 1878 in Tennessee, having married Minerva Rivers; SARAH H., born 3 July 1808 in Davidson County, Tennessee, died unmarried 20 August 1828; ANTHONY T., born 18 July 1815, died 23 July 1880 in Arkansas, having married Caroline H. B. Hitt; ALBERT, born 30 April 1811 in Williamson County, Tennessee, died 4 July 1901 in Tennessee, married 1st in 1837 a Miss Richardson, and 2nd Anna P. Walton; JOHN HOWELL, born 11 November 1817 in Williamson County, Tennessee, died 3 August 1905 in Mississippi, having married 1st Virginia Richardson, and 2nd in 1843 Mary Locke; JOHN H., born 20 June 1820 in Williamson County, Tennessee.

Mary Stevenson Scruggs, daughter of Finch and Nancy (Thomas) Scruggs, was born 3 November 1794 in Cumberland County, Virginia, and died 29 April 1881 in Mississippi. She married William R. Barksdale by whom she had several sons and a daughter, Narcissa. Narcissa married Alexander Barksdale on 21 August 1823 (sic).

Allen Franklin Scruggs, son of Finch and Nancy (Thomas) Scruggs, was born 3 November 1803 in Buckingham County, and died 10 September 1902 in Missouri. He married 1st Mary A. Kittrell, 2nd Sarah Jane Hitt, 3rd Harriett H. Hitt, and 4th Margaret P. Honey.

THE SHEPARD FAMILY

The Shepard family of Buckingham County is said to have borne these arms, found in an old Shepard book dated 1751. The arms were: Ermine, on a chief Sable, three poleaxes Argent. Crest: On a mount Vert, a stag courant regardant ppr., attired Or, Motto: Nec timeo, nec sperno. The arms were granted in 1574.

110

SAMUEL SHEPARD lived in Southeast Buckingham County and served in the Revolution. He had at least one son: SAMUEL, Jr.

SAMUEL SHEPARD, Jr., son of Samuel, was born c.1772, and married Susannah Holman, daughter of John Holman (who was appointed a judge by Governor Botetourt, c.1768-1770) by his wife a Miss Yancey.

Samuel Shepard of Buckingham and John Holman of Cumberland conveyed land in Cumberland County to Robert and John Yancey (Cumberland County Deeds Book 12, p. 489).

Lt. Col. Charles Yancey of Buckingham County, commander of the 1st Virginia Regiment in the War of 1812, was a frequent visitor in the Shepard home. The Shepards and the Yanceys called each other cousin.

Samuel Shepard and his wife, Miss Yancey (sic) were the parents of: BURWELL; CARROLL, who married a Miss Smith - Brown; HARRIETT, who married Henry Garnett; JULIET, who married Andrew Amonet; MARIA, who married Len Bosher of Henrico County; MAGARIA, who married Fleming Casey; WILLIAM E.

BURWELL SHEPARD, son of Samuel, married Elizabeth Guthrie, and was the father of: ELIZABETH; AMARANDA E.; NAPOLEON B.; THADDEUS D.; GENEVA, who married Leach Phillips; CERVANTES A., and EDWERTA A.

CARROLL SHEPARD, son of Samuel, married a Miss Smith - Brown. He was the father of: JOHN, who married a Miss Loving and moved to Tennessee; WILLIAM, who was a member of the State Legislature prior to the war, was defeated by Philip McKinney, and then ran a law school near Buckingham Court House; SUSAN; ANNE.

WILLIAM E. SHEPARD, son of Samuel, married Lauzianne Guthrie, and was the father of: JAMES, C.S.A.; BETTY, married Mr. Kish; JOHN, of Co. F., Va. Inf., C.S.A., captured at Rich Mountain and killed at Petersburg, June 1864; WILLIAM B., Troop G, 3rd Va. Cavalry, C.S.A.; SAMUEL MONROE, of Co. F., Buckingham Institute Guards, 20th Va. Inf., C.S.A.. killed at Gettysburg in 1863; and EDWARD POINDEXTER.

NAPOLEON B. ("Pitt") SHEPARD, son of Burwell and Elizabeth Guthrie Shepard, was in Co. I, 2nd Regt., Va. State Reserves, C.S.A., in July and August 1864.

THADDEUS D. SHEPARD, son of Burwell and Elizabeth (Guthrie) Shepard, enlisted 10 March 1862 at Buckingham in the Co. K, 4th Regt., Virginia Cavalry, C.S.A. He was captured at Kelly's Ford, Va., on 17 March 1863, imprisoned at Old Capitol Prison, Washington, D. C., and delivered to the Confederate agent at City Point on 29 March 1863. He did not live long after the war.

EDWARD POINDEXTER SHEPARD, son of William E. and Lauzianne (Guthrie) Shepard, was a lieutenant in Co. C, 25th Battalion, Va. Inf., C.S.A. He married Georgianna Guthrie, and had at least one son: MILLER.

MILLER SHEPARD, son of Edward Poindexter and Georgianna (Guthrie) Shepard, was born 9 April 1862, and married Sarah Jane Gannaway, who was born 26 January 1868. She was descended from John Gannaway who served in the French and Indian Wars.

See: William Shepard, "Shepard and Other Buckingham Families," William and Mary Quarterly, 2nd series, VI, 151-153.

THE STRATTON FAMILY

Jane Baugh Stratton, wife of David Molloy, was a daughter of Peter Stratton (who moved to Buckingham County from Powhatan County) and his wife Mary Steger (born 2 September 1764), and granddaughter of Peter and Jane (Baugh) Streger of Powhatan County. She was descended from Joseph Stratton of James City County, who was a member of the House of Burgesses from 1628 to 1632 and himself a descendant of the Strattons of England.

See: William Shepard, "Shepard and Other Buckingham County Families," William and Mary Quarterly, 2nd series, VI, 152-153.

THE TALIAFERRO FAMILY

JOHN TALIAFERRO, a physician and a minister, married about 1755 Mary Hardin, daughter of Henry and Judith (Lynch) Hardin. John and Mary lived in Pittsylvania County, Virginia, until about 1779 when they moved to Surry County, North Carolina. In 1776 John Taliaferro organized a company of minute men, and was made captain.

John and Mary (Hardin) Taliaferro were the parents of: RICHARD, born 1756; ROSE, married Joseph Porter; ELIZABETH, married Levi Pruitt on 22 October 1778; ANN, born c.1768, died 1864, married Johnathan McCrary; CHARLES, died 1838, married 1st Sallie Burroughs and 2nd Dicie Tucker; BENJAMIN, born 1763, married Ada Snow; JUDITH, married in 1848 Shadrack Franklin; MARY, married Mr. Mercer; BETHLAND; LUCY, born 29 May 1780, died 28 February 1848, married John Lawrence Jones in 1797.

RICHARD TALIAFERRO, son of John and Mary (Hardin) Taliaferro, was born 1756 and died 15 March 1781 in Buckingham County, at the Battle of Guilford Court House. He was a Revolutionary Soldier and a member of the Volunteer Riflemen from Surry County. He married Dorcus Perkins and had issue: JEAN; MARY HARDIN; and JUDY.

See: Schenck, History of North Carolina, 1780 - 1781, p. 301.
The Monument on the Battlefield.
Lewis W. Rigsby, Historic Georgia Families, 1925-28 (Repr. Baltimore: Genealogical Publishing Co., 1969), pp. 116-118.
The Huguenot, Publication No. 13, p. 139.

THE TINDALE/TINDALL FAMILY

Thomas Tindale (or Tindall) was in Goochland County as early as 1728. The 1774 will of Thomas Tindall of Albemarle County and the Fluvanna Records, 1777, list Thomas Tindale and Benjamin Tindale of Buckingham County. Hatcher and Benjamin Tindall had land on Slate River and Hunt's Creek in Buckingham. Washington Tindall was probably a close relative of Claiborne West as he left legacies to the latter's two oldest sons, Thomas and Benjamin West.

See: Goochland County Deed Book 1, p. 17.
Albemarle County Will Book 2, p. 313.

THE WALKER FAMILY

The Rev. Jesse Walker was a native of Buckingham County, born 9 June 1766. He married Susannah Webly. He traveled throughout North Carolina, East Tennessee, and later went to West (now Middle) Tennessee, and served in the Nashville Circuit of the Methodist Church.

He was a local minister and resisted many attempts to persuade him to enter the itinerant ministry on the grounds that it would not be fair to his wife. He changed his mind after two of his children died.

In 1802 he was received into the Western Conference and served in the Tennessee and Kentucky Circuits until 1806. He then went to Illinois, and may be considered the "Father of Methodism in Illinois." He went as a missionary to the Missouri Conference, which at that time included all of Missouri and Illinois.

Jesse Walker had a daughter, Jane, who married her cousin, Rev. James Walker, nephew of her father.

James Walker, nephew of Rev. Jesse Walker, was a native of Tennessee and served under General Andrew Jackson at New Orleans in the War of 1812. After that War and the removal of his family to Illinois, he became a Methodist minister.

See: Minutes of the Missouri Conference.
Almer M. Pennwell, Methodist Movement in Northern Illinois, 1942, pp. 16 - 21.

THE WEBB FAMILY

Henry Gaines Webb was born 1867 in Hawkins County, Tennessee, and married Sarah (Sally) Lucinda Wolfe. He was a son of Gabriel W. and Phoebe (Young) Webb, and grandson of Theodoric and Catherine (Mattox) Webb, both born in Buckingham County, Virginia, in the 18th century. Henry Gaines Webb left Tennessee before Charles Edwards (his son ?) was born in 1897. Henry had a brother (probably a twin) who lived and died in Knox County, Tennessee.

See: The Eastern Kentuckian, (March 1977), vol. XI.

THE WEST FAMILY

The will of Delaware West, dated 4 January 1810 and proved in Norfolk, City, Va., on 28 February 1810. He gave all his estate to his brother John West and named his niece Elizabeth Seaton.

John West married Elizabeth Seaton (aunt of William Winston Seaton, whose Biography furnished this information) and had issue: THOMAS.

Thomas West, son of John and Elizabeth (Seaton) West, was a member of the House of Delegates from Campbell County, Virginia, 1799 - 1801, and married Elizabeth Blair Bolling. She was a daughter of Robert Bolling of "Chellowe," Buckingham County, Virginia, and granddaughter of Col. John and Elizabeth (Blair) Bolling, and great-granddaughter of Dr. Archibald Blair.

See: "The West Family," Tyler's Quarterly (1925), VI, 117.
J. Hall Pleasants, "The Gorsuch and Lovelace Families," Virginia Magazine of History and Biography, (Oct. 1917), XXV, 432.
"Bolling of Virginia," Virginia Magazine of History and Biography (July 1914), XXII, 352.
Wyndham Robertson, Pocahontas, Alias Matoaka, And Her Descendants, 1887 (Repr.: Baltimore: Genealogical Publishing Company, 1968).

THE WHITE FAMILY

Henry White, living in Bedford County, Virginia, had moved there from Buckingham County. In his will, 1802, he ordered that his debts be paid, and named his son Jacob White, son William White, and granddaughter Judith David. He mentioned "sons and daughters." Sons Jacob and William were to be executors, and the will was witnessed by Chas. Gwatkins, Fell LeSuer, and Julius Hatcher, Sr. The will was dated 12 August 1800 and proved 1802.

Jacob White, private and then captain in the Virginia Line during the Revolutionary War, was born 20 October 1765 in Buckingham County, and died 2 June 1832 in Bedford County, Virginia. He married 1st, in 1785 in Amherst County, Hannah Spiers, born c.1769, died 11 January 1816. He married 2nd in Bedford County in 1816 Nancy Oglesby.

Jacob White, son of Henry White, and Revolutionary soldier, was the father of: SALLIE, born 18 August 1787, married David Douglas; JOHN A., married Elizabeth Robinson; NANCY R., born 1789, married 1st Abraham Robinson and 2nd Jessie Spinner; JACOB WASHINGTON, born 5 March 1792, married Matilda Buford; REBECCA H., married Charles Lewis David; ELIZABETH, married Henry Hatcher; WILLIAM ALLEN, born 1800, married 1st Caroline Poindexter and 2nd Nancy McDaniel Reese; SAMUEL D., settled in Simpson Coimty, Kentucky; MARY (POLLY), born 13 March 1801, married Julius W. Hatcher; CATHERINE, married Thomas Hatcher; HENRY MILTON, born 13 January 1803, married Mary Gwatkin; EDNA, married Moses Penn; EDITH S., married Gabriel S. Fisher.

Mary (Polly) White, daughter of Jacob, was born 13 March 1801, and married Julius Wooldridge Hatcher, on 28 January 1817 in Bedford County, Virginia. Julius W. Hatcher was born 1794 in Chesterfield County, Virginia, and died 1876 near Franklin, Williamson County, Tennessee. Among the children of Julius and Mary (White) Hatcher was: ETHELBERT HENRY.

Ethelbert Henry Hatcher, son of Julius and Mary (White) Hatcher, was born 18 January 1818 in Bedford County, Virginia, died 25 January 1853 in Columbia, Maury County, Tennessee. On 1 January 1843 he married near Nashville, Davidson County, Tennessee, Louisa C. Graves, born 12 August 1817 in Montgomery County, Kentucky, died 6 November 1897 at San Louis Pretese, Mexico. The couple resided in Nashville. Ethelbert Henry Hatcher was a minister. He and his wife had at least one son: JOHN WATSON.

John Watson Hatcher, son of Ethelbert and Louisa (Graves) Hatcher, was a minister like his father. He was born 3 January 1845, and died 16 January 1878. On 2 July 1868 he married Alice Grissim Hawkins, born 1849 in Lebanon, Wilson County, Tennessee, where she died 14 April 1885.

See: The Huguenot, Publication no. 14.
H. H. Hardesty and Co., Historical and Geographical Encyclopedia (Chicago: 1883), p. 434.
D.A.R. Lineages of members, national numbers 173356 and 210706.

THE WOODSON FAMILY

Jacob Woodson had a grant of 390 acres in Buckingham County, adjoining land of Chiles, Richard Holland, Flemsterd Ranson, and James Coleman (Land Office, Treasury Warrant no. 19831, issued 10 October 1783 and 29 July 1789).

William Woodson, formerly of the City of Richmond, now of Buckingham County, on 18 May 1821 conveyed to Charles Ellis and John Allen 153 acres of land in Goochland County, adjoining the land of John Trentian, David Ellis, amd William Webbert, etc. (Goochland County Deed Book 25, p. 14).

Jacob Woodson and wife Mary, William Johnson and wife Elizabeth, Stephen Woodson and wife Sarah, Thomas Woodson and wife Elizabeth, all of Goochland County, and Jacob Woodson, Jr., and wife Mary, of Buckingham County, on 26 April 1803 conveyed to Benjamin Woodson of Goochland County 200 acres of land bounded by lands of William Harris, Philip Pleasants, and Robert Morris (Goochland County Deed Book 2, p. 624).

John Woodson, planter, of Cumberland County, on 24 February 1797, sold to Edward Vawter 150 acres of land in Cumberland and Buckingham Counties, part of a tract formerly owned by John Woodson. (Cumberland County Deed Book 8, p. 55).

Shadrack Woodson and wife Susannah, of Buckingham County, on 14 November 1780 conveyed to Isaac Bryant 220 acres in Buckingham and Cumberland Counties, adjoining land of John Carnon, Isaac Bryant, and others, being the same land conveyed to the said Shadrack by his father William Woodson. (Cumberland County Deed Book 6, p. 94).

William Woodson, late of Buckingham County, now of Cumberland County, owned in fee simple 200 acres of land on the branches of Randolph's Creek in said Buckingham County. The land is now in the possession of John Bagby. Drury Woodson, son of William, claimed the land was his by reason of a gift. Jesse Woodson, another son of William, claimed his father had promised him 100 acres on the occasion of his (Jesse's) marriage. An agreement was reached between William, Drury, and Jesse. Also mentioned was Shadrack Woodson, another son of William. The agreement was signed by William Woodson on 17 March 1783. (Cumberland County Deed Book 6, p. 149).

Tucker Woodson of Goochland County, on 17 May 1778 conveyed to John Matthews 400 acres in Buckingham and Cumberland Counties, on Randolph's Creek, adjoining the land of Alex. Trent, Randolph, and others. (Cumberland County Deeds, Book 6, p. 28).

Jacob Woodson of Buckingham County, on 14 February 1763 sold to Robert Moore 260 acres in Cumberland County, being part of a greater tract granted on 11 April 1732 to William, Joseph, and John Woodson, and by them conveyed to the said Jacob Woodson on 22 July 1751. (Cumberland County Deed Book 3, p. 383).

John Woodson (son of John Woodson of "Carter's Ferry"), in his will called himself John Woodson of Bear Garden, Buckingham County. He died without issue, and in his will, proved 28 May 1832 in Cumberland County, named his sister Nancy Deane, nephew Francis B. Deane, niece Elizabeth wife of Robert Irving, dec., children of sister Sally Overton, and surviving children of dec. sister Elizabeth Kennon. Francis B. Deane, Sr., Randolph Harrison, John B. Cocke, and nephew Francis B. Deane, Jr., were executors. William Woodson and Carter H. Bradley were witnesses.

William Woodson was born at "Rosebank," the Cumberland County home of his father, Capt. Charles Woodson, on 28 March 1784. His mother was Judith Leake. William's uncle Drury, conducted a school near the plantation, "Red House."

Daniel and Jacob Woodson, sons of Capt. Obadiah Woodson, lived in the southwestern part of Buckingham County. Daniel married Elizabeth, daughter of John Jones who resided in Buckingham County. Daniel and Elizabeth (Jones) Woodson had a daughter, Elizabeth (Betsy) Ann, who was the third wife of Claiborne Dandridge West.

See: Henry Morton Woodson, Historical Genealogy of the Woodsons and Their Connections (Memphis: The Author, 1915), pp. 194-195, 302.
    "Woodson Family," William and Mary Quarterly, 1st series, XI, 52.
    Edward P. Valentine, The Edward P. Valentine Papers, 4 vols. (Richmond: 1927), pp. 1841-2, 2040.

CHAPTER SIX

MISCELLANEOUS NOTES

LAND GRANTS AND DEEDS

Edward Maxey had 400 acres in Buckingham County on Slate River, at mouth of Great Creek, surveyed 24 March 1764.

Nathaniel Maxey had 300 acres in Buckingham County, between lands of Crouch, Walker, and Widow Gilliam surveyed (Virginia State Archives).

Anthony Agree had 400 acres in Buckingham County on the branches of Green Creek surveyed 10 July 1767 (Virginia Land Office, Patent Book 37, p. 1).

John Worley had 183 acres in Buckingham , on the branches of Wreck Island Creek, adjoining lines of David Rogers, 3 May 1780. The land was transferred to Worley by Norty Gordon (Virginia Land Office Patents).

Silas Whorley has 92 acres in Buckingham on branches of Wreck Island Creek, crossing Stovall's Road and adjoining land of Wm. Duiguid, William Gilliam, Charles Witt, and Thomas Doss, on 1 March 1781. John Worley was the assignee of Thomas Doss, who received the grant in 1772. (Land Grant Book D, p. 603).

Charles Maxey had 400 acres on Little Phillips Creek in Buckingham, 16 April 1783 (Land Patent Book 11, p. 689).

Charles Maxey had 50 acres on Juland Creek on 29 May 1788, and 400 acres on Sycamore Island Creek in 1789 (Virginia Land Office, Richmond).

Nathaniel Maxey in 1796 received 300 acres on Holladay River, Buckingham County (The Holladay River now forms part of the boundary between Buckingham and Appomattox Counties, which were separated in 1845) (Virginia Land Office).

William A. Lightfoot of Buckingham, and wife Caroline, in 1839 deeded a lot in Williamsburg, which had been owned by William Lightfoot, then by his son Philip John Lightfoot, and then to the latter's devisees. Philip John Lightfoot married Mary Ann (?) and died without issue (His will, 16 June 1819 - 15 July 1819). The deed refers to a cause entitled Lewis & c. VS. Blakey & c., 1835, in the Henrico County Superior Court of Law and Chancery, in which a division was made of Philip John Lightfoot's property. ("Lightfoot Family", William and Mary Quarterly, 1st ser., III, 109).

Drury Woodson, Shadrack Woodson, and Jesse Woodson were sons of William Woodson. According to an agreement dated 17 March 1783 in Cumberland County, these three agreed about 200 acres in Buckingham County. William Woodson of the fourth generation married Sarah Allen. Jesse Woodson, son of William, lived in Buckingham County. His nephew Joseph, probably son of Jesse's brother Shadrack, lived in Caswell County, North Carolina.

Daniel Moseley and wife Martha of Buckingham, Rezin Porter and wife Mary, William Cook and wife Elizabeth, and Jane and Rebecca Pettus of Prince Edward County, in a deed recorded 16 October 1809 sold John Pettus of Prince Edward County, for £ 300, 261 acres in Prince Edward County where the late Stephen Pettus lived and which he devised by his will to the above named daughters. (Prince Edward County Deed Book 14, p. 312).

Stephen Pettus of the State of Tennesse, on 5 August 1809, sold James Watt of Buckingham, for £ 439 237 acres of land in Prince Edward, being part of the land where Stephen Pettus once lived and which he devised by will to the said Stephen Pettus. Thomas C. Martin, Samuel Shepherd, William Preston, and John C. Owens witnessed the deed, which was recorded 16 October 1809 (Prince Edward County Deed Book 14, p. 313).

The next group of abstracts, taken from Albemarle Surveys, are thought to refer to land in Buckingham County.

William Allen of Albemarle County conveyed to William Hunt Allen 650 acres on both sides of the Slate River, 9 September 1748.

William Duiguid of Albemarle County conveyed 156 acres on the south side of Fluvanna River to Thomas McDaniel of St. Anne's Parish, in 1748.

William Allen of Albemarle County conveyed 394 acres, both sides of Slate River, and both sides of Glover's Road, and both sides of Horn Quarter Road, on the heads of the branches of Randolph's, Hatcher's, and Joshua's Creeks, to John Allen on 9 September 1748.

Edmund Wood and wife Mary, of Albemarle County conveyed 595 acres on a branch of Hatcher's Creek of Willis' River, to Robert Tomson of Goochland County, 8 September 1748.

William Noland of Albemarle conveyed 200 acres on Arthur's Creek of Slate River to Thomas Blakey of Goochland County on 8 September 1748.

* * * * * * *

Thomas Jackson, planter, and wife Ann of Louisa County, Nicholas Miller, planter of Hanover, David Anderson merchant of Hanover and wife Elizabeth, Ann Duiguid of Powhatan County, widow, William Duiguid of Buckingham, merchant, and wife Lucy, William Johan and wife Mary of Louisa County, Ann Miller of Hanover widow of Charles Miller, dec., all appoint Am. Anderson of American Square their attorney to recover from Richard Neave of New Broad Street, London, an account of the estates of Dr. Josiah Cole and Wm. Mowatt (See: William and Mary Quarterly, 1st series, XXII, 122; and XXV, 186).

Valentine Childress of Powhatan County, Virginia, granted power of attorney to Christopher Robinson of Cumberland County, on 28 July 1800, to handle all claims as heir and legatee of Valentine's father, Thomas Childress, of Buckingham County, dec., providing him to transact business in his name and to sell and convey property. (Cumberland County Deed Book 8, p. 369).

Walter Davis and wife Sally (Morton) of Powhatan County, on 1 January 1800 sold to William Anderson of Buckingham County, one-half acre of land being lot no. 10 in the Town of Cartersville (Cumberland County Deeds, Book 8, p. 339).

Robert Anderson and wife Mary of Cumberland County on 3 February 1796 sold to Joseph Carrington for £ 556, 380 acres in Cumberland and Buckingham Counties on the south side of Hatcher's Creek, on which they lived.

Charles Bryant of Cumberland County on 9 October 1835 conveyed property including 680 acres on which he lived, slaves, and books. The deed mentions that Bryant had two daughters: Mary Ann who married Reuben Boatwright, and Susan who married William Anderson, Jr. Boatwright lived in Buckingham County. (Cumberland County Deed Book 9).

A deed dated 14 December 1816 states that Robert Brown, dec., owned a tract of land in Buckingham and Cumberland Counties, and after his death it descended to his sons Nathaniel and Samuel. Nathaniel Brown, Mary Brown, and Samuel Brown conveyed the land to John Akers of Patrick County, Virginia for $100. (Cumberland County Deed Book 17, p. 361).

Philip Jacob Irion od Bedford County sold 400 acres in Culpeper County to William Allen of Buckingham, and is indebted to Allen. Indenture was dated 2 September 1784. (Culpepper County Deeds, 1785- 1787, Book N(?).).

John and Mary Phelps of Buckingham in a deed of 2 October 1786 to Robert Blank of Goochland County, mention Phelps' Falls on the Fluvanna River in Fluvanna County (Fluvanna County Deed Book 2, p. 194).

John Fearn of Buckingham County and wife Elizabeth on 19 August 1776 conveyed to George Carrington, Jno. Nicholas, and Samuel Jordan, Trustees appointed by the Commonwealth of Virginia for paying away £ 5000 to John Ballendine and John Revely for the purpose of erecting and carrying on a blast furnace situated on Phelps Creek. For £ 350, 127 acres on Phelps Creek being part of the tract where John Fearn now lives...lower side of the main road leading to Slate River...line of Thomas Fearn and line of William Walker and Richard Blanks, eastwardly by the line of Hartwell Cocke, southwardly and westwardly the said John Fearn's land. The deed was signed by John Fearn and Elizabeth Fearn, and witnessed by John Bernard, William Cannon, William Binnon, Richard (X) Blanks. The deed was proved in Buckingham County on 10 February 1777 by Wm. Cannon, William Binion or Binnon, and Richard Blanks, and attested by Rolfe Eldridge, clerk, copy of R. Eldridge, Jr., deputy clerk. (Virginia Executive Papers).

William Walker of Bedford County and wife Elizabeth on 19 August 1776 conveyed to George Carrington, John Nicholas, and Samuel Jordan, Trustees appointed...(as above), for £ 95 200 acres on the branches of Bear Garden Creek granted to William Walker by patent 26 September 1768. The deed was signed by Wm. (X) Walker, and witnessed by Hardin Perkins, Benjamin Cottrell, Wm. Gates, and Anthony Murry. It was acknowledged in Buckingham County on 14 October 1776 by William and Elizabeth Walker, and attested by Rolfe Eldridge, clerk. (Virginia State Archives, Richmond; see also The Virginia Genealogist, vol. XVI).

Robert Patterson entered a claim on 29 October 1795 for Charles Patterson of Buckingham County, Virginia, for 5625 acres on the waters of the North Fork of the Licking and Salt Lick Creek, Mason County, Kentucky; 3rd rate land. Patterson also entered a claim for 4000 acres on the first large creek emptying into the Ohio above Big Bone Creek, Campbell County; 2nd rate land. (Non-Resident Land, Franklin County, Ky., Kentucky Certificate Book, Register of The Kentucky State Historical Society, XXIV, 109).

Price Curd on 11 Nov. 1795 entered a claim for John Curd for 1000 acres of land lying on Licking and on the south side of Indian Creek, Bourbon County, Kentucky; 2nd rate land. He also entered a claim for 1000 acres in Shelby County, on the waters of Brashare Creek; 2nd rate land. He also entered a claim for William Curd of Buckingham County for 1000 acres on the waters of Elkhorn, supposed to be in Scott County, Ky.; 2nd rate land. Signed by Price Curd. (Non-Resident Land Owners, Certificate Book of Kentucky, Kentucky State Archives; also The Register, vol. (?), p. 111).

Charles Smith and wife Nancy of Price Edward County, on 15 March 1779, sold to Seth Cason of Buckingham County, for £ 1000 Virginia money 325 acres in Prince Edward County on the branches of Vaughan's Creek. (Prince Edward County Deeds, Book for 1778 - 1783, p. 115).

John Ussery and wife Elizabeth of Anson County, North Carolina, sold to William Leak of Buckingham County for £ 170 Virginia currency two tracts of land north of the Peedee: 1st, a grant to Thomas Holmes made 7 April 1749, conveyed by Holmes to Thomas Coleman who bequeathed it to his son John Coleman, who sold it to Peter Brister who sold it to John Ussery, 100 acres, on 22 January 1762; 2nd, a tract granted to Samuel Parsons who conveyed it to Haten or Haden Morris. The will was proved January 1770 by William Mask, and witnessed by John Skinner, Solomon Gross, and William Mask (Anson County, North Carolina, Deed Book, Book 7, p. 262 ; in McBee, Abstracts of Anson County, N. C., Vol. I, p. 50).

Peter Hale of Buckingham County, Virginia, on 26 August 1818, conveyed to Daniel Alexander of Smith County, Tennessee, for $2600.00, land on the Main East Fork of Stones River, being the same land Charles Kavanagh conveyed to Hale on 16 September 1817, and being the land whereon William H. Robertson now lives, and adjoining the lands of Bradford and Edwards. Peter Hales signed, and L. Anderson, Wm. Ledbetter, Isaac Ledbetter, and Stephen Hall witnessed the will. (Rutherford County, Tennessee, Deed Book L, p. 304, no. 255).

William Wright, son and heir of Henry Wright of the State of Georgia, Archibald Wright, Gabriel Wright, and William Gells and his wife Mary, of Buckingham County, Virginia, legatees of George Wright, the elder, dec., of the one part, on 10 February 1804, for £ 287, sold to William Wright and Henry Ransome of Cumberland County, Virginia, 200 acres of land devised by the said George Wright, the elder, to be sold by his executors, being the same land where Elizabeth Armostrong formerly lived, and whereon George Wright formerly lived. William Wright was administrator of Henry Wright of Georgia. Deed recorded 27 August 1804. (Cumberland County Deed Book 9, p. 425).

Thomas Donoho of Caswell County, North Carolina, sold to Frederick Sanders of Buckingham County, Virginia, the same land which the State of North Carolina had granted to Donoho for his military service. (Smith County, Tennessee, Deed Book B, p. 46).

Thomas Jackson of Louisa County, Virginia, and wife Ann, Nicholas Mills of Hanover County, David Anderson of Hanover, merchant, and his wife Elizabeth, Ann Duiguid of Powhatan County, widow, William Duiguid of Buckingham and wife Lucy, William Hogan of Louisa County and wife Mary, and Ann Mills, widow of Charles Mills, appoint Wm. Anderson of America Square, City of London, their attorney to recover from Richard Neave of New Broad Street, London, an account of his administration of the estates of Dr. Josiah Cole and Wm. Mowat. (William and Mary Quarterly, 1st series, XXI, 144).

John Dew of Davidson County, Tennessee, on 25 December 1807, sold William M. Allen of Buckingham County, Virginia, 226 acres of land on the Cumberland River in Davidson County. (Davidson County Deeds, Book E, p. 273).

Silas Flournoy of Buckingham County, Virginia, on 4 March 1807, sold to Daniel Williams of Davidson County, Tennessee 599½ acres of land on the south side of the Cumberland River in Davidson County. (Davidson County Deeds, Book E, p. 328).

Thomas Sanders of Davidson County and wife Mary, for $ 2000.00 sold to Archibald Austin of Buckingham County, land in Buckingham County, known as Sanders' "old place," where the said Sanders formerly lived in Buckingham County, on both sides of the North Fork of Slate River, including 400 acres. Thomas and Mary Sanders signed the deed. (Davidson County Deeds, Book G, p. 437).

Henry Binkley of Davidson County, Tennessee, on 10 June 1826, sold to Edward C. Watson of Buckingham County, 50 acres on Sycamore Creek granted to said Binkley by the State of Tennessee in September 1825. (Davidson County Deeds, Book R, p. 693).

Prettyman Merry of Buckingham County, on 14 November 1811, appointed James Sanders of Sumner County, Tennessee, his attorney to sell land in Sumner County on east side of Drake's Creek, deeded to Merry by John Roberts, and sold by Maj. William Buckner by power of attorney to William Dotson (Sumner County, Tennessee, Deed Book 6, p. 133).

Prettyman Merry of Buckingham County, Virginia, on 16 April 1812, for $1200.00 sold to Nancy W. Douglass, Jincey H. Dodson, Betsey M. Dodson, Polly W. Dodson, William Dodson, Edward L. Dodson, children and heirs of L. Dodson, dec., land on Drake's Creek, Sumner County. (Sumner County, Tennessee, Deeds, Book 6, p. 145).

Ambrose Lipscomb of Overton County, Tennessee, gave power of attorney to Wesley Huddleston of Buckingham County, Virginia, as executor of his brother Josiah Lipscomb, dec., to receive portion of estate due said Ambrose, 31 October 1817. (Overton County Deeds, Book C, p. 21).

NEWSPAPER ITEMS

Col. Joel Watkins, a Revolutionary soldier, died in Buckingham County on 5 July 1824, aged 66 years. (Enquirer, 3 August 1824).

Benjamin Whitehead, Sr., died in Buckingham County on 25 July 1838, aged 78 years. He was a Revolutionary soldier. (Whig, 3 August 1838).

Josiah Chambers advertised he had taken up a mare and a colt in Buckingham County. (Virginia Gazette, 31 May 1780).

William Palmer of Buckingham County advertised that in December 1773 he bought three negroed from John Hawkins, now deceased, then of Hanover County. He gave two bonds for payment, and has paid off one of the bonds. He wishes to locate the holder of the other bond. (Virginia Gazette, 23 May 1780).

William Ronald advertises for sale 600 acres of land in the lower end of Buckingham County, adjoining the "voted tract of right land" of George Webb, Esq. Apply to Mr. John Hay in Richmond or to sd. Ronald in Powhatan County. (Virginia Gazette, 11 November 1780).

Thomas Anderson of Buckingham County advertised for rent 150 acres of land on the James River in the lower end of Amherst County, 80 miles above Richmond, with dwelling for overseer, 30 or 40 acres of land opposite part of aforesaid land in Buckingham County, with a dwelling of two rooms on a floor, and an adjoining plantation with a ferry across the river, with house for overseer. (Virginia Gazette, 18 November 1780).

William Clark advertised for three slaves who were at the surrender of York, and offers a reward to any person that will bring the slaves to him in Cumberland County. He also states he will sell or rent a plantation in Buckingham County, the plantation is in good order for cropping, and has a fine young orchard on it. (Virginia Gazette, 12 January 1782).

Reuben Puryear died 30 August 1838, aged 75 years, in Buckingham County. He was in the Revolution, enlisting in the Continental services in 1777, and continued there until July 1781, when he was honorably discharged. He is survived by a widow and two children. (Whig, 4 September 1838).

Capt. John Flood, Sr., died 16 August 1826, aged 68 years in Buckingham County. He was in the Revolutionary War. (Whig, 5 September 1826).

TAX LISTS

Lewis Wilkinson had 1 slave and 3 horses; removed to Buckingham County (New Kent County Delinquent Tax Payers List, 1787 - 1790; for 1789).

Henry Davenport removed to Buckingham County (Cumberland County Delinquent Tax Payers List, "it being a list of Insolvents and Removals returned by John Lee, Deputy Sheriff, for Henry Skipwith for the year 1788).

Benjamin Hopkins removed from Cumberland County to Buckingham County (Ibid.)

William Minton removed from Cumberland to Buckingham (Cumberland County List of Insolvents and Removals for the year 1788, returned by George Carrington, Deputy Sheriff, for Henry Skipwith of Cumberland).

Jesse Tally removed from Cumberland County to Powhatan (Ibid.).

Langhorne Walton removed from Cumberland to Buckingham (Ibid.).

Yewen Cardin, owning 1 horse, removed from Powhatan to Buckingham County (List and account of persons who have removed from the County of Powhatan chargeable with taxes for 1787...).

John Cardin, Jr., owning 1 horse, removed to Buckingham (Ibid.).

Mary Gannaway, owning 1 negro, to Buckingham County (List of Insolvents returned by John Watson, Deputy Sheriff for William Bibb late of Prince Edward County, Virginia, in Revenue Tax for 1788).

The following names were found in a list of Delinquent Tax Payers, 1787 - 1790, for Buckingham County, for 1787 revenue tax returned by Wm. R. Bernard, Deputy Sheriff for J. Bernard, Sheriff of Buckingham County):

William Gates, owned 5 horses, gone to Kentucky.

Jesse Hamilton, owned 1 horse, gone to Kentucky.

Edw'd Hersey, owned 3 horses.

Nicholas Morris, owned 2 slaves and 4 horses, deceased.

George Rye(?), owned 1 horse, moved to Charlotte County.

Langhorn Walton, owned 1 slave and 2 horses, to Cumberland County.

James Ayres James, owned 2 horses, to Cumberland County.

The above list was sworn to at a court held for Buckingham County, and was ordered to be certified to the Auditor of Public Accounts. Matthew Branch, D. C.

Dudley Brooke, Jr., "moved to Buckingham," in a list of insolvents in the revenue tax for 1789.

The return of revenue for Cumberland County in 1789 shows the following names:

Wilson Davenport, Buckingham County.

Amos Lepperd (?), Buckingham County.

Elliott Vawter or Vauter, Buckingham County.

* * * * * * *

BRITISH MERCANTILE CLAIMS

Benjamin Howard's estate shows £ 328.7.7 3/4 by account, Albemarle Store, George Keppen & Co. Howard died in 1772 and left a daughter, who married Thomas Anderson, and Howard left a very valuable estate. Anderson died in Buckingham County in 1800. (British Mercantile Claims in Virginia, in the Virginia State Archives).

Thomas Smith, living in Buckingham County, and "said to be very poor" had a £ 21.113 bond in Petersburg Store (British Mercantile Claims, 1775-1803).

David Morris, a resident of Cumberland or Buckingham County, has an account of £ 6.1.9½ account in Cumberland Store (Ibid.).

Benjamin Tyndall, £ 56.10.0, Richmond Store; Tyndall died about twelve months ago, and his son Benjamin is possessed of vouchers to show that the debt is paid. He lived in Buckingham County. (British Mercantile Claims, 1775 - 1783, p. 102).

Acuklang(?) Austin, owned £ 135.18.6¼. The debt has been paid by James Lyle of Manchester, as in possession of Archibald Austin of Buckingham, relinquishing the war interest. (Ibid.)

Robt. Glover owed £ 24.15.4½, Manchester Store. Glover died several years ago and his executors have since paid the debt to James Lyle of Manchester, except for the war interest, voluntarily relinquished by Lyle. (British Mercantile Claims, 1783).

James Pattison owed £ 55.12.11¼, Manchester Store. A suit has been brought, and the court has ordered the debt to be paid by William Daniel, attorney-at-law, at court next July in Buckingham County (Ibid.).

Thomas Pattison owned £ 146.3.2 3/4, Manchester Store. John Chambers of Buckingham and William Cabell of Amherst now have the books and papers of Benjamin Jourdin, lately dec., who they say has already paid the debt (Ibid.).

George Chambers, £ 3.13.2, Cumberland Store; Judgement. The debt has been relinquished and execution issued 13 May 1773, and no return. The plaintiffs may yet get their money if they pursue the proper remedy (Records of Buckingham Court).

William Gregory, £ 23.2.7, Cumberland Store. Judgement has been obtained in Buckingham Court and the money paid to William Daniel, except the interest, which has been relinquished. (British Mercantile Claims, 1783).

Miles Gibson, £ 7.12.4¼, Cumberland Store. Judgement is obtained in Buckingham Court, and the money will soon be paid.

Judith Bell, £ 231.6.1, Warwick Store. Judgement had been obtained several years ago in Federal Court, and long after the judgement Judith Bell died, leaving David Bell as her executor. David Bell qualified in Buckingham Court, advertised, and sold all the property. He moved to Kentucky, and is now deceased, owing £ 437.14.10¼, also at Warwick Store. Two suits have been alternately instituted in Federal Court about 5 or 6 years ago, one against Henry Bell as heir at law of David Bell, but since no assets were found, a second suit was brought against him upon an assumption, which was not proved, and the case was discharged. David Bell, dec., was not able to pay this debt at the time it was contracted, much less was the estate able in 1783. David Bell held his wife's estate as tenant by courtesy.

John Benning, £ 15.10.1½, Manchester Store. Benning, who lived in Buckingham County, paid the debt and moved to the westward.

Thomas Word owed £ 104.4.6¼ in Buckingham Court. The defendant has arranged with James Lyle, Sr., of Manchester to pay this debt, as also a debt due Henderson, McColl, and Company by installments. 1783. (British Mercantile Claims, 1779 - 1803).

John Coleman, £ 4.12.11½. Judgement in Buckingham Court; execution returned, ready to satisfy the debts and costs.

WILLS AND ESTATES

21 June 1813, Logan County, Kentucky. Henningham Bernard, late of Buckingham County, later of the City of Richmond, died leaving as legatees: daughter Anne, Henningham C., Judith, friend Joshua Fry of Kentucky, Paul J. Carrington, Joseph Carrington of Virginia in trust for daughter Elizabeth Wells, wife of Willis Wells (or Wills), and the heirs of her body. Executors were Joshua Fry, Joseph Carrington, and Paul J. Carrington. Witnesses were: E. Carrington, Eliza Ann May, and Adeline Albert (Logan County, Kentucky, Will Book A, p. 285).

John Mackghee owned land in Buckingham County. His will was proved in Hanover County on 25 July 1828. In it he described himself as living in St. Paul's Parish, Hanover County, and named his children: Lewis, Mary (Polly) Barker, Nancy Acre, Joseph Macghee, Susannah Livesay, Sally Mosby Livesay, Patsy Gathright and Catherine Talley. Executors were: Maj. Thomas Starke, Bowling Starke, and son Joseph Mackghee. He mentioned land in Buckingham County. ("McGehee Family," William and Mary Quarterly, 1st ser., XXV, 284).

Thomas Snoddy's will, 21 May 1839 - August 1839, was proved in Jefferson County, Tennessee. In it he named children Mary Moyers, Nancy McDonald, John D. Snoddy, son Edward Blackburn Snoddy, Hannah Snoddy, Jane M. Snoddy, John Edward Snoddy and Carey Snoddy, Harriot Nowel McDonald and Hannah Mc-Donald, not yet 18 (are granddaughters), daughter Grissey Margaret Snoddy, brother Carey Snoddy, dec., father John Snoddy, dec. Legacies were also left to: Thomas Snoddy Edgar, Thomas Snoddy Moser, Thomas Andrew Snoddy, John Anoddy McDonald, and Thomas Davis Snoddy. Will mentions land in Buckingham County, Virginia. (Jefferson County, Tennessee, Wills, 1826 - 1840, p. 543).

The will of Alexander Stinson was proved in March 1782 Court of Caswell County, North Carolina. In it he stated his daughter Nancy was to have land in Buckingham County, Virginia. He also named his wife Sarah, referred to any unborn child, referred to personal estate left him by his grandfather Childress. Executors were his wife Sarah and his father John. (Caswell County, North Carolina, Deeds, Book A, 1781 - 1782, p. 182).

Thomas Pleasants of Goochland County, in his will stated that one-third part of 157 acres in Buckingham County, including the mill seat near the mouth of Island Creek, purchased of Jeremiah Whitlow in partnership with William Duiguid and James Webster be disposed of (E. P. Valentine Papers, p. 975).

The will of Edward Cason of Buckingham County, Virginia, was proved in Prince Edward County in 1784. He left 400 acres in Buckingham to his son Seth, and 20 acres in Spottsylvania to his son William. His son Thomas was to have the land in Spottsylvania where he formerly lived. He also mentioned 100 acres in Spottsylvania County, where he was now living. (Prince Edward County Will Book, 1754 - 1784, p. 343).

Henningham Bernard, dec.; inventory and appraisal. John Latham and William Loving and James Wilson were appointed, agreeable to the court. The estate was divided among William R. Bernard (wife Anna), children of Elizabeth Willis, Henningham C. Bernard Copeland, Judith Bernard Merewether (Logan County, Kentucky, Will Book A, p. 296). See 1st entry in this section, above.

The will of Joseph Bondurant of Buckingham County, dated 1 August 1806, names wife Agnes, negroes Dock, Tom, Daniel, Ben, Sucky, Phyllis, and Amy, son Joseph, son Edward, son William, daughter Ann Maxey, daughter Mary Gyers, daughter Betty Perkins, daughter Lucy Landrum. Executors were to be: Charles Maxey, Nathan Ayers, Bray Ford, and James Wilson. The will was witnessed by Robert Moseley, Jr., Daniel Moseley, Thomas Austin, and John Hubbard. (See The Huguenot, Publication no. 13, p. 132).

The will of William Perkins, 8 March 1822 - 8 June 1822, was recorded in Davidson County, Tennessee. In it he named his wife Susannah, daughter Eliza Fearn Perkins (under age); daughter Sally Price Scales, grandchildren America Cannon and William Perkins Cannon, and son Nicholas Perkins. Daniel Perkins, Samuel Perkins, and Thomas Edmiston were to be executors. (Davidson County, Tennessee Will Book 8, p. 104).

BIOGRAPHICAL SKETCHES

BERNARD: William Bernard of Gloucester County (will made 1704) had a son Robert alive in 1732. The name Bernard is also found spelled Barnard and Barnett. Richard Barnard was a vestryman of Petsworth Parish in 1677 (Vestry Book). Mr. William Bernard was church warden in 1695. Peter Bernard of Gloucester was a captain in the Revolution. His brother and heir John Bernard of Buckingham County was sheriff there in 1781, and married Henningham, a daughter of Col. George Carrington. Captain Peter Bernard had a sister, Margaret, who married George Carrington in 1764 (William and Mary Quarterly, 1st series, III, 41).

CHAMBERLAYNE: Dr. Lewis W. Chamberlayne married Martha Burwell Dabney on 11 April 1820. She was born 15 September 1802. He was a son of Edward Pye Chamberlayne of King William County, Virginia. Dr. Chamberlayne was a prominent physician at Richmond, and was one of the founders of the Medical College. Lewis and Martha (Dabney) Chamberlayne's daughter, Parke, married Dr. George Bagby of Richmond, a native of Buckingham County, and a writer and lecturer of some note (William and Mary Quarterly, 1st series, IV, 103).

BALLENDINE: Thomas William Ballendine, member of Phi Neta Kappa Society at William and Mary College was a son of John Ballendine of Prince William County, who owned a large iron foundry in Buckingham County, used during the Revolution. (William and Mary Quarterly, 1st series, IV, 249).

CANNON: William Cannon of Mt. Ida, Buckingham County, Virginia, went to Tennessee c.1807 - 1812. (William and Mary Quarterly, 1st series, IV, 206).

MIMS: David Mims, Jr., married Martha Duiguid and died leaving a will in Goochland County, 1786. Many of their descendants settled in Todd County, Kentucky. In Buckingham County there was a place called Duiguidsville, and as early as 1812 there was a tobacco warehouse there called "Horsleys."

CAMM: Some of the descendants of John Camm, President of William and Mary College, located in Buckingham County. John Camm, third son of the president, is recorded in an account by Dr. Thomas H. Ellis of Powellton, West Virginia, from family and county records. John Camm was born 2 December 1775, studied law, after 1794 removed from Amherst County for practice, and clerk from 1814 until his death in 1818. He committed suicide in a fit of temporary insanity. There is an amusing tradition about him. He went bald at a very early age, and the court crier, who seems to have been facetiously inclined, was wont to summon the clerk to his duties at the courthouse door with cries of: "John Camm! John Camm! Little baldheaded man! Little baldheaded man!" Camm married Elizabeth Powell, daughter of Thomas Powell who was known as "Gentleman Tom," to distinguish him from "Shoemaker Tom" Powell of another family. Elizabeth Powell's mother was Betsey Thomas, daughter of Cornelius Thomas of Albemarle County, Virginia. Bishop Meade mentions the Thomas family as having been prominent since before the Revolutionary War. The Powells were prominent in Amherst County for over a hundred years, several members of the family going to Congress. The name is now extinct in Amherst, but every Amherst family of note has Powell blood in its veins. There is a tradition that the Powells were closely related to the Powells of Loudon and Fauquier Counties. Elizabeth Powell Camm died 25 January 1867. She and her husband, John Camm, were the parents of six children: Elizabeth (of whom later), Nancy who married Jack Anderson, Sally who married Benjamin Donald, Mary who married William L. Saunders, Emma who died unmarried, and Robert Camm.

Elizabeth Camm, daughter of John and Elizabeth (Powell) Camm, married Dr. David Patteson of Buckingham County, and they had several children, of whom Reuben B. Patteson was a graduate of the University of Virginia, and assistant surgeon of the 19th Mississippi Regiment (L. Q. C. Lamar, Lieutenant-Quartermaster). Reuben B. Patteson died from exposure at Fort Donelson.

Sallie D. Patteson, daughter of Dr. and Mrs. David Patteson, married Dr. Samuel B. Scott of Bedford County, Virginia, and died leaving issue.

Camm Patteson, son of Dr. and Mrs. David Patteson, married Miss Mary Mills, and lived in Buckingham County. He was a lawyer and a member of the House of Delegates.

David R. Patteson, son of Dr. and Mrs. David Patteson, died at the age of 19 from camp fever, in 1862.

Annie A. Patteson, daughter of Dr. David Patteson, married Dr. A. B. Hartsook.

Bettie C. Patteson, daughter of Dr. David and Mrs. Patteson, married Benjamin C. Hartsook.

John A. Patteson, seventh child of Dr. David and Mrs. David Patteson, served as a private in the 4th Virginia Cavalry. He died at 17 from exposure in the Battle of the Wilderness.

Jno. Hampton Patteson, eighth child of Dr. and Mrs. David Patteson, died in infancy. His brother, Robert C. Patteson, also died in infancy.

Kate, the tenth child of Dr. and Mrs. Patteson, resided in Buckingham County. She married Geo. W. Patteson, probably a relative.

S. S. P. Patteson, eleventh child of Dr. and Mrs. Patteson, was a lawyer from Richmond.

Jesse Patteson, the youngest child of Dr. and Mrs. Patteson, died in infancy. (See William and Mary Quarterly, 1st series, IV, 278).

PATTESON: The Patteson family was prominent in Buckingham County. The following members sat in the Virginia legislature and conventions. David R. Patteson, Nelson County, was in the House 1812-13, 1813-14, and 1825-26. Camm Patteson was from Cumberland and Buckingham Counties, and was in the House 1893-94, and in the Senate, 1904-06. Charles Patteson, Buckingham County, served in the Convention of 1776-88, in the House, 1776, 1777, 1781-82, 1784-85, 1787-88. David Patteson of Buckingham County was in the House 1806-07, 1807-08, 1808-09, snf 1809-10. Reuben B. Patteson, from Buckingham County, was in the House 1821-22, 1822-23, 1823-24, 1824-25, 1825-26, 1826-27, 1827-28. William N. Patteson, Buckingham County, was in the House, 1831-32, 1832-33, and 1833-34.

ARMISTEAD: Hannah Armistead's will named granddaughter Hannah. This Hannah was the first wife of Miles Cary of "Pear Tree Hall." Their children, named in Judith Robinson's will, were: 1) John Cary, born c.1745, named in

the wills of his grandmother and aunt, died 1795, having married first Sally
Sclater and second Susanna, daughter of Gill Armistead of New Kent; 2) Robert
Cary, also named in the wills of his aunt and grandmother, died in Buckingham
County about 1763; 3) Rebecca Cary, married Rev. Miles Selden who died in
1785; 4) Elizabeth Cary, married Benjamin Watkins; and 5) Judith Cary, born
after her father's death, named in her grandmother's will, named John
Robinson, and herself left a will, 6 March 1768 - 27 January 1769. John and
Judith (Cary) Robinson had a son, Starkey Robinson. (William and Mary Quar-
terly, 1st series, VI, 228).

During the War of 1812, Samuel M. Armistead was drafted at Buckingham
Courthouse for the 100th Regiment of said county in February 1814, and served
for six months in Capt. John Hays' company of Col. Edward Jones' 5th Virginia
Regiment. On 16 October 1850 he applied for a bounty land grant, from Buckingham, and on 22 October 1855 applied again from Sullivan County, Tennessee,
giving his age as 75 and 83 years respectively. In the 1850 application he
stated that his papers were carried to the State of Tennessee in 1817 and he
had not heard of them since then (War of 1812 Bounty Land Warrant No. 78035-
120-55, at National Archives, Washington, D. C.). The 1850 Census of
Buckingham County showed Samuel Armistead, 72, and Lucy Armistead, 62, as
natives of Campbell and Prince Edward Counties, respectively. In the 1860
Census of Sullivan County, Tennessee, "Lucreasy Armistead," age 74, was
living with Hiram and Rebecca A. Jones, both born in Tennessee (Sullivan
County, Tennessee, 1860 Census, p. 18, no. 126). Lucy Armistead's will,
proved 11 April 1864, left her property to her daughter Rebecca Elizabeth
Jones, wife of Hiram Jones (Sullivan County Will Book # 1, p. 28). Lucy
named as contingent heirs, "the daughters of my three sisters, viz; Nancy
Williams, Rebecca Runnels (Reynolds), and Polly Russell." The marriages of
these three (Cannifao?) sisters are recorded in Campbell County, Virginia.

One Jesse Armistead died before October 1839, when Thomas Taylor of Smith
County, Tennessee, was named administrator of the estate of Jesse M. Armistead
who died intestate. An inventory and accounting of sales were recorded; among
those credited with purchases were: the widow, and S. A., J. M., J. A., and
John Armistead. (Smith County, Tennessee, Inventory Book # 4, pp. 541, 557,
60).

Jesse M. Armistead was in Cumberland County in 1808 when he witnessed
Susannah Gaulding's consent for the marriage of her daughter Polly to William
A. Burton (D.A.R. Magazine, vol. 65, p. 43).

In 1810 a Jesse Armistead was on the Cumberland County tax roll for 1
tithable, but he did not appear in 1809 or 1811. He is probably the same
Jesse who was on the Buckingham County personal and real property rolls
between 1811 and 1818 with 149 acres in fee, on Wrick Island, and joining the
land of Meshac Boaz. The land was conveyed to Thomas Coleman, according to
the 1819 roll, and Jesse Armistead disappeared from the Buckingham County
rolls. By the time of the 1820 Census he was in Smith County, age 26-45,
with three boys and one girl under 10, and three slaves. He is not in Smith
County in the 1830 Census, but he was probably in the vicinity. In 1833 the
Smith County Court refused to pay Jesse Armistead for a "bridge across Voden's
Spring Branch...it appearing to the court that the bridge had not been built
by him according to his contract..." In 1839 the commissioners decided "to
lay off and set apart provisions out of the stock on hand for the use and
support of the widow and family of Jesse Armistead, dec'd." (Smith County
Min. Book, 1831-33, p. 415; Minute Book, 1835-41, pp. 409, 428, 451; Smith
County Inventory Book # 4, 1836-40, p. 557).

Jesse Armistead's widow, Martha, was born c.1790 in Virginia, and was
head of a family in Smith County in 1850 and 1860. Jesse and Martha were the
parents of the following children living in 1850: 1) Alexander, born c.1815
in Virginia; 2) John A (?), born c.1819 in Va.; 3) Julia Ann, born c.1820, Va.;
4) Joseph I., born c.1822, Tenn., married Judith Boulton or Bolton; 5) Elizabeth, born c.1824, Tenn., married James Bolton; 6) Jesse M., born c.1829,
Tenn.; 7) Martha S., born c.1833, Tenn.; and 8) Thomas J., born c.1834, Tenn.

In 1820 William and William H. Armistead were in Smith County, Tennessee.
In 1850 William B., born c.1806 in Powhatan County, and Nancy, born c.1807 in
Buckingham County, were in that county in 1850, with their children: Robert H.,

126

Anthony, Sallie C., and Egbert. In 1820 Smith County, Tennessee, was the home of a William and a William H. Armistead.

Many articles on the Virginia Armisteads have contained information on the family in Smith County, Tennessee.

GREGORY: William Gregory, born 1788, in Buckingham County, married 1st Nancy Fuqua, who died in 1820; married 2nd Nancy Robinson in 1829; and moved to Missouri in 1832.

BRANCH: Anthony Martin Branch, born 16 July 1823 in Buckingham County, died 3 October 1867 in Huntsville, Texas.

RATHER-WOMACK: G. W. Rather married Mary Chamberlain Womack, born 24 September 1817, in Buckingham County, and died 14 April 1860 in Huntsville, Texas.

DANCE: Stephen Dance, son of Thomas Dance of Chesterfield County, and of Dinwiddie County, on 5 April 1751, was conveyed by his father, the said Thomas Dance, 150 acres of land, part of the tract whereon the said Thomas Dance then lived, to include the houses and to be laid off so as to join the lines of John Robertson, Joseph Gill, and Humphrey Taylor. The witnesses were Matthew Mayes, Henry Dance, and Richard Griffin (Chesterfield County Court Records, Deed Book 1, p. 199). In April 1771, Stephen Dance and his wife Phoebe of Dinwiddie County were parties to an indenture tripartite by which the land on which Stephen's father, Thomas Dance, had lived was sold. On 25 March 1767 Stephen Dance advertised in Purdie and Dixon's <u>Virginia Gazette</u> that he had several tracts of land for sale, one in Buckingham County (late the property of Allen Tye), and described himself as living in "Dinwiddie County about 14 miles above Petersburg." Stephen Dance died 2 May 1784, and his wife Phoebe (maiden name unknown) died 31 May 1781. A deed in Chesterfield County dated 11 March 1783 reveals that Stephen Dance took as his second wife the widow of Daniel Gill, Sr., of Chesterfield County (Deed Book 10, p. 183).

See: article on Dance family in <u>William and Mary Quarterly, 1st series,</u> XXVI, 52.

HARRISON: Benjamin Harrison died in 1761 leaving a wife Priscilla. On 5 October 1776 Priscilla Harrison of Cumberland County conveyed to her son Benjamin, "for love and affection," 100 acres of woodland on Willis River, being a part of 600 acres devised to her by her late husband, Benjamin Harrison, deceased. At the same time she conveyed to her other son, Cary Harrison, 100 acres of woodland.

Cary Harrison, son of Benjamin and Priscilla, married Sarah Langhorne, nee Bell, widow of John Langhorne.

Benjamin Harrison, son of Benjamin and Priscilla, died 25 August 1811 in Buckingham County. His daughter Nancy married William Shelton Lewis of Pittsylvania County. The land tax records of Buckingham County indicate "Estate of Benjamin Harrison," beginning in 1812.

See: Cumberland County Deed Book, V, p. 497.
<u>Tyler's Quarterly</u>, VII, 286.

WYCHE: James Wyche, son of Peter of George of George of Henry, was born 25 December 1785 in Brunswick County. On 21 April 1806 he married Pamela Evans of Buckingham County. They had issue: John Jenkins, Martha Hendricks, William Evans, Peter Peters, Perry Wayne, Ira Thomas, Elizabeth Jenkins, Louisa Young, George Edward, Robert Henry, Cyril Franville, Beverly Granville, and Benjamin and Charles Humphreys Wyche. In 1825 James Wyche removed to Granville County, North Carolina, where he lived until his death on 28 March 1845. He served several times as representative from Granville County in the State Legislature. At the time of his death he was a member of the Senate. He was first president of the Raleigh and Gaston Railroad, an office he held until his death. Pamela Evans, his wife, was born 28 February 1789 in Cumberland County, resided for a while in Brunswick before her marriage, and died 28 February 1869 in Granville County, North Carolina. She was a daughter of Lieutenant William Evans of the Continental Army.

See <u>William and Mary Quarterly, 1st series</u>, XIII, 216.

ROBINSON: Robert Robinson married Rachel Pate, daughter of Matthew Pate, and had a son named Robert who died young, and another son, Thomas, who married a widow lady in Charles City County. Her married name had been Backus, but her maiden name was Boyce and she was a sister of a Major Boyce. Thomas and his wife had two children: William and Rachel.

William Robinson, son of Thomas, resided in Petersburg in 1813, and was unmarried. His sister Rachel married a Captain Pully of Isle of Wight County, by whom she had a son John and a daughter named Ann, and perhaps others.

Rachel Pate Robinson, widow of Robert, married as her second husband a Mr. John Warrington, then of Williamsburg, and a native of England, and by him she had several children: John, married Mary Thelabald(?) of Norfolk, who survived him (John died 28 December 1829 at his farm on Mason's Creek in Norfolk County); Nancy Warrington died unmarried; Sarah Hatfield Warrington who lived in Norfolk; Becca Warrington, married William Nice of Richmond, a native of Pennsylvania, by whom she had a daughter who was living in the upper part of Virginia; Polly Warrington married James Marshall of Hanover County, with whom she removed to Buckingham County and by whom she had several children: William, John, and Ulysses, and perhaps others.

See: William and Mary Quarterly, 1st series, XII, 198.

GAY: William Alexander Gay, sixth in descent from Pocohantas of Powhatan Counties, and a son of Capt. William Gay, married Lucy Harrison Coupland. He was a vestryman of Southam Parish, Cumberland County.

See: Wyndham Robertson, Pocahontas, Alias Matoaka, and Her Descendants 1887, (Repr.: Baltimore: Genealogical Publishing Co., 1968)
Cumberland County Deed Books 9, p. 437, and 18, p. 89.
Cumberland County Will Book 5, p. 32.

DAVIS: William F. Davis, Sr., of Buckingham County, aged 76 on 8 January 1851; served as corporal in Capt. Walter L. Fontaine's Company, 8th Regt. of Virginia Militia, commanded by Charles Wall Cole in the War of 1812. He volunteered for service in Buckingham County at William Newton's in 1814 and was discharged from Camp Carter in 1814 for being sick. His discharge from the camp was signed by commanding officer William Jackson, Jr. David J. Woodfin of New Canton, Mecklenburg County, Virginia, on 8 February 1853 wrote to James E. Heath, Esq., stating that William F. Davis of Buckingham County had filed an application in February 1851 for Bounty Land for service in the War of 1812. William F. Davis died 18 May (no year stated-ED) leaving neither widow nor minor child, but left an adult son, Thomas N. Davis, who inherited his whole estate. /s/ Thomas N. Davis, Buckingham Co., Virginia.

Chapman Davis of Buckingham County on 16 May 1854 gave power of attorney to John G. Gilliam, J. P. Davis stated he was age 76 in 1855, and that he had been a private in the company of Capt. Walter L. Fontaine, 8th Regt., Va. Militia, commanded by Brig. Gen. John H. Cocke, in the War of 1812. He stated that he had been drafted at Buckingham County, Virginia, on 28 August 1814, and had been given an honorable discharge at Camp Carter on 19 February 1818. His declaration for bounty land was witnessed by John W. Fisher and William T. Davis, and sworn to by John I. Gilliam, J. P., on 6 May 1851. Chapman Davis appointed W. W. Forbes his attorney in Buckingham County in 1855.

WOODROF: Hardin Woodrof or Woodroof, son of David Woodrof, Sr., was an orphans. His guardian was James Nevil, of Amherst County, about 1759. Hardin served in the Revolution, and first declared for a pension when he was 72 years of age, was in either 1828 or 1829, placing his year of birth at 1756 or 1757. He was a corporal in Capt. James Burton's Company, 1st Va. Regt. He married in Buckingham County, on 11 October 1784, Sally Gunter, born 1760, daughter of Thomas Gunter. She died in Buckingham County on 23 January 1833. Hardin and Sally (Gunter) Woodrof had at least one child: a daughter mentioned in the pension papers in 1843 as being the wife of Daniel O. Bass of Buckingham County.

See: Virginia Magazine of History and Biography, XXXVI, 78.

HARRIS: James Harris of Buckingham County, born 1752, died 1836, and a Revolutionary Soldier, married Patte (?) (1755 - 1840). He lived for a short time in Patrick County, Virginia, before moving to Floyd County, Kentucky.

James and Patte (?) Harris were the parents of: Lucy, Sally, Fanny, and James Harris.

See: The East Kentuckian, (1965), vol. I.

CORNETT: William Cornett was born in 1761 in Henrico County, and died on 26 November 1836 in Perry County, Kentucky. He was a son of John Cornett of Buckingham County and married 1st Rhoda Gilliam, and 2nd Mary Everage. He settled on Bull Creek in what is now Perry County. Mary Everage Cornett died 28 January 1852. William had four children by his first wife and seven by his second wife. He was the father of: John, Arch, Lucy, Elizabeth, (and by his second wife) Robert, Bustard, Roger, Nancy, Rachel, Samuel, Joseph E.

JONES: William S. Jones of Buckingham County had a son William, Jr., who was the father of James Saunders Jones. James married a daughter of Thomas and Elizabeth Blair (Bolling) West of Campbell County, Virginia. (The Virginia Genealogist, III, 179).

ROBERTS: John Roberts was born in Buckingham County aboyt 1759. His first wife is unknown and he married Nancy Adkins as his second wife. He guarded prisoners through Tennessee and helped to build Fort Nashborough. He settled in Kentucky, but was killed in Tennessee (The Virginia Genealogist, vol. VII).

PERROW: Daniel Perrow lived in old King William Parish as late as 28 September 1761. On that date he sold 100 acres of land on the south side of James River to Benjamin Weaver (Cumberland County Deed Nook 3, p. 205). Prior to this time he had acquired land in newer regions. He gave to his infant grandson land on Beaver Creek in Bedford (later Campbell) County. He followed his sons Charles and Stephen into Buckingham County. He is shown on the tax lists for personal property between 1783 and 1789. In 1790 the tax list shows "Estate of Daniel Perro." Daniel and his wife Marie had issue: Charles, born 5 September 1728; Daniel, born c.1731; Stephen, born 20 November 1735; Mary, born c.1738.

Charles Perrow, son of Daniel and Marie, was born 5 September 1728. His godparents were his paternal grandmother and her second husband ("Antoine Rapine and his wife"), and was named for his paternal grandfather. He married Francoise Guerrant, daughter of Daniel and Francoise (L'Orange) Guerrant. Charles died in Buckingham County in 1797. (See: Brock, p. 82, and King William Parish Register).

Daniel Perrow, son of Daniel and Marie, was born about 1731, and died prior to 19 April 1758. He married Celia Battersby, daughter of William Battersby.

Stephen Perrow, or "Etienne," son of Daniel and Marie, was born 20 November 1735. He married in 1778 Elizabeth Fleming, daughter of David Fleming. Stephen died in Campbell County about 1791. (See Brock, p. 92, and King William Parish Reg.).

Mary Perrow, daughter of Daniel and Marie, was born about 1738, and married in 1756 Pierre Guerrant, Jr., born 1737, died 1819, son of Pierre and Magdalene (Trabue) Guerrant, and nephew of her brother Charles' wife, Francoise Guerrant. (See "Perrault - Perrow Family," in Virginia Genealogist, VIII, 71).

JOHNS: James Johns, a Revolutionary Soldier, married about 1771 in Buckingham County, Mary Gannaway, one of twelve children of John and Mary (Gregory) Gannaway, Jr. John Gannaway, Jr., of Albemarle and Buckingham County, married Mary Gregory c.1746. Their children were: William, John, Catherine, Thomas, Gregory, Mary, Robert, Frances, Edmund, Sally, Elizabeth, and Susannah, and probably one called Money.

WATSON: Henry and Powhatan Watson left Buckingham County for Charlton County, Missouri, between 1830 and 1840.

TUCKER: Pleasant Tucker, born Cumberland County, 1776, left Buckingham County in 1823, and died 22 April 1854 in Noxubee County, Mississippi. In his will he named the following children: James A. (died in McMinn County, Tennessee); Thomas M. (died 17 November 1887 in Lowndes County,

Mississippi); William A.; Mildred A. (married a Mr. Whitehead); Mary Amanda (married 1st Mr. Gilmer, and 2nd Wm. M. Gilkey, and lived in Pickins County, Alabama about 1850); Pleasant W.; Nancy H., (married a Mr. Hart); Frances V. A. (married James S. Lull or Sull, lived in Lowndes County, Mississippi, in 1850); and John A. Tucker.

PERKINS: William Perkins, Jr., was named in the commission of the peace, and took the oath of appointment on 10 May 1779 (Virginia Executive Papers for 1779, Virginia State Archives in Richmond).

William Perkins, Jr., and Josias Jones, on the motion of Jeremiah Whitney, Gent., Sheriff, were admitted as his Under Sheriffs. (Ibid.)

PUTNEY: Ellis Washington Putney, 4th child of Richard and Sarah (Ellis) Putney of Surry County, Virginia, married Frances Fearn, and lived in the lower end of Buckingham County. (The Virginia Genealogist, XVI, 318).

LEWIS: Thomas Lewis, born c.1745, died in 1806 in Buckingham County. He married Agnes Walker Jones, widow of William Jones (killed at the Battle of Guilford Courthouse during the Revolution) and daughter of James Walker who lived in Buckingham. Agnes is said to have lived to 102 years of age. Thomas and Agnes (Walker) Lewis had a son, Henry Lewis, who married Elizabeth Morton Woodson, daughter of Capt. Jack Woodson. Henry and his wife moved to Missouri about 1819.

CHASTAIN: John Chastain and wife Mary (O/Brien) married in Buckingham County in the 1760's. They later moved to Pendleton District, South Carolina, where he died after 1803. (Virginia Genealogist, XXIII).

HARRIS: Giles Harris, born 1720, died 1750 of Hanover County, married Mrs. Elizabeth Gray Chandler, and they had three sons: Edmond, born 1770, married Rhoda Arnold; John Claiborne, born 1772, died 1862, married Polly Gannaway; and Obediah, born 1774, married Elizabeth Walker. They were all residents of Buckingham County.

HARGRAVE: Hezekiah Hargrave or Hargrove was a Revolutionary Soldier. He applied for a pension on 25 September 1832 in Nelson County, Virginia. The application contains both spellings of the name. Hargrave stated he had eleven periods of service, beginning in 1775 as a minute man under Capt. Nicholas Cabell, and continuing until 1781, when he was ordered to go to the siege of York, but was forced to hire a substitute on the way after being bitten by a rattlesnake in Buckingham County. He was often told by one of his aunts that he was born on 21 February 1748 in Caroline County. The bond for the marriage of Hezekiah Hargrove and Susannah Murphey, widow, was dated 8 September 1772 (Rev. War Pension Application S-5481; Amherst County, Virginia, Marriage Bonds).

SANDERS: Samuel Sanders was a descendant of Stephen Sanders who married Elizabeth Moseley and settled on Jim Creek. The Sanders or Saunders plantation tracts were north of Willis River, adjoining on the west Benjamin Morris' land, and on the east Edward Curd's line.

CARY: Archibald Cary married Mary, daughter of Richard Randolph of Curles. Richard's father bought nearly all the land on James River after the Indian massacre of 1622 from Richmond, down, as shown on Bishop Madison's map. In 1787 Archibald Cary owned much land in Buckingham County. "Cary's Wood" was built on one of his grants, four miles north of Dillwyn (Edward P. Valentine, The Edward P. Valentine Papers, 1927, p. 244).

TALLEY: Charles Talley is thought to have married Sarah Wade. His son was Benjamin Talley, born 12 May 1798. Benjamin married Judith A. Chastain. (D.A.R. Magazine, March 1957, p. 328).

HUDDLESTON: George Augustine Huddleston, son of George and Lucy (Winston) Huddleston, was born in Buckingham County, Virginia. The Huddleston family came to Virginia from England about 1760. (Thomas McAdory Owen, History of Alabama and Dictionary of Alabama Biography, 1921, p. 856).

FRY: William A. Fry of Buckingham County was a son of John Fry, formerly of Albemarle County. John was entitled to bounty land in right of his father Joshua Fry's military service under the former Colony of Virginia, under the royal proclamation of 1763 (Lyman Chalkley, Chronicles of the Scotch-Irish Settlement in Virginia, Extracted from the Original Court Records of Augusta County, 1745 - 1800, 3 vols., 1912; Repr.: Baltimore Genealogical Publishing Company, 1974, II, p. 58).

MATHEWS: Thomas Mathews of Buckingham County in his lifetime contracted with Thomas Upton of Kenawha County to purchase a tract of land on Great Kenawha. In 1789 he sent his sons Thomas and R. Lott, and one Jarred Doling to the land to prepare it to live on. Thomas Mathews, Sr., died in March 1799, aged 78 years. His heirs at law were: James Doling and wife Sarah, Young Lee and wife Jemima, Andrew Bogies and wife Diana, John Self and wife Bershaba, Joseph R. Lott, and Thomas Mathews.

Thomas Upton died without children. He left a will, and the following heirs: brother Joseph Upton, John Couch and wife Rebecca, Thomas Maupin and wife, John Maupin ad wife Nancy, Fleming Cobb, and Thomas Cobb. Rebecca, the wives of the Maupins, and Fleming and Thomas Cobb are either sisters or children of sisters of said Thomas Upton.

Joseph Thomas deposed in Kenawha on 20 January 1807 that he was closely acquainted with Thomas Mathew from 1784 to 1797 when Joseph went to Kenawha. John Kersey, formerly from Albemarle, also deposed. Josiah Harrison deposed on 3 February 1807 that in 1790 he came to Kenawha. Upton then lived near the mouth of David's Creek.

Thomas Upton's will, 2 January 1794 - 7 May 1794, named nephew Fleming Cobb; brother Joseph Upton; nephew Thomas Cobb, son of Thomas Cobb of Buckingham County; brother Joseph's sons Thomas, Joseph, Elia, and Elijah Upton; Judia Cobbs and Naapin, daughters of Thomas Cobb; Rebeckah Thomas, daughter of Rebeckah Crench; Maria Toler, daughter of Thomas Cobb; Nanny Cobbs, daughter of Thomas Cobbs.

On 13 June 1790 Thomas Upton of Kenawha County executed a deed to Thomas Davis of Lincoln County, Kentucky.

See Mathews vs. Upton, O. S. 122, N. S. 422, circuit court papers of Augusta County, Virginia, partly abstracted by Chalkley and published in his Chronicles of the Scotch-Irish..., II, 117.

MORRIS: Robert James Morris, son of Samuel, was born 28 July 1820 in Buckingham County, Virginia, married before 1850, and died 17 April 1901 in Buckingham County. He married Susannah L., daughter of John Osborne. Susannah was born 1819 in Prince Edward County, and died 24 November 1890 in Buckingham County. Robert and Susannah had a daughter, Mary Etta Virginia Morris, born 2 February 1855 in Buckingham County, and died 20 October 1922 ("John McGee" MSS. File, Tennessee State Library, Nashville).

WHITE: Henry White of Buckingham County went to Bedford County after the Revolutionary War, and died there in 1802. (William and Mary Quarterly, 2nd series, III, 49).

JORDAN: Col. Samuel Jordan of "Seven Islands," Buckingham County, was a member of the House of Burgesses from that county. (Virginia Magazine of History and Biography, XXIII, 325).

JEFFERSON: Randolph Jefferson, youngest brother of President Thomas Jefferson, and his only brother to survive infancy, was born 1 October 1755, and died 7 August 1815. He resided in Fluvanna County, and married on 30 July 1780 his cousin Anne Lewis, daughter of Charles and Mary (Randolph) Lewis, Jr. It is stated in The Virginia Magazine of History and Biography, VII, 326, that he married Mitchie B. Pryor, daughter of David B. Pryor of Buckingham. If this is true, she was a second wife. Randolph Jefferson had a twin sister, Ann Scott Jefferson. She married Hastings Marks.

EARLY: The Diary of Rev. John Early, states (16 September 1807): "to brother Thompson's for dinner and there spent the day with the dear people. That night went to Brother Walker's and stayed all night. Next day he went with me to William Staples on James River, Buckingham, to a two day meeting...."

CHAPTER SEVEN

PLANTERSTOWN

"An Act to Establish Several Towns," Passed by the General Assembly, January 15, 1798: Be it enacted by the General Assembly, that twenty-five acres of land, the property of Ichabod Hunter and John Epperson, lying at the Cutbanks in the County of Buckingham, shall be, and they are hereby invested in

William Perkins, Jr.	Henry Flood
Charles Yancey	Nathaniel Lancaster
John Johns	Robert Kelso
Joel Watkins	Anthony Winston
Daniel Moseley	Stephen Pettus

Gentlemen, trustees, to be by them or a majority of them, laid off into lots of half an acre each, with convenient streets, shall be and is hereby allowed the owners of lots in Planterstown, in Buckingham County, to improve the same in the manner required by law."

In 1930 while searching for the graves of Claiborne West and wife Betty Ann Woodson (Epperson), the author found Mr. Irving Davie living in the old Claiborne West home. In his possession was an old account book for the years 1802-1803, kept by John Epperson at his tobacco warehouse and general store on the Appomattox River, Buckingham County, Virginia, at the place of settlement called Planterstown. John Epperson's wife was Elizabeth (Betty) Ann Woodson. Epperson was killed in a stage coach accident about 1806. The widow married Claiborne West and they removed to near Hopkinsville, Kentucky. After Mr. West died his widow married as her third husband Col. Davie of North Carolina. Irving Davie allowed the author to make a copy of the old book, which in quite lengthy and carried a number of duplications of names. In order to save space the author has copied only those names shown in the book.

Adcock, Joseph	Cary, Robert (dec.)
Akers, John, Sr.	Cason, William
Akers, Klkbn(?) of John	Chamberlayne, Edwd. P.
Akers, William of Franklin Co.	Chamberlayn, Wm.
	Childress, John B. T.
Anderson, David	Childress, John
Arnold, Davis.	Childress, Drury
Ball, Isham	Coleman, Stephen
Baird, Arche	Cox, Edward
Baker, John	Cox, Thomas
Bernard, William R.	Curd, Benjamin
Biscoe, H. L.	Curd, Edward
Blackbourne, James	Curd, John
Brooke, Dudley	Curd, Joseph, Sr.
Buchannan, John	Davenport, Anne
Carter, George, Jr.	Duncan, George
Carter, Henry	Elcan, Lion

Eldridge, Rolfe
Epperson, Joseph
Epperson, James
Faris, Richard
Farley, David
Ferguson, Robert
Fuqua, Gabriel
Flood, Henry
Flood, Moses
Flowers, William
Fore, Joseph
Francis, Eliza
Francis, Elizabeth
Francis, Susanna
Gaines, Bernard
Galding, Jacob
Gannaway, Gregory
Gannaway, John, Jr.
Garrett, William
Gilliam, C.
Gilliam, Isham
Gilliam, John, of John
Gilliam, James
Gilliam, Patsy
Gilliam, William
    (for William Jones, Jr.)
Glover, Stephen
Gregory, Thomas
Guerrant, Daniel
Guerrant, William
Hare, G.
Harris, Edmund
Harris, Obe.
Harrison, B.
Harvey, Daniel
Harvey, Ellison
Harvey, Jeffrey
Harvey, Stephen
Hendrick, Elijah H.
Hendrick, John
Higginbotham, J.
Hobson, Lawson
Holland, Mrs.
Hooper, Benjamin

Hooper, George
Hooper, James
Hooper, Stephen
Hooper, William
Huddlestone, George
Irvine, Wm.
Jeffriss, Jesse
Jeffriss, Nathaniel
Jeffriss, M.
Jeffriss, William
Johns, Anthony
Johns, Edmund
Johns, Glover
Johns, William
Johns, John
Johnston, Peter
Johnston, William
Jones, Arthur
Jones, Charles
Jones, Daniel, son of J. A.
Jones, Edward
Jones, Josias
Jones, John
Jones, Lewellyn
Jones, William
Jones, William, Jr.
Jones, William, son Robin
Jones, William, son Robert
Jones, Samuel
    (per L. Wilkinson)
Laforrest, Aubin
Layne, Gabriel
Lewis, Thomas
    (per son Henry)
Lipford, Amos
Loyd, Joshua
Lumpkin, Anne
Maddox, Davis
Maddox, Michael
Martin, T.
Matteuer, Dr.
Medley, F.
Miller, John
Molly, William

Morgan, John
Morris, Benjamin
Morris, Hudson
Morris, John, son of
    Nathaniel
Morrow, John
Mosby, Sary
Moseley, Charles, Sr.
Moseley, Daniel
Moseley, Edwd.
Moseley, Garland
Mottley, John
McClaird, Daniel
McCormack, Benjamin
McCormack, David
McCormack, Stephen
McCraw, William
McMurray, John
Nelson, Elijah
Nicholas, Joshua
Oglesby, David
Oliver, John
Palmer, John
Parker, James
Patterson, N.
Perkins, George
Pittman, I.
Price, John
Pollock, Allen
Pollock, Robert
Ridgeway, Richard
Robertson, N.
Routon, N.
Sanders, Daniel J.
Sanders, James
Sanders, John, son of Rob't.
Sanders, Robert
Sanders, sons of Samuel
Sanders, Samuel, Sr.
Sanders, William
Sayler, Martin
Scott, S.
Scott, Saymer
Seay, Abner

Seay, William
Setlief, Abraham
Scott, Moses
Smith, Jeffrey
Smith, John
Smith, Uriah
Stinson, Arche
Stinson, John
Sweeney, Hoses
Taggott, John
Tapscott, George
Taylor, George
Ternan, James
Tyree, William
Wadmore, William
Walke, Thomas
Walker, James
Walker, John
Warner, David
Watkins, Spencer
Watt, James
West, Claiborne
Wilkinson, E. J.
Wilkinson, L.
Williams, Samuel
Wills, Willis
Willis, Eston
Wilson, James
Winston, Isaac
Wood, Jacob
Wood, Thomas, Sr.
Woodall, William
Woodson, Blake B.
Woodson, Daniel
Wooldridge, Joseph
Wooldridge, Thomas
    (carpenter)
Wright, Pryor
Wright, Saymer
Wright, Benjamin
Warehouses and business
mentioned in the account
Dean's Warehouse
Epperson's Warehouse

Johnson's Warehouse

Brown-Reives & Co.

Dunlop-Pollock & Co.

Epperson and Scott

Faris & Cheadle

Farrar & Lackland

Hodgson & Hunter

Hughes, Allen, & Co.

W. Irvine & Co.

Jones, John, & Co.

Robert and Allen
    Pollock & Co.

Shanks & McRea, per
    Scott & Co.

S. Scott & Co.

Willis Wills & Co.

Estates mentioned in
the account:

Estate on Willis's for
    taxes

Estate, Hunter & Epperson

Estate, Nathaniel
    Jeffries, dec.

Estate, William
    Jeffries, dec.

A., Jac. 37
A., Thad 37
Abbot, George 7
Abbott, Benjamin 47
Abraham, Jacobs L. 41
Abram, Elizabeth 80
Abrums, Elizabeth 80
Acheson, Minnie 108
Acre, Nancy 123
Adams, Catherine 89
   Polly 58
   William 31, 40
Adcock, Anderson 7
   And'n 31
   Carter 31
   Edmund 27
   George 7, 31, 68
   Henry 3, 31
   Jno. 31
   John 3, 7, 31, 47, 69
   Joseph 3, 7, 31, 133
   Mary 54
   Polley 69
   William 31
   Winnie 48
Adkins, Nancy 129
   Peter 7
Agee, (?) 95
   Mr. 108
   Anthony 3, 7
   Bushrod 95
   Chloe 95
   Frank 95, 108
   Hercules 31
   Isaac 3, 7
   Jacob 31
   James 3, 7, 31, 95
   John 3, 7, 31, 47
   John R. 95
   Joseph 31
   Joshua 7
   Mary Faure 95
   Mathew 7
   Matthew 3
   Moody 95
   Robert 95
   Van Lew 95
   William 7
   Wm. 7
Agle, Cloe 47
Agree, Anthony 117
   James 31
Akers, Blackburn 3
   Eliza 31
   Jno. 31
   John 3, 7, 31, 47, 118,
     133
   Klkbn 133
   Lewis 31
   Susan 31
   Th. 33
   William 3, 31, 133
   Wm. 7

Albert, Adeline 123
Alexander, Daniel 119
   James 101
   James M. 49
   Jno. M. 49
Alk, Th. 33
Allen, (?) 7, 38, 118, 136
   Daniel 80
   Elizabeth 7, 80
   Ethel 94
   George 40
   George Hunt 3, 7
   Jane R. 78
   John 7, 114, 118
   Mary 31
   Mary Evelyn 97
   Samuel 31, 49
   Col. Samuel 31
   Sarah 117
   William 31, 118
   William Hunt 3, 31, 118
   William M. 120
   Wm. Hunt 7
Alott, Benjamin 41
   George 41
Alvis, Ashley 40
   Charles 40
   David 41
Alvord, Martha 101
   Patsy 101
Ambros, Ambrose 40
   Henry 40
Ambruse, Ambrose 13
Amet, Judith 75
Amith, Henry 5
Ammette, Judith 75
Ammonet, John 7
Ammonett, Judith 75
Ammonette, Judith 75
Amnett, Judith 75
Amonet, Andrew 111
   Mary 47
   Reuben 31
   Wm. 47
Amonett, William 31
Amos, Clough 31
   Fra. 31
   Francis 31
   Frank 7, 31
   James 3, 31
   Obe 31
   Reuben 31
Anderson, Am. 118
   Ann 8
   Benjamin 3
   Charles 3
   Capt. Charles 31
   David 3, 8, 118, 120, 133
   Edmund 31
   Elizabeth 118, 120
   Henry 8, 31
   Jack 125

Anderson, James 3, 31, 47
   Jeffry 31
   John 31, 40, 67
   L. 119
   Martha M. 71
   Mary 118
   Matthew 31
   Micajah 8
   Nathaniel 8
   Polly 86
   Richard 31
   Robert 118
   Sally 47
   Thomas 31, 121, 122
   Capt. Thomas 54
   William 3, 8, 31, 47, 118
   Capt. William 54
   Wm. 120
Andley, William M. 49
Anglea, Adria 3
   William 3
Anglin, Adrain 8, 24
   Adran 8
   Adrian 8
   Isaac 8
   Jos. 8
   Philip 8
   William 8
Anlen, Philip 3
Ansley, William M. 49
Anthony, Capt. 58
Apperson, (?) 37
   Jacob 31
   Sterling G. 54
Arbuckle, (?) 56
Archer, Charles 31
Armistead, (?) 126
   Alexander 126
   Anthony 127
   Egbert 127
   Elizabeth 126
   Gill 126
   Hannah 125
   Jesse 126
   Jesse M. 126
   John 126
   John A. 126
   Joseph I. 126
   Julia Ann 126
   Lucreasy 126
   Lucy 126
   Martha 126
   Martha S. 126
   Nancy 126
   Robert H. 126
   Sallie C. 127
   Samuel 126
   Samuel M. 126
   Susanna 126
   Thadeus 31
   Thomas J. 126
   William 126, 127

Beverly, Robert 76
  William 4.
Bibb, William 121
Bigbie, William 41
Binford, Narcissa 103
Binion, Martin 3
  William 1, 3, 119
Binkley, Henry 120
Binnon, William 119
Binns, John 9
  Martin 9
Binon, William 9
Birk, John 4
Birks, Charles 9
  John 9
Biscoe, H. L. 133
Bishop, Stephen 32, 50
Black, Ben 96
  Charles 86
  David E. 96
  Keziah 86
Blackborn, James 32
Blackbourne, James 133
Blackburn, Jacob 9
  James 4
  John 9, 20
  Lambeth 4
  Lambuth 9
  Thomas 9
  William 4
Blair, Allen 49
  Dr. Archibald 113
  Francis P. 89
  James 81
  Montgomery 89
Blakey, (?) 117
  Ann 73
  Ann Haden 73
  Catherine 73
  Churchill 73
  George 73
  John 73
  Joseph 73
  Reuben 73
  Robert 9, 41
  Sarah 73
  Sarah George 73
  Susanna 73
  Thomas 4, 9, 41, 73, 118
  William 73
  Wm. 9
Blalock, John 50
  Polly 50
Blank, Robert 118
Blankenship, Elijah 32
  Gad 32
  J. 32
Blanks, Craddock 85
  Richard 9, 119
  Robt. 32
Bledsoe, Jesse 89
Blunt, Betsy 69
Boage, Robert 19
Boatright, Reuben 32
Boatwright, Daniel 4
  Jesse 9
  Reuben 118
Boaz, Archibald 9
  Daniel 10
  Elizabeth 32, 57
  Jas. 32
  John 41
  Meshac 126
  Meshach 57
  Meshack 10, 32, 57
  Thomas 10
Boaze, Daniel 4
  Edmund 4
  Thomas 4

Bocock, Dr. 73
  John 10, 41
  John H. 73
  Thomas S. 73
Bogies, Andrew 131
  Diana 131
Bois, Maj. 65
Boler, Capt. Leonard 53
Boling, Archibald 41
  Susan 91
Bolling, Archibald 10, 73
  Elizabeth Blair 113
  Jesse 32
  Col. John 113
  Lenaeus 32
  Pocahontas Rebecca 78
  Powhatan 32, 74
  Robert 4, 73, 74, 78, 113
  Col. Robert 10
Bolton, James 126
  Judith 126
Bondurant, Agnes 124
  Darby 10, 32
  David 10
  Edward 124
  F. 41
  Ja. 32
  Jno. 32
  Joel 9
  John 10
  Joseph 124
  R. M. 103
  Robert 107
  Thomas 32
  Thomas M. 86
  William 41, 124
Bones, John 49
Bonner, Minerva 83
Bootwright, James 11
  Jesse 22
Bosher, Len. 111
Bostick, (?) 57
  John 4, 10
Boswell, Dr. 89
Botetourt, Gov. 111
Boulton, Judith 126
Bowles, David 10
  John 18, 82
  Nancy 82
Bowling, Col. 62
Bowman, (?) 77
  Delifaiette 80
  John 49
  John Anderson 80
  Willie P. 80
Boyce, Maj. 128
Braddock, (?) 89
Bradford, (?) 119
Bradley, Carter H. 115
  Do. 41
  John 13, 41
  Joseph 4
  Martha 104
  Richard 41
  Stephen 41
  Terry 3
  Thomas 4
  William 4, 41
  Wm. 10, 16
Bradly, Wm. 10
Brady, Jos. 10
Bramer, James 3
  John 3
Brammer, James 10
  John 10
Branc, Cal. 37
Branch, (?) 75
  Col. 74
  Anthony Martin 74, 127

Branch, Archerhel 41
  Arthur 74
  Bolling 31, 75
  Charles 74
  Christopher 74
  Edward 74
  Elizabeth 74, 75, 81
  Elizabeth Archer 81
  Hannah 74
  Harriet Eveline 74
  Harris 74
  Henry 74
  Hopkins 74
  James Heath 74
  John 74
  Dr. John 74
  Jonathan 41
  Martha Winnifred 74
  Mary 74, 84
  Mary Jane 74
  Mary Marshall 74
  Mary Susan 75
  Matthew 32, 47, 74, 75, 122
  Midley 74
  Oliver 74, 75
  Peter 74
  Polly 75
  Robert Guerrant 74
  Samuel 74
  Capt. Samuel 74
  Sarah 74, 75
  Sarah Elizabeth 74
  Thomas 74, 75, 81, 83
  William 75, 83, 86
  William Daniel 74
  Winifred 74
Bransford, Benjamin 32
  Elizabeth 75
  James 75
  John 32, 75
  Judith 75
  Thomas 32, 75
Brashears, Polly 58
Brashere, Margaret 98
Brashers, Margaret 58
  Robert 58
  Robert S. 58
  Sampson 58
Brashier, Margaret 98
  Robert 98
Breckenridge, John 77
  Dr. John 76
  Joseph Cabell 77
  Lettecia Preston 77
  Mary Hopkins 77
Breedlove, William 8
Brent, Lucy 82
Bridgewater, Chesley 31
Brister, Peter 119
Bristow, James 10, 48
  Thompson 25
Brittain, Elizabeth 66
Broadeater, Julia A. 83
Brock, Mary 66
Brooke, Catherine 76
  Catherine Fauntleroy 86
  Dudley 122, 133
  Edmund 76
  Elizabeth 76
  Prof. St. George Tucker 76
  Humphrey 76
  Lydia Bushrod 76
  Mary 76
  Robert 76, 86
  Robin 76
  Sarah 76
  Susannah 76
  Thomas 29
Brookes, Lieut. John 54

Dotson, William 120
Douglas, David 113
  James 14
  John 5, 14
  William 83
Douglass, John 14
  Nancy W. 120
Downer, Sarah 82
Drake, Joel 33
  John Briton 80
  Matilda Caroline 80
Drew, Dolphin 1
  Col. Dolphin 14
  Thomas Haynes 14
Drinkerd, Archibald 42
  Dancey 42
Druen, Samuel 33
  William 33
DuBreuille, Anthony 98
  Dr. Christoffe 98
  Jean Antoine 98
  Marianne Dutoi 98
Dugar, Capt. 52
Duguid, Capt. William 49
Duiguis, (?) 62
  Ann 14, 118, 120
  Anne 5
  George 62
  Joyce 79
  Lucy 118, 120
  Martha 124
  William 118, 120, 123
  Wm. 14, 117
  Capt. Wm. 69
Duncan, Articinica 83
  Charles 33
  Edward 83
  Edw'd 33
  Elizabeth A. 83
  Fleming 47
  Fleming W. 33
  Frederick W. 83
  George 33, 133
  Jacob 33
  Jerome B. 83
  Jesse 33
  Joel 83
  John 33
  Joseph C. 83
  Metter B. 83
  Ouslaw G. 83
  Richard 83
Dunham, James 25
Dunimon, Daniel 49
Dunkin, James 14
  John 5, 14
Dunkum, Ellis 108
  Gratz E. 108
  Irene 108
  James 107, 108
  Mary Archie 108
  Olney 108
  Susan 108
  Virginia 108
  Willie 108
Dunlop, (?) 136
Dunne, Miss 102
Dupuis, Jane 105
Durfee, Amanda Jane 92
Durham, John 14
  William 5, 14
Durram, James 25
Durrum, Phebe 60
  William W. C. 60
DuVal, Dr. 107
Duval, Philip 64
  Philop 42
  Samuel S. 42
  William 64

Duval, Capt. William 64
  Maj. William 64
Duvall, (?) 64
  Claiborne 64
  William 64
Early, Rev. John 131
Easley, Warsham 6
  William 3, 14
East, Ezekiel 14
  Thomas 42
Easter, Sarah 75
Edens, Alexr. 9
  James 14
  John 5, 14
Edgar, Thomas Snoddy 123
Edins, James 6
  John 23
Edmiston, Thomas 124
Edmundson, Sarah 91
Eds, B. 32
Edwards, (?) 65, 119
  Archibald 33
  Jesse 11
  Martha 65
  Nehemiah 34
  Thomas 65
Edw'd, Prince 33
Eklis, Sarah 107
Elcan, Lion 34, 40, 133
Eldredge, Mary 75
  Thomas 75
Eldridge, (?) 84
  Mr. 2, 84
  Courtney Tucker 84
  David Walker 84
  Geo. 84
  George Wythe 84
  Jane Pocohantas 84
  Martha Bolling 84
  Mary Meade 84
  Nancy Meade 84
  R. 119
  Ro. 33
  Rolfe 1, 14, 33, 84, 99,
    119, 134
  Susan Meade 84
  Susanna 84
  Susanna Walker 84
  Thomas 84
  Thomas Kidder 84
Elerson, Thomas 42
Elgin, John 42
Ellett, Zachariah 14
Elliott, Col. 64
Ellis, Charles 114
  David 114
  Edith 96
  Edward 107
  Dr. Thomas H. 124
Ellsome, Thomas 14
Elsom, Thomas 22
  Wm. 98
Enix, James 49
Epperson, (?) 133, 135, 136
  Betty Ann Woodson 133
  Elizabeth Ann Woodson 133
  Francis 14
  George 13, 14
  James 134
  John 33, 40, 133
  Joseph 5, 13, 14, 134
  Littleberry 5, 14
  Susanna 4
Eppes, Sarah 90
Etherage, Mary 58
  Polly 58
  Sally 58
Evans, Mr. 19
  Ambrose 6

Evans, Catherine 87, 88
  George K. 99
  George Kemper 99
  Henry 6
  John Henry 99
  Joseph 6, 22
  Pamela 127
  Robert 14, 33
  Capt. William 33
  Lieut. William 86, 127
Evansson, Joseph 6
Everage, Mary 58, 129
Everett, John 83
  Susan 83
Evett, John 6
Evins, Thomas 6, 14
Evitt, Thomas 14
Evitts, Nehemiah 14
Ewing, Lieut. Wm. 69
Fallwell, Henry 6
  William 6
Falwell, (?) 54
  Henry 22
  James 54
  Wm. 15
Fambrough, Benjamin 5
Fanning, Harry 25
Farguson, Archibald 42
  Dougald 42
  Edward 15
  Joel 15, 42
  John 15, 42
  Moses 15, 42
  Robert 42
  Thomas 42
  Wm. 15
Faris, (?) 136
  Charles 34
  Jacob 42
  Richard 134
  Silvanus 42
  Valentine 42
Farley, David 42, 134
Farmer, Jeremiah 6
  Lieut. John 55
Farrar, (?) 136
Farrow, Thomas 34
Fasher, Neager 53
Fauntleroy, Mary 76
  William 76
Faure, Pierre 78
Fawell, Elisha 42
  Richard 42
  William 42
Fearn, Elizabeth 118, 119
  Fanny 85
  Frances 107, 130
  George 34
  Jane 85
  John 1, 6, 15, 84, 85, 107,
    118, 119
  Leanna 85
  Leanna Lee 107
  Mary 85
  Mary Burton 85
  Mary Lee 84
  Robert 85
  Col. Robert 85
  Samuel 85
  Thomas 15, 85, 119
Ferguson, Edmund 34
  Joel 15
  John 15, 34
  Moses 15
  Robert 134
  Robertl. 34
  Samuel 77
Ferrow, Charles 107

Ferrow, Frances Guerrant 107
   Mary 107
   Molly 107
Feutchenberger, Mary Lee 96
   Otto 96
   Rosa 96
Fields, Joh. 15
   John 15
Fiest, G. Robert 96
Filbates, Edward 34
Fird, John 15
Fisher, Gabriel S. 114
   John W. 128
Fitch, Samuel 34
Fitxhjawald, John 29
Fitz, Charles 42
Fitzgerald, John 49
FitzJarrell, James 6
Fleatwood, Thomas 53
Fleetwood, (?) 53
   John 53
   Moses 52, 53
   Thomas 53
Fleming, Col. 62, 63
   Capt. Charles 54
   Col. Charles 54
   David 129
   Elizabeth 98, 129
Flood, Henry 8, 133, 134
   Capt. Henry 42
   John 6, 15, 42
   Capt. John 121
   Moses 42, 134
   Noah 42
   William 42
Flournoy, (?) 85
   Alfred 85
   David 85
   Eliza 85
   Jordan 85
   Martha 85
   Silas 34, 78, 85, 120
Flover, Gartie Hood 92
Flowers, (?) 65
   Andrew 15, 42
   Andrews 6
   Ann 65
   Ann Jarot 65
   Anna 65
   Anna Jarot 65
   Anthony 65
   Arthur 65
   Betsy 65
   Deliela 65
   James 34, 65
   John 6, 42
   Joseph 34
   Judy 65
   Maggie 65
   Mary 42
   Polly 65
   Ralph 15, 42
   Rosanna 65
   Rowland 34, 65
   Rowland J. 65
   Sally 65
   Samuel 42
   Sarah 47
   William 6, 65, 134
   Rev. William 42, 65
Flud, John 15
Foard, Rich'd 15
Fontaine, Col. 60
   Capt. Walter L. 128
Forbes, Alexander 34, 47
   Peter A. 2
   W. W. 128
Ford, Capt. 50
   Addison J. 86

Ford, Ambrose 86
   Ann 78, 86
   Boaz 15, 34, 86
   Bray 124
   Daniel 86
   Elisha 34
   Eliz 15
   Hannah 86
   Jack 86
   James 6, 15, 78, 79
   Joel 34, 86
   John 86
   Joseph 34
   Judith 86
   Peter 6, 48, 86
   Polly 86
   Ruth 86
   Salley 34
   Sally 86
   Salon 86
   Samuel 86
   Sarah 86
Forde, Richard 15
Fore, Joseph 134
Forsee, Stephen 6
Forsey, Francis 42
Forster, William 42
Fosee, Lawson 88
Foulks, Joel 55
Fowler, William 74
France, Henry 99
Francis, Eliza 134
   Elizabeth 134
   John 34
   Susanna 134
   Thomas 53
   Wm. 15, 29
Francisco, (?) 86
   Benjamin Morris 86
   Catherine Fauntleroy 87
   Eva 86
   James Anderson 86
   Mary B. 86
   Peter 76, 86, 87
   Ptere 86
   Robert L. 86
   Susan Brooke 87
Franklin, Hen. 20
   Henry 17
   John 6
   Lewis 75
   Shadrack 112
Frazer, James 57
Frealand, Mace 42
Freeland, Mace 6, 15
Freeman, Isaac 42
   Peater 42
   Wm. 28
Freland, Rob't. 15
Fresheur, Micajer 52
Fretwell, Frances 101
   Leonard 101
   Richard 101
   William 101
Fry, John 130
   Col. John 6
   Joshua 123, 130
   Margaret 110
   Martha 110
   William A. 130
Fulkerson, W. M. 58
Fuller, Frank D. 83
Fuqua, Gabriel 34, 134
   Jos. 4
   Joseph 15, 34
   Mo. 34
   Nancy 127
   Robert 34
   Stephen 34

Fuqua, William 6, 15, 34
   Wm. 15, 34, 47
Furlong, John 15
   Robert 20
G., Jno. 37
Gaines, Barnet 43
   Bernard 43
   Col. Daniel 79
Galding, Freeman 34
   Jacob 134
Gallahon, Terry 16
Gallaway, Wm. 15
Galle, Terry 15
Galleway, Terry 34
   Wm. 34
Galloway, Eliza 91
   Phebe 60
Gannaway, Maj. 57
   A. 88
   Betsey 88
   Betsy 87
   Betty 87
   Burrell 87, 88
   Catherine 87, 129
   Edmund 87, 88, 129
   Elizabeth 129
   Frances 87, 88, 129
   Gregory 15, 87, 88, 129, 134
   Grigory 43
   Hannah 87
   John 6, 15, 17, 34, 87, 88, 111, 129, 134
   John E. 87, 88
   Marmaduke 34, 87, 88
   Martha 87
   Mary 87, 121, 129
   Mary Gregory 129
   Meney 87
   Money 87, 88, 129
   Polly 130
   Richard 88
   Richard Woodson 103
   Robert 34, 87, 129
   Sally 87, 88, 129
   Sarah 87
   Sarah Jane 88, 111
   Susanna 88
   Susannah 87, 129
   Theodorick 87, 88
   Theodorick C. 88
   Thomas 34, 87, 88, 129
   Warren 88
   William 87, 88, 129
   William G. 88
   Wm. 15, 34
   Woodson 88
Gardner, James 34
Garland, Jesse 34
   John B. 10
Garnet, Amsted 43
   John 43
Garnett, Armistead 65
   Edward 18
   Henry 111
   Nathaniel 34
   W. 34
Garratt, Charles 15
   John 16, 29
   Stephen 16
   Thomas 16
Garrett, John 10
   Lucy 95
   Thomas 34
   William 134
Garrit, Stephen 48
   Susannah 48
Garrott, Ann 65
   Anna 65

Garrot, Charles 6, 47
  Stephen 6, 48
  Thomas 6
Garrott, Anthony 34
  Charles 16, 34, 95
  Chloe Agee 95
  Cloey 95
  Elijah 34
  Henry 11
  Isaac 34
  Jno. D. 34
  John 77
  Joshua 34
  Lucy 95
  Margaret 95
  Nancy 95
  Stephen 34, 43
  Thomas 43
  William 34
  Wm. 34
Garthard, John B. 16
Gary, (?) 71
  John 43
Gates, (?) 53, 62, 86
  Allen 34
  Charles 16
  Elijah 16
  Hezekiah 16
  William 6, 16, 121
  Wm. 119
Gathright, Miles 64
  Obadiah 64
  Patsy 123
Gaulding, Polly 126
  Susannah 126
Gay, John 14
  Capt. William 128
  William Alexander 128
Gearin, Capt. Peter 65
Gells, Mary 119
  William 119
Genkins, John 16
  Joseph 16
George, Mary 83
  Robert 73
  Sarah 73
Gevandin, John 65
Gevedann, John 66
  Mary 66
Geveden, John 6
Geverann, John 65
Gevidan, John 65, 66
  Mary 65, 66
  Shadrack M. 66
Gevodin, Thomas 34
Gibson, Edward 6, 16
  John 6, 16
  Labon 43
  Lucy 93
  Miles 16, 42, 123
  Thomas 6
  William 16, 101
  Wm. 16
Giddeon, Francis 21
Gilbert, John Wyatt 49
Giles, Josiah 60
  Capt. Wm. 50
Gilkey, Wm. M. 130
Gill, Daniel 127
  Joseph 127
Giller, Gilliam 88
Gillespie, Martha 71
Gillett, James 70
Gilley, Charles 16
  Francis 16
Gilliam, (?) 81
  Miss 102
  Widow 117
  Arch. 23

Gilliam, C. 134
  Charles 16
  Isham 34, 134
  James 134
  John 16, 34, 134
  John G. 128
  John I. 128
  Patsy 134
  Rhoda 129
  Richard 34
  Richard Curd 34
  Susanna 34
  William 6, 34, 88, 117,
    134
  Wm. 16
Gillom, David 43
  Ditto 42
  James 42
  John 42
  Richard 43
Gills, Judith Lancaster 87, 88
  William 34
Gilmer, Mr. 134
  Lieut. John 49
Gipson, (?) 101
  John 34
  Miles 54
  Th. 34
  William 34, 101
  Wm. 34
Gist, (?) 89
  Ann 89
  Christopher 89
  Elizabeth V. H. 89
  Henry Cary 89
  Judith 89
  Nathaniel 89
  Capt. Nathaniel 101
  Col. Nathaniel 62
  Sarah Howard 89
  Thomas Cecil 89
Giuguid, William 42
Givin, George Holms 6
Gleaves, John G. 83
Glenn, William 107
Glover, (?) 118
  Anthoney 43
  Anthy. 16
  Chesley 43
  Edmond 16, 43
  John 6, 16, 34, 43
  Joseph 16
  Mary Ann 107
  Phineas 89
  Robert 6, 16, 107
  Robt. 122
  Samuel 6, 16, 34, 66, 89,
    92
  Stephen 43, 134
  Susan 107
  Thomas 34
  William 34, 107
Godfree, (?) 16
Godfrey, John 43
Godsay, Thomas 6
Godsey, Augustine 16
  Austin 16
  Thomas 16
Goff, John 6, 34
  William 34
Goings, Moses 12
Golden, Julius 49
Goldsby, Charles 11
Goleher, Charles 43
Golloday, Mr. 100
Goode, Col. 55
  Maude 108
  Robert 81
  Col. Robert 55

Goode, William 55
Goodman, Mary 95
Goodwin, Frances Annie 87
Gordan, Knotley 6
Gordon, Motley 16
  Northly 16
  Norty 117
Goss, Benjamin 17
  James 6, 17
  William 47
Gossett, Willie Virginia 96
Gotherd, John B. 42
  Shadrick 42
Gott, William 16
Gouge, Rachel 99
Gough, Mr. 95
Gowing, Wm. 30
Goyan, William 42
Gratz, Benjamin 89
Graves, Louisa C. 114
  Mary 82
  Rebecca 75
Gray, Alexander Trent 89
  Elizabeth Randolph 90
  Harriet Ann Wherry 90
  James 89
  John Taylor 89, 90
  Julia Randolph Trent 89
  Julian 90
  Mildred W. 90
  Susannah 90
  Susannah Crenshaw 90
  William 90, 100
Grayson, Sophonisba E. 78
Green, Hugh 6
  Joseph 27
Greene, Gen. 64, 104
  Nathaniel 86
  Gen. Nathaniel 86
Greenhill, (?) 74
Gregg, Edward 75
Gregory, Mary 129
  Samuel 34
  Thomas 17, 134
  Ens. Thomas 57
  William 17, 34, 122, 127
Griffin, Reuben 49
  Richard 127
  Techariah 47
  Thomas 49
  Zachariah 16
  Zechariah 47
Grifin, Zachariah 42
Grigg, William 100
Griggory, William 6
Griggs, E. T. 83
Grigory, Edmond 42
  Thomas 42
Grisham, Lee 17
Grizle, Henry 34
  William 34
Gross, Solomon 119
Grymes, Mary B. 86, 87
Guanaway, John 17
Guarrant, Daniel 6
  Peter 6, 62
Guerrant, (?) 40
  Daniel 129, 134
  Capt. Daniel 107
  Francoise 129
  Francoise L'Orange 129
  Janie 47
  Jno. 17
  Capt. John 34
  Magdalene Trabue 129
  Peter 17, 34, 40, 47
  Pierre 129
  Stephen 34, 103

148

Patteson, Capt. Charles 54, 62
  Charles Mart. 45
  David 23, 125
  Dr. David 125
  Mrs. David 125
  David R. 125
  Rev. Davis 45
  Edward 44
  Geo. W. 125
  James 23, 45
  Jas. 44
  Jas. G. 60
  Jesse 125
  Jno. Hampton 125
  John 23, 44, 45, 61
  John A. 125
  Kate 125
  Littleberry 23
  Martha 79
  Peater 45
  Peter 23
  Reuben B. 125
  Robert C. 125
  S. S. P. 125
  Sallie D. 125
  Tarleton 45
  Thomas 23, 62
  William 44
  William N. 125
  Wm. 23
Pattison, Charles 37
  Capt. David 37
  James 122
  John 37
  Thomas 37, 122
Patton, Capt. 59
Payne, Barnett 23
  Benja. 27
  Benjamin 22
  Catherine 105
  Catherine G. 105
  Ella Susan 105
  G. B. 105
  Geo. M. 105
  George B. 105
  George M. 105
  Ida 105
  James A. 109
  Joseph 23
  Marion L. 105
  Rosa L. 105
  Rosalie 105
  Rodaline 105
  Sallie Penn 105
  Sara Penn 105
  Susan M. 105
  Virginia Morton 105
Peak, Henry 23
  Jeffery 23
  Jeffry 38
  Philop 44
  Samuel 4
  William 23
Pearcy, James 69
Peasley, Robert 23
  William 23
  Rev. William 1
  Wm. 23
Peck, Rev. Will 61
Peek, Aaron 23
  Absolom 23
  John 23
  Jonathan 23
  Wm. 23
Peel, Mrs. William L. 75
Pen, Rawly 23
Pendleton, (?) 69
  Ben 15

Pendleton, Benja. 23
  Benjamin 44
  James 44
  John 23
  Mace 44
  Micajah 69
Penn, Catharine G. 105
  Catherine G. 105
  Edmond 105
  George 44
  Jane 105
  Moses 114
Pennington, Abel 58
Perkins, Capt. 60
  Betty 124
  Daniel 124
  Dorcus 112
  Eliza Fearn 124
  Frances 71
  George 135
  Harden 1
  Hardin 23, 37, 104, 119
  Capt. Hardin 37
  Henry 30
  John 45
  John W. 23
  John Watkins 23
  Nicholas 124
  Price 37
  Samuel 45, 124
  Susannah 124
  Walker 22
  William 23, 45, 124, 130, 133
  Capt. William 62
  Col. William 45
  Wm. 23
  Capt. Wm. 49
Perro, Daniel 129
Perrow, Charles 24, 37, 129
  Daniel 24, 129
  Daniel Battersby 24
  David 24
  Etienne 129
  Guerrant 37, 40
  Marie 129
  Mary 129
  Stephen 24, 129
Perry, G. 32
  Tandy K. 78
Pescud, Edward 87
Peters, Edmund 24
  Lt. Edmund 62
Peterson, Capt. 62
Pettus, Elizabeth 76
  Jane 117
  John 117
  Rebecca 117
  Stephen 117, 118, 133
Phelps, Alexander 44
  Charles 45
  James 44
  John 24, 118
  Josiah 24
  Mary 118
  Richard 44
  Rich'd. 24
  Robert 44
  Thomas 24
  William 44, 47
  Wm. 24, 44, 45
Phenix, John 51
  William 51
Phillips, (?) 55
  Edna 108
  George 49
  Leach 111
  Richard 6
Pickins, Joshua 104

Pierce, James 69
Piercy, Betsy 69
  Elizabeth 69
  James 69
Pillow, Jerome 85
Pinketham, Rebecca 80
  William 80
Pittman, I. 135
Pittmon, John 45
Plant, James 44
Pleasants, Col. 58, 59
  Philip 114
  Thomas 123
Plunkett, Adeline 106
  Ambrose 106
  Benjamin 106
  Cyrena 106
  Elizabeth 106
  Frances 106
  James 106
  John 106
  John Hill 106
  Jonathan 106
  Mildred 106
  Mildred Hawkins 106
  Nancy 106
  Nancy Ann 106
  Napoleon 106
  Nelly Rucker 106
  Sally 106
  Sarah 106
  Tabitha 106
  Taliaferro 106
  Washington 106
  William 106
  William Rucker 106
  Willis 106
  Willis Rucker 106
  Winifred 106
Poindexter, Caroline 114
Pollard, Benja. 40
  Benjamin 37
Pollett, Elizabeth R. 78
Pollock, (?) 136
  Allen 135, 136
  Robert 135, 136
Polly, Hiram 52
Poor, Capt. William 62
Poore, Elisha 45
Pope, Col. John 64
Porter, Capt. 51, 61
  Isaac 98
  Capt. Isaac 50
  Joseph 112
  Mary 117
  Rezin 117
Powel, William 99, 100
Powell, Elizabeth 125
  Gertrude 97
  Capt. Robert 93
  Thomas 125
  William 49
Powers, Stephen 65
Pratt, Bryce M. 2
Preston, William 118
Pretchard, John 24
Price, Parson 55
  Elizabeth 82
  Rev. Henry 70
  James 48
  John 37, 135
  Joseph 89
  Thomas Johnson 37
  Dr. Wilson 37
Prichard, John 24
Pride, Francis 24
  Winifred 100
Prince, John 37
Prinn, E. 39

Pritchard, John 44
Prosser, Capt. Thomas 64
Pruitt, Levi 112
Pryar, Banister 37
   David 37
   Langston 37
Pryde, Daniel 28
Pryer, David 24
   Edmond 24
   Edward 24
   Edw'd 24
   John 9
   Sarah 24
   William 24
Pryor, (?) 106, 107
   Baynton 106
   Daniel 106
   David 37, 106, 107
   David B. 131
   Frank 106
   John 106
   Judge John C. 106
   Langston 106
   Leonard 106
   Medora 106
   Mitchie B. 106, 107, 131
   Nicholas B. 107
   Nicholas Ballow 106, 107
   Susan 106
   Capt. William 106
   Dr. William S. 106
   Zachariah B. 106
   Zane 106
Pucket, Cheatham 37
   Douglas 38
   Robert 24
Pullin, Elizabeth Ann 80
Pully, Capt. 128
   Ann 128
   John 128
Punch, Mary 81
   Page 81
Purdy, Thomas 88
Puryear, Reuben 37, 121
Putney, Mr. 85
   Ann 108
   Ann Haseltine 107
   Annie H. 94
   Benjamin 107
   David 107, 108
   Duke 108
   Elizabeth 107, 108
   Elizabeth Ann Taylor 108
   Ellis 37, 107, 108
   Ellis W. 95, 107, 108
   Ellis Walker 108
   Ellis Washington 107, 108, 130
   Fanny 85, 108
   Frances 107
   Frances Fearn 107
   Fulton 108
   Isaac 108
   Isaac B. 107
   J. Norman 108
   James 107
   James Lee 108
   Jno. 37
   John 107
   Julian E. 108
   Kemper 108
   Lelia 108
   Lewis 107
   Lucy Ann Haseltine 95
   Mary 107, 108
   Mary Alice 108
   Mary Ann 107
   Mary Ann Glover 95, 108
   Mary Elizabeth 95, 96, 107

Putney, Mary Glover 95
   Mollie 95, 96
   Rebecca 107
   Rebecca Ann 107
   Richard 107, 108, 130
   Richard Ellis 107
   Robert 108
   Sally Bryant 107, 108
   Samuel 107, 108
   Samuel Fearn 107, 108
   Sarah 107, 108
   Sarah Bryant 107
   Sarah Ellis 107, 130
   Susan 107, 108
   Thornton 108
   Virginia Alice 107, 108
   Walker 108
   Wesley Taylor 108
   William 107, 108
   William Witt 108
   Willie 108
   Zenobia 108
Qualls, David 24
   John 24
Radford, Benjamin 45
   James 45
   John 24, 29, 45
   Reubin 45
   Thomas 108
   William 45
Raglin, James 38
   John 45
Railey, Philip 24
   Shelton 17
Rakes, Anthoney 45
   Charles 16, 24
   David 24, 45
   Elisha 45
   Henry 24, 45
   John 45
   William 24, 45
Ramsey, James 38
Randall, Col. 61
Randolph, (?) 115, 118
   Beverly 81
   Elizabeth 89
   Henry 49
   Isaetta C. 91
   Jane 74
   Dr. L. C. 91
   Mary 130
   Richard 74, 81, 130
Ransome, Henry 120
Ranson, Flemsterd 114
Ransone, Flamsteed 24
   Flemstead 38
   Henry 24
   Jno. D. 38
   William 38
Rapine, Antoine 129
Rather, G. W. 127
Rawlins, Henry 38
Rayley, Wm. 24
Read, Clement 38
Reagan, Athalonia 109
   Dixie 109
   Erasmus 108, 109
   Jeremiah 109
   John Fletcher 109
   Landon Carter 109
   Launa 109
   Laura Amner 109
   Mary Lee 109
   Nancy Mize 109
   Pan Dora 109
   Racheal 109
Redd, Capt. 50
   John 24
   Thomas 24

Reece, William 38
Reed, Elliot 49
Reese, Nancy McDaniel 114
Reid, Col. John 76
Reives, (?) 136
Rembert, J. C. 105
Renne, Stephen 24
Renno, John 24
   Stephen 24
Renolds, Archer 24
Revely, John 119
Reves, John 24
Reynolds, Archelus 24
   Charles 24, 108
   David 11, 38
   Moses 24
   Rebecca 126
Rhodes, Fannie 109
   Francisco 109
   Jacintha 109
   John 109
   John D. 109
   Lucy Ann 109
   Ryland 109
   Sarah 109
   Sidney 109
   Tyree 109
   Virginia 109
   William 109
Ri, J. 46
Rice, Davenport 38
Richardson, Capt. 58
   Col. 58
   Miss 110
   Agnes 81
   Ann 81
   Maj. Dudley 80
   Elizabeth 81
   Frances 81
   Isham 81
   John 81
   Martha 81
   Mary 81
   Mary Curd 81
   Richard 38
   Sarah 81
   Stanup 19
   Susannah 81
   Virginia 110
Richerson, Robert 45
Riddle, Capt. 61
   Capt. Isaac 61
   Peyton 38, 40
Ridgeway, James 25
   John 25
   Phebe 25
   Richard 25, 38
Riggan, James M. 83
Right, Augustine 25
   John 25
Ripley, Richard 38
Rippy, Richard 25
Rivers, Minerva 110
Rives, Robert 46
Roadman, William C. 67
Roark, James 49
Roberson, James 28
Roberts, Maj. 60
   John 45, 120, 129
Robertson, Hugh 45
   James 27
   Jeffrey 88
   John 127
   Lieut. John 54, 55
   Mary 25
   N. 135
   Nicholas 38
   Rhoda 88
   Richard 25

Willis, Eston 135
    Jno. 49
    John 49
    Meshack 30
    Willis 46, 77, 123, 136
Wilson, James 39, 124, 135
    Mary 91
    Nacy 107
Winemiller, Noah 71
Winfree, George 30
    Reuben 74
Winfrey, Henry 39, 70
    Hill 39
    John 70
    Philip 70
    Sally Lucy 101
    Samuel 39
Wingfield, Charles Jackson 96
    Stonewall Jackson 96
Wingo, John 30
Winkfield, Thomas 46
Winniford, Judith 40
Winston, Anthony 30, 40, 133
    Capt. Anthony 57
    Judge Anthony 86
    Edm'd. 99
    Isaac 135
    William 40
Witmer, Margaret 97
Witt, Ben 30
    Charles 117
    Littleberry 49
Witz, John 40
Wm., Alexr. 30
Wolfe, Sally Lucinda 113
    Sarah Lucinda 113
Womack, Mary Chamberlain 127
Wood, Gen. Abram 92
    Edmund 40, 118
    Henry 76
    Jacob 135
    Jno. 40
    Jonathan John 70
    Josiah 3
    Margaret 92
    Mary 92, 118
    Owen 40
    Ro. 40
    Suckey 63
    Thomas 19, 30, 40, 135
    William 56
Woodall, David 30, 39
    Isaac 39
    James 30
    Jno. 39
    Obediah 39
    William 30, 39, 135
Woodfin, David J. 128
    Elizabeth 108
Woodford, Gen. 60
Woodrof, David 128
    Hardin 128
    Sally Gunter 128
Woodroff, Hardin 46, 67
    Capt. John 46
    Nathaniel 5
Woodroof, Hardin 128
Woods, James 77
    Samuel 109
Woodson, Alexr. 30
    Anderson 10, 102
    Benjamin 114
    Betsy Ann 115, 133
    Blake B. 135
    Capt. Charles 115
    Daniel 115, 135
    Drury 114, 115, 117
    Drusilla 87
    Elizabeth 114

Woodson, Elizabeth Anderson 87
    Elizabeth Ann 115, 133
    Elizabeth Jones 115
    Elizabeth Morton 115
    Col. Hugh 86
    Capt. Jack 130
    Jacob 30, 40, 114, 115
    Jesse 30, 114, 115, 117
    John 15, 30, 81, 86, 87,
        114, 115
    Joseph 115, 117
    Judith 87
    Judith Jane 88
    Judith Leake 115
    Martha 87
    Mary 114
    Miller 86
    Capt. Obadiah 115
    Sarah 114
    Shadrack 30, 114, 115, 117
    Stephen 114
    Susannah 114
    Thomas 114
    Tucker 30, 115
    William 30, 40, 114, 115,
        117
    Wm. 30
Woodward, Jeremiah 14
Woody, Henry 46
    Susannah 63
Wooldredge, John 46
Wooldridge, Charles 39
    Henry 30, 40
    John 40
    Joseph 40, 135
    Thomas 39, 135
Woolridge, Nancy 82
Wooten, Elizabeth 70
    George W. 70
    Jack 70
    James 70
    John R. 70
    Josiah 70
    Nancy 48
    Nancy Roper 70
    Polly 70
    Rhoda 70
    Robert A. 70
    Sally 70
    Turner 70
    William 39, 40
    William H. 70
Wootten, James 101
    Joseph 40
Word, Banjemin 39
    George Washington 40
    Peter 13
    Thomas 40, 123
Worley, John 5, 9, 117
    William 27
Worthen, Sarah 84
Wright, (?) 30
    Mr. 102
    Archibald 40, 119
    Augustine 30
    Benjamin 49, 135
    Elizabeth 87
    Gabriel 40, 119
    George 30, 119, 120
    Henry 119, 120
    James 46
    John 46
    Minos 49
    Moses 62, 70
    Peter 30
    Pryor 135
    Randolph 30
    Robert 46
    Saymer 135

Wright, Stephen 48
    Thomas 11, 30, 46
    Thos. 30
    William 46, 119, 120
Ws, W. 33
Wst, Jno. 33
Wyche, Benjamin 127
    Beverly Granville 127
    Charles Humphreys 127
    Cyril Franville 127
    Elizabeth Jenkins 127
    George 127
    George Edward 127
    Henry 127
    Ira Thomas 127
    James 127
    John Jenkins 127
    Louisa Young 127
    Martha Hendricks 127
    PamelaEvans 127
    Perry Wayne 127
    Peter 127
    Peter Peters 127
    Robert Henry 127
    William Evans 127
Wynn, Thomas H. 73
Yancey, Miss 111
    Charles 46, 67, 133
    Lt. Col. Charles 111
    John 111
    Robert 111
Young, John 56
    Lloyd B. 67
Younger, Kenard 61
Zachary, Bartho 30
    John 30

                SINGLE NAMES

Amy, negro 124
Ann 82
Ben, negro 124
Daniel, negro 124
Dilly, slave 103
Dock, negro 124
Elizabeth 92, 94, 100, 110
Hannah 87
Jane 82
Joyce 79
Littleberry 67
Margaret 100
Marguerite 96
Mary Ann 117
Mary Jane 96
Matoaka 74, 113
Patsey 102
Patte 128
Phyllis, negro 124
Pocahantas 74, 113
Pocohantas 74, 128
Polly 58
Polly, slave 103
Sallie 103
Sally 58, 87, 88
Sarah 95
Sarah, slave 103
Sarah Sanderson 103
Sucky, negro 124
Terry 48
Tim, slave 103
Tom, negro 124
Tom, slave 103
Travis, negro 103
William 88

162